מסורה

ArtScroll Mesorah Series

Rabbi Nosson Scherman/Rabbi Meir Zlotowitz
General Editors

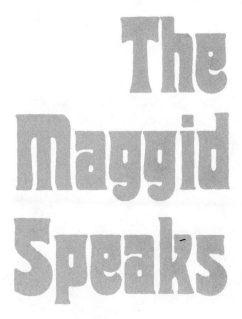

The Maggid Speaks

The Maggid

by Rabbi Paysach J. Krohn

Published by

Mesorah Publications, ltd

Speaks

Favorite Stories and Parables of
Rabbi Sholom Schwadron shlita,
Maggid of Jerusalem

FIRST EDITION
First Impression . . . February, 1987
Second Impression . . . April, 1987
Third Impression . . . June, 1987
Fourth Impression . . . August, 1987
Fifth Impression . . . October, 1987
Sixth Impression . . . December, 1987
Seventh Impression . . . November, 1989
Eighth Impression . . . November, 1990

Published and Distributed by
MESORAH PUBLICATIONS, Ltd.
Brooklyn, New York 11232

Distributed in Israel by
MESORAH MAFITZIM / J. GROSSMAN
Rechov Harav Uziel 117
Jerusalem, Israel

Distributed in Europe by
J. LEHMANN HEBREW BOOKSELLERS
20 Cambridge Terrace
Gateshead, Tyne and Wear
England NE8 1RP

Distributed in Australia & New Zealand by
GOLD'S BOOK & GIFT CO.
36 William Street
Balaclava 3183, Vic., Australia

Distributed in South Africa by
KOLLEL BOOKSHOP
22 Muller Street
Yeoville 2198
Johannesburg, South Africa

THE ARTSCROLL MESORAH SERIES®
THE MAGGID SPEAKS

ISBN
0-89906-230-X (hard cover)
0-89906-231-8 (paperback)

Typography by Compuscribe at ArtScroll Studios, Ltd.

Printed in the United States of America by Noble Book Press
Bound by Sefercraft, Quality Bookbinders, Ltd. Brooklyn, N.Y.

הרב שלום מרדכי הכהן שבדרן

שערי חסד, ירושלים

בס״ד

בכי טוב פ׳ מקץ ה׳ דחנוכה תשמ״ז

אל מע״כ חביבי יקירי הרב וכו׳ פסח יוסף קראהן נ״י (בנו של ידידינו הדגול, האהוב לכל, הבלתי נשכח, הרב הגדול נעים הליכות, נחמד ונעים, רב פעלים ועמוד החסד, מוה״ר אברהם זעליג ז״ל, מוהל בק׳ נו יארק רבתי).

אחדשה״ט, שמחתי מאד לשמוע כי ספרך אשר הכנת ועמלת בו ביתר שאת ויתר עז לפרסם בפני קהל ועדה ישראל קדושים הם סיפורי מעשיות ומשלים הרבה מגדולי ישראל עיני העדה בדורנו ומלפני כמה דורות. אשר קיבצת מה ששמעת מאתי בע״פ ובכתב בכמ״ק זה עשרים ואחד שנה עוד בהיותי בבית אביך ז״ל, ואמך הרבנית תחי׳ (אשר כפי שאמרת לי גם נעזרת על ידה בעריכת הספר הזה בכמה דברים בשיפור הלשון וסיגנונו). ולא עוד! אלא שעיטרת פעמים רבות בסיפור מעשה או משל בדברי מוסר קצרים לפניו או לאחריו להורות הדרך מהו הפועל יוצא מאותה מעשה משל ומליצה. ונכון הדבר מאד אשר עשית כן. אשריך וטוב לך!

והנני חותם ברגשי גיל ושמחה רבה שזכית במצוה גדולה ועצומה כזאת לזכות את הרבים — בפרט המון העם אשר לא ידעו ולא הכירו אף מעט מהרבה גדולי הדור — ונתת להם עינים!

בהוקרה וברכה מרובה!

ידידך באהבה!

שלו׳ מרדכי הכהן שבדרן

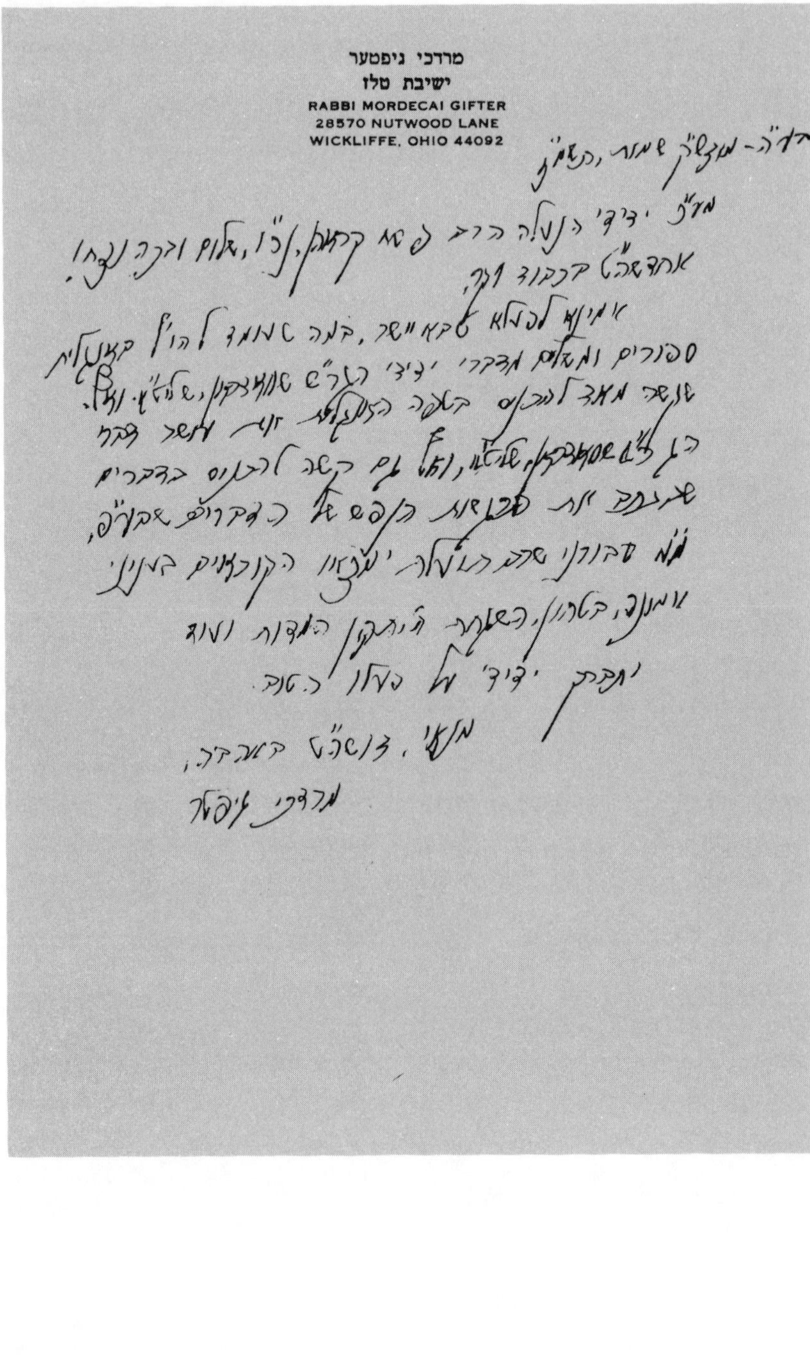
מרדכי גיפטער
ישיבת טלז
RABBI MORDECAI GIFTER
28570 NUTWOOD LANE
WICKLIFFE, OHIO 44092

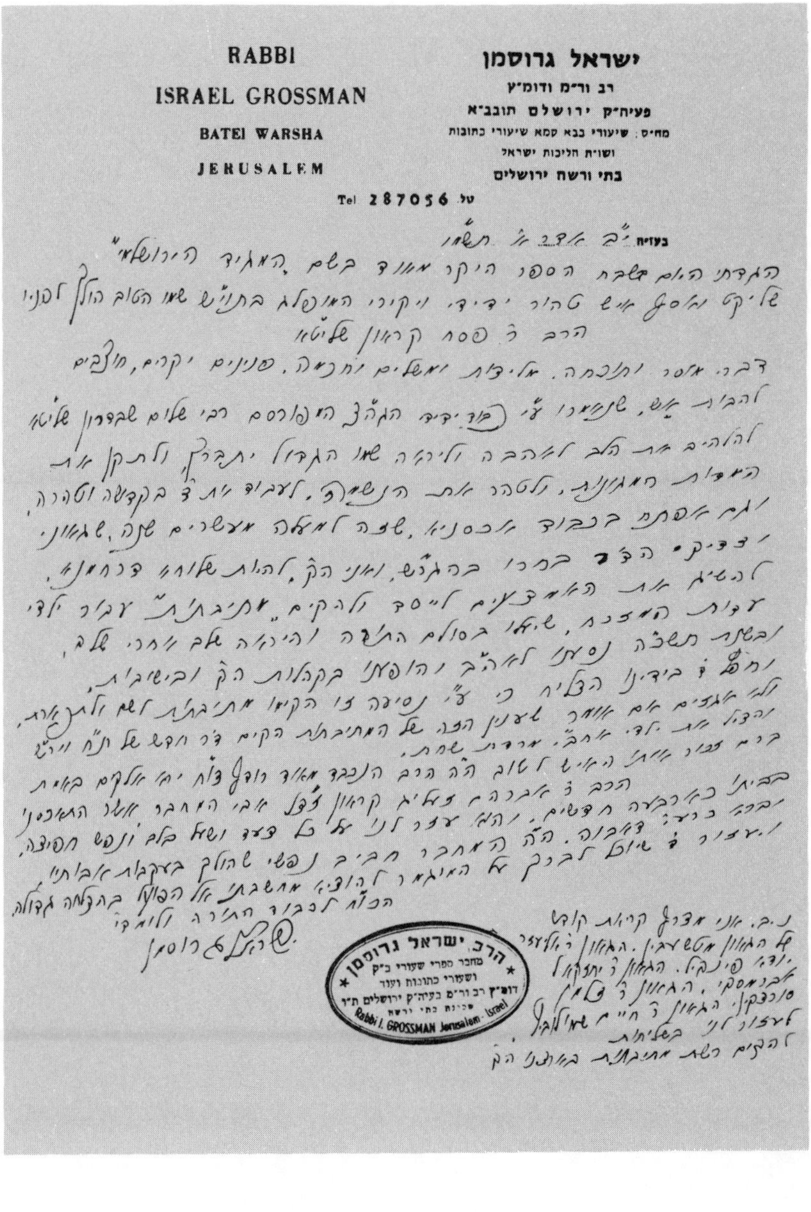

RABBI
ISRAEL GROSSMAN
BATEI WARSHA
JERUSALEM

ישראל גרוסמן
רב ור״מ ודומ״ץ
פעיה״ק ירושלם תובב״א
מח״ס: שיעורי בבא קמא שיעורי כתובות
ושו״ת הליכות ישראל
בתי ורשה ירושלים

Tel **287056** טל.

בעזה״י

הגהתי היום בשבת הספר היקר מאוד בשם "המגיד הירושלמי"
שליקט ואסף איש טהור ידידי ויקירי המופלג בתו״ש שמו הטוב הולך לפניו
הרב ר׳ פסח קראון שליט״א
דברי מוסר ותוכחה. אגדות ומשלים וחכמה. פנינים יקרים, חוצבים
להבות אש, שנאמרו ע״י כבוד ידידי הגה״צ המפורסם רבי שלום שבדרון שליט״א
להלהיב את הלב לאהבה וליראה שמו הגדול יתברך, ולתקן את
המדות האנושיות, ולטהר את הנשמה, לעבוד את ד׳ בקדושה וטהרה,

[illegible]

הרב ישראל גרוסמן
מחבר הספרי שיעורי ב״ק ושיעורי כתובות ועוד
דומ״ץ רב ור״מ בעיה״ק ירושלים ת״ו
שכונת בתי ורשה
Rabbi I. GROSSMAN Jerusalem - Israel

דוד קאהן

ביהמ"ד גבול יעבץ
ברוקלין, נוא יארק

בס"ד

כבוד יקירי וחביבי, רחימא דנפשאי
הרב ר' פסח יוסף
נרו יאיר ויזרח

בקשת ממני מכתב ברכה לרגל הופעת ספרך החדש באנגלית "מגיד מירושלים" בו מובאים סיפורים ומשלים שיש ללמוד מהם מוסר ודעת ששמעת מהגאון הצדיק רב שלום מרדכי הכהן שבדרון שליט"א, מהמשפיעים הב' גדולים בדורנו. הנני מזכיר בזה שאותן הרגשות שהבעתי במכתב ברכה לספרך הראשון על ברית מילה שייכות הן בכפל כפלים כאן. ספרך הנוכחי אינו ספר שעומד בפני עצמו אלא בבחינה אחת הוא המשך של ספרך הראשון. כיצד?

אם נשתמש בספריך ככלי מדידה של יחסיך לאביך ז"ל נתאר הראשון כעבודת הגימור לעצמת אביך, שטרח ואסף וקיבל חומר רב על עניני מילה ואתה באת וחיברת חיבור למופת ופעלת בזה הגשמה לחלומו. מאידך גיסא מספרך השני מתקבל מתוכו אהבה עזה והתקשרות להגה"צ מירושלים שיש לתאר עבודתך שהשקעת בו כעבודת המשך, שבזה הנך ממשיך היחס של חיבה והערצה של אביך ז"ל לכבוד הגה"צ מירושלים יבלח"ט.

אין ספק אצלי שהנחת רוח שגרמת לנשמת אביך ז"ל בהפצת חיבור זה עולה היא על הקורת רוח שטעמה נשמתו מחיבורך הראשון שהלא הנביא שהבטיח ליהושע כהן גדול שיתקיימו בניו אחריו אמר (זכריה ג-ז) "ונתתי לך מהלכים בין העומדים האלה", והבן הממשיך בדרכי אביו יותר קרוב הוא לתואר של "מהלך" מהבן הגומר עצמת אביו.

ואומר לך כה לחי, וכשם שזכית להרבות כבוד שמים בחיבורך הראשון כן תזכה בחיבורך הזה לעורר לבות ישראל לדרישת רבינו יונה (שע"ת שער ב' אות כב) לעמל התורה, להתבונן ביראת ה', לתיקון המידות, להשיג מעלות היראה והאהבה, ולחשוב מחשבות איך יגדיל ויאדיר מצוות להיות לנפשם סגולה ואוצר, אמן כן יהי רצון.

בעתירת אוהבך דורש שלומך והצלחתך
כל הימים
דוד קאהן
ערב חנוכה תשמ"ז

Table of Contents

Author's Preface

I present this work to the public with a deep sense of gratitude to Hashem for having allowed me to complete a work that blends two dynamic forces in Jewry today: the ArtScroll Mesorah Series and the renowned *Maggid* of Jerusalem, R' Sholom Schwadron, who continues to inspire Jews throughout the world with his vibrant stories and parables.

When R' Sholom first mentioned to me the possibility of publishing his stories and parables, I was swept with excitement. For more than twenty years I, like thousands of others the world over, have thrilled to the exuberance of his *drashos* (sermons), with their anecdotes and episodes. I have seen him electrify audiences large and small with his narratives and moving *Maggid's* "melody". I have witnessed his vivid descriptions that make people — scholars and students alike — laugh and cry. I have watched how he thunderously exhorts and movingly inspires both adults and youngsters. Thus, for me to have been given the opportunity to record R' Sholom's most memorable tales and have them published by ArtScroll is truly an honor and a privilege.

I am grateful to Hashem that He allowed me, through working on these stories, to gain insight in the lives and ideals of many of the great *tzaddikim* of the last few hundred years. From the great mass of available material, I hope I have chosen well and done justice to R' Sholom and the personalities about whom he speaks. I am equally grateful that I have been able to spend much time with R' Sholom, both here and in *Eretz Yisrael,* in preparing this work. He is an exceptional person whose private life is as inspirational as his public life.

May I point out that this is the first time many of these stories have been made available to the non-Yiddish/Hebrew speakng public. And although I realize that inflections and nuances are often lost in the translation, and that the written word cannot capture R' Sholom's unique and memorable manner of delivery, yet beneath his flamboyance, dramatics and melody, there is always a deep message — he is a master not only in *how* he speaks, but in *what* he says; he is electrifying not only for his delivery, but for the thoughts he conveys — thus, be it a parable or a story, much can be gained, even from the translated, written version.

Acknowledgments

Because Rav Sholom feels strongly that a *sefer* such as this could elevate the readers' commitment to Torah and *mitzvos,* heighten their *yiras Shamayim* and provide insights to the thoughts of *gedolim,* he gave this project endless hours of his time. He enhanced the *sefer* by telling me new stories, amending those I thought I knew and adding perceptive insights to those I had already written. I had constant access to his own tapes and notes, and I shall always treasure the voluminous special correspondence that we shared through tapes and letters over the past two years.

I must inject a note on a point about which Rav Sholom feels very strongly. Namely, this volume is not meant to be a historical work. It contains both stories that Rav Sholom has heard and stories that he himself experienced. He has always transmitted these stories as faithfully as possible. Nevertheless, other versions may exist. In some, the same incident involves different people; in others, the details differ. The primary objectives in the retelling of these stories are the basic truths they teach us; the inspiration the reader can derive from them; the insight they provide regarding the great minds and personalities of the *tzaddikim* and *gedolim* of yesterday; and an appreciation of the level of intimacy that Hashem shares with the most beloved of His people. For all this Rav Sholom devoted much time and effort to this project. I am thankful to him beyond words.

I am also grateful to many others who graciously provided the tapes from which many of the stories and parables in this volume were culled. Foremost among them is Rabbi Eli Teitelbaum, founder of the Dial-a-Shiur program, which presents Rav Sholom's recorded weekly *drashos* on the weekly *sidros*. Rabbi Avrohom Kanarek introduced me to *Ner L'meah*, an Israeli organization which stocks hundreds of tapes from a variety of speakers. Among them are Rav Sholom's Hebrew talks to Sephardic *baalei teshuvah*. Mr. Erwin Grunhut allowed me access to his extensive personal library of Rav Sholom's tapes. Also helpful were the tapes of Rav Aharon Kohn, Rav Yosef Teitelbaum, and Reb Hillel Wolfson, and the copious notes of Rav Ozer Yonah Kushner. This work has been enhanced by the generosity of these individuals.

I am indebted to Rabbi and Mrs. Mordechai Tropper, Rabbi Chaim Dovid Ackerman and Mrs. Reggie Levi-Tovbin who read the manuscript and added perspective and comments. Rabbi Lipa Brenner and Rabbi Hirsch Goldwurm were helpful and informative regarding the historical background of many selections. Mrs. Tziona Bin-Nun edited the entire work with skill and perception. I am grateful to them all.

It has been my good fortune to consult regularly with my *rebbi* and *moreh derech*, Rav Dovid Cohen, whose perceptive insights and advice to me in all aspects of this work were invaluable.

My mother, Mrs. Hindy Krohn, שתחי׳, has been involved with me on this project since its inception. Her eloquence of phrase and her talent for clear and concise writing were of immeasurable help as we worked together on this book. Working on these stories and parables, many of which she heard at her own gracious table, has given her much satisfaction. I am gratified that my mother had a significant share in bringing this project to fruition, and I know that Rav Sholom shares this sentiment.

Over the last decade, ArtScroll/Mesorah Publications has established itself as the leader in English-language Torah literature. Under the helm of Rabbi Meir Zlotowitz and Rabbi Nosson Scherman, ArtScroll has opened vistas of Torah to "those thirsty for the word of Hashem," with lucid expositions of numerous facets of Torah study and Jewish history. It is a privilege for me to be affiliated with this exemplary group of individuals.

The staff at ArtScroll is a unique blend of individuals whose talents mesh to inspire Jews throughout the world. In addition to those mentioned above, I was fortunate to benefit from Rabbi Avie Gold's meticulous attention to detail and clarity, Mrs. Simie Korn and Menucha Marcus' phototypesetting, Shimon Golding and Shmuel Klaver's marketing skills, Sheah Brander's graphic genius, Eli Kroen's layout talents, Mrs. Faygie Weinbaum and Mrs. Judi Dick's proofreading; and the other members of the Mesorah staff: Lea Freier, Mrs. Esther Feierstein, Esther Zlotowitz, Yosef Timinsky, and Yehudah Neugarten.

Finally, I give thanks and praise to my wife Miriam and our children for their encouragement and enthusiasm throughout this project. For each of us this project has been a learning experience. May Hashem grant us the privilege to serve Him by reaching the standards of the *tzaddikim* and *tzidkanios* in these pages.

אלקים שמע תפלתי האזינה לאמרי פי

Paysach J. Krohn
Kew Gardens, N.Y.
February 1987

פסח יוסף קראהן
מוצאי שבת ק׳ ט״ו בשבט תשמ״ז

INTRODUCTION –

The Maggid of Jerusalem: Personal Encounters

◆§ *What is a Maggid?*

What is a *"maggid"*? Literally the word *maggid* means one who narrates an incident or event. For hundreds of years, the term *maggid* has meant someone who serves the Jewish community as a preacher. In many communities he was an appointed public servant, like the *rav* (rabbi) or *dayan* (religious judge), whose function was to chastise and admonish, encourage and exhort. An appointed *maggid* was known in Hebrew as the *maggid d'massa,* or in Yiddish as the *shtodt maggid,* both meaning "town preacher." Later, the term *maggid* came to refer to itinerant speakers who traveled from town to town. Whether they traveled or not, *maggidim* came to be known for their exceptional skills in oratory and their fearlessness in speaking out against evils, regardless of how influential the perpetrator might be. An itinerant *maggid* such as the renowned eighteenth-century *maggid* of Dubno (1740-1804) or the celebrated nineteenth-century *maggid* of Kelem (1828-1899) would come into a town, meet with the community leaders and find out what aspect of Judaism needed addressing.

Was the *chevra kadisha* (burial society) functioning properly? Was the *bikkur cholim* (society to care for the sick) serving those who needed it? Was there proper Sabbath observance? Were people setting aside time for Torah study? Were they honest in business? His information in hand, the *maggid* was ready for his *drashah.* Almost every man, woman and child would crowd into the designated hall, usually the largest synagogue in town, quite often on a Friday night or Shabbos afternoon, where the *maggid* would address the public.

Unlike the more intricately reasoned sermons of the *rav*, the *maggid* utilized many stories and parables to make his point. At times his heated oratory would become exuberant and exciting. But perhaps most memorable of all were the beautifully haunting melodies with which the *maggid* flavored his *drashah*. At times his song added a loving warmth to his words and at times, it injected fire to his fearful rebuke.

Whatever the melody, it was like a colorful background, on which the *maggid* painted the verbal portrait of his *drashah*.

R' Sholom Schwadron: The Man

During the forty years of his public speaking career, R' Sholom has come to epitomize the itinerant *maggid*. Throughout countless towns and cities in *Eretz Yisrael*, Europe and America, R' Sholom's distinctly deep and resonant voice, incessant *joie de vivre*, exaggerated gestures and exclamations of "*Pilay ployim* (wonder of wonders)! *Noyroh noyro'oys* (awesome of awesome)!" and hearty, friendly countenance have become familiar and legendary.

A grandson of the nineteenth-century *gadol hador* whose name he carries — R' Sholom Mordecai Hacohen Schwadron of Brezhan, Galicia (1835-1911), also known as the *Maharsham* — R' Sholom was born in Jerusalem, to R' Yitzchak and Fraida Leah Schwadron. Little Sholom'ke, as he was called in his childhood, was tragically orphaned at the age of seven when his father passed away. With his widowed mother he lived through a period of wrenching poverty, and for a while had to reside in an orphanage in Jerusalem. He attended a *talmud torah* in the Me'ah Shearim section of Jerusalem, and after his *bar-mitzvah* attended the Lomzer Yeshivah Ketanah in Petach Tikvah where two years later he came under the tutelage of the sainted R' Elya Dushnitzer (1876-1949), the *mashgiach* of the Yeshivah Gedolah. Sholom'ke was there until he was seventeen.

After the horrifying Arab pogrom in 1929 that decimated the Slabodka Yeshivah in Chevron, its *roshei hayeshivah* there — R' Moshe Mordechai Epstein (1866-1933) and his son-in-law R' Yecheskel Sarna (1895-1969) — moved the yeshivah to Jerusalem, where they renamed it Yeshivas Chevron. Numerous *bochurim* sought to enter the Yeshivah, and Sholom'ke was one of those accepted. He studied there for seven years and became the *talmid muvhak* (esteemed pupil) of the *mashgiach*, R' Leib Chasman (1869-1935), who had been *rav* and *rosh yeshivah* in Stutchin, Poland, before settling in *Eretz Yisrael.*

R' Sholom married Leah Auerbach (who passed away in 1977) the daughter of R' Chaim Yehudah Leib Auerbach (1886-1954), *rosh yeshivah* of Shaar HaShamayim, the Kollel for the study of *Kabbalah* in Jerusalem. The *rebbetzin's* brother, יבל"ח, R' Shlomo Zalman Auerbach — the *rosh yeshivah* of Yeshivah Kol Torah in the Bayit Vegan section of Jerusalem — is one of the foremost *gedolim* of our time.

After his wedding R' Sholom joined the Kollel Ohel Torah under the auspices of the Chief Rabbi, R' Yitzchak Isaac Halevi Herzog (1888-1959). He later became the *mashgiach* of Yeshivas Tiferes Tzvi, the secondary division of Yeshivas Chevron, and eventually became the *rosh yeshivah* of Yeshivah Oholei Shem. In 1946, he published his first *sefer,* the responsa of his grandfather, *She'ailos Ut'shuvos Maharsham.* Since then, he has written, annotated, and edited more than twenty-five *sefarim,* primarily the works of his grandfather, covering the gamut of *halachah* (religious law), *drush* (homiletics) and *mussar* (ethics).

Although R' Sholom has drawn from many *tzaddikim,* both the well known and those who shunned the public eye, his three primary teachers in *mussar* were: R' Elya Dushnitzer, R' Leib Chasman, and later, R' Elya Lopian (1872-1970), the *mashgiach* in the Yeshivah of Kfar Chassidim. Indeed, the noted *mussar* tracts *Ohr Yahel* by R' Leib Chasman and *Lev Eliyahu* by R' Elya Lopian were written and edited by their *talmid,* R' Sholom.

The teaching *(Avos* 1:4) that "one should drink with thirst the words of sages" aptly applies to R' Sholom with regard to these three giants of *mussar.* He absorbed, studied and contemplated their every word and nuance, and he repeats them with awe and reverence.

Even before he was married, his unusual talent for public speaking became widely known. He has addressed every kind of gathering: conference, convention, *teshuvah* assembly, *simchah* or — Heaven forbid — funeral. For more than three decades he has been the regular Friday night *darshan* in the noted Zichron Moshe *shul* in Jerusalem.

His presence is electrifying. When he walks into a room, everything stops. A crowd gathers around him, eager to greet him and anxious to hear whatever he has to say. It may be a new story, a humorous comment, a sharp insight or just a warm and friendly greeting. Soon, those on the perimeter of the circle are questioning those toward the center as to exactly what he said and what he meant.

By the time he has finally made his way to the pulpit to begin his talk, many ideas have crossed his mind. He has often remarked, "Whenever I have to speak, I plan one *drashah* at home, on my way to the *shul* I think of a second one, and when I am at the *bimah* I find that I end up saying a third one."

Often during a *drashah*, R' Sholom will introduce a seemingly unrelated story or thought by noting, "R' Elya Lopian once instructed me that if I am speaking publicly and suddenly a thought or particular story comes to mind it is a sign from Heaven that it was meant to be delivered to this specific audience because it is what they need to hear." It is no wonder that listeners are always attentive, for with R' Sholom there is no such thing as a "standard" *drashah*.

He delivers two different types of talks. When his audience is made up exclusively of *yeshivah bochurim* he is demanding, serious and somber. He elucidates a firm principled outlook on life, with a serious discussion of man's role and responsibility in this world.

To *baleibatim* (the general public) he delivers what he calls a *drashah* of *Mesillas Yesharim* (the classic *mussar* work) in the tune of a Purim song. In other words, the message is strong, but he softens it with pleasantries, stories, and self-deprecating humor. Whoever comprises his audience, his objective is to stir them towards introspection and improvement.

R' Sholom is famous for the hearty laughter he evokes from his listeners. An outsider seeing only the audience would find it hard to imagine that they are listening to an esteemed *rav* from *Yerushalayim.* The humor is intended to get people to laugh ... at themselves. It is to illustrate the folly of the real-life situations in which people become snared by acting without sufficient forethought.

An incident in his youth gives us an insight into his approach to public speaking. When he was only thirteen, one of his classmates organized a group that would meet every *Shabbos* afternoon. They called it *Bimas Hadrashos* (pulpit sermons) and its purpose was to practice public speaking.

Like a *maggid,* a boy would stand at the *bimah* wrapped in a *tallis,* and address his classmates on the *sidrah* of the week.

The very first speaker on the very first week, was the spritely orphan boy, "Sholom'ke." He strode up to the *bimah,* brimming with confidence, filled with aspirations for the future, and began.

> I would like to start with a parable that I hope someday to be able to say to a large audience, at a real *drashah* in a huge *shul.* A father had two children who were both very sick. The doctor prescribed bad-tasting medicine, and they both refused to take it. The father began talking to the older child and explained to him the severity of his illness and the importance of the medicine. "If you refuse to take it, you could — Heaven forbid — end up in the hospital. You would miss playing with your friends." And so on, and so on. Being an intelligent, mature child, the boy finally relented and took the awful-tasting medicine.
>
> With the second, much younger, son, however, the father did not even begin to talk about the medication. Instead he began to play with him, engaging him in delightful conversation. Then the father told him a joke. The boy smiled. Soon the father told an even funnier joke and the boy began laughing. As his mouth opened in hearty laughter, the father slipped the medicine in and before the boy knew it, he had swallowed the medicine.
>
> A person watching the father's behavior might think that

he loved his younger child more than the older one. With the first, he was stern and strict, while with the second he took so much time playing and getting him to laugh and almost "enjoy" the medication. The truth, of course, is that the older child was more mature and thus the father could appeal to him logically, explaining to him the facts of the illness. The second child was too young to respond to the threat of going to a hospital. He might even think it would be fun! His father's only choice was to find a roundabout way to administer the medicine.

The same is true of our generation. The *maggidim* of former times could go straight to the point. There was no need to make an audience laugh and soften them up with pleasantries. People were receptive to *mussar* and reproof. Nowadays, though, if you try to force *mussar* upon people, most will resist it. If you are rebuking them, they will resent your attitude and not accept your words. But if they are loosened up with laughter, their hearts and minds become receptive even to words of reproof and instruction.

Now, more than half a century later, R' Sholom says, "It was true then when I was a child, and even more so today."

Today, every Friday night, hundreds of men, women and children gather in the old Zichron Moshe *shul* in Jerusalem, to hear a *drashah* by the famed *Maggid* of Jerusalem, R' Sholom Schwadron. It is a ritual that people despite inclement weather, have followed for decades.

From the alleys, streets and avenues of Jerusalem, tourists and residents, Ashkenazim and Sephardim, gather to be inspired by, and to laugh and cry with R' Sholom. But perhaps most of all, they come to be in the presence of a warm, loving *talmid chacham,* a robust gentleman who is like everyone's grandfather. His friendly countenance, his easy laugh and charming words embrace the audience; they are magnets that have drawn hundreds of thousands of people to hear him in his forty years of public speaking.

Though he makes his listeners feel comfortable, he opens their minds and hearts to repentance. He makes no attempt to hide his own deepfelt emotions and sensitivities. He laughs and cries easily, he admonishes and praises whenever necessary. His powerful and booming words hammer home like a pile driver, but his thunder is always followed by a refreshing bit of sunshine, never leaving his audience angered or with the bitter taste of rebuke.

Most of his listeners know that R' Sholom is steeped in *mussar* and *halachah*. His words often reflect the thoughts of *tzaddikim* who lived in the generations before him. Possessed of a keen and retentive mind, always ready to listen to a good story, he elicits from his listeners their own stories, some poignant, some fascinating, which eventually find their way into his own repertoire. To R' Sholom, a story is a jewel to be collected, treasured, and polished — and to be displayed at the appropriate moment.

Children and adults flock to listen to R' Sholom. He walks up to the *bimah*, kisses the *aron hakodesh*, removes his *shtreimel* as the crowd subsides into respectful silence. They are about to hear another *drashah* from the *Maggid* of Jerusalem, an individual who is an institution known and loved by Jews throughout the world.

לְמַעַן אַחַי וְרֵעָי, אֲדַבְּרָה נָּא **שָׁלוֹם** בָּךְ

This book was written not merely with admiration for a public figure, but with reverence for a man who has meant so much to so many members of my family. For twenty years R' Sholom has shared our joys and sorrows. He has comforted us in sadness and rejoiced with us in happiness. From near and from afar, he has stood beside us like a father and grandfather. People often wonder how our family became so close to R' Sholom. The story is worth retelling, because it reveals *hashgachah pratis* (Divine Providence), portrays human nature at its best, and demonstrates the rewards awaiting those who "make their home a meeting place for *talmidei chachamim*" (See *Avos* 1:4).

A Son Comes Home

In 1962, my cousin Chaim Dovid Ackerman was returning to the United States after two years of study at Chevron Yeshivah in Jerusalem. On the way he stopped off to spend two weeks in London with yeshivah-mates from Chevron.

On Chaim Dovid's first Friday in London, he learned that R' Sholom Schwadron would be speaking that night in a *shul* in Stamford Hill. Knowing R' Sholom from his *drashos* in Jerusalem and as the *baal tefillah* for the *Yamim Noraim* (High Holy Days) in the Chevron Yeshivah, my cousin decided to attend the *drashah* that Friday night.

At the *drashah*, R' Sholom spoke about the weekly *sidrah*, *Vayigash*, and told of another son in another era who was on his way to meet his father.

> Joseph was preparing to greet Jacob, whom he had not seen in twenty-two years. We can barely imagine the longing they both felt as they moved closer to the rendezvous. In describing their first meeting in over two decades, Rashi observes, "יוֹסֵף נִרְאָה אֶל אָבִיו — Joseph appeared before his father" (*Bereishis* 46:29 s.v. וירא).
>
> Why does Rashi stress the obvious?
>
> My *rebbi*, R' Leib Chasman, explained that Rashi is revealing that Joseph's primary intent was not to gratify his enormous personal yearning to see Jacob again. Rather, his wish was to give Jacob the ecstasy of seeing his long-lost son. His first concern was כִּבּוּד אָב, *honoring his father*, providing Jacob with the happiness of seeing the child he thought was no longer alive. This is what Rashi meant by the seemingly obvious "Joseph appeared before his father."

My cousin sat awestruck. It was as if R' Sholom was addressing only him. His parents too, longed to see him after two years of separation. They could not have been thrilled with his London detour. He reacted to the *drashah*. Sunday morning he took the first flight out to America, "to appear before his parents".

At a small gathering in our home in Chaim Dovid's honor, my

father asked him, "We weren't expecting you for two weeks. Why the sudden change?"

Chaim Dovid told us about the penetrating words of the *Maggid* of Jerusalem that had compelled him to act.

"If R' Schwadron ever comes to America," my father said softly, "I'd want to meet him and have him as a guest in our home."

Little did we realize the significance of my father's words.

◈§ *Travelers*

In the summer of 1964, my parents sent me to the Fifth *Knessia Gedolah* of Agudath Israel in Jerusalem. During my six-week stay, I became friendly with Rafael Brenner, of Chinuch Atzmai/Torah Schools for Israel. Before leaving for the United States, I told him, "If you are ever in America, please make sure to be with us for a Shabbos." That simple invitation led to my family's second encounter with the *Maggid* of Jerusalem.

Four months later, Rafi Brenner was in America and accepted the invitation. During the *Shabbos* meals he spoke of his work with Chinuch Atzmai. My father asked whether his work ever brought him into contact with R' Sholom Schwadron. "Of course I know him. In fact he will be coming to America this week, together with R' Yisrael Grossman of Jerusalem." Then Rafi added, "I don't know where they will be staying but I am certain that R' Menachem Porush of the Agudah has already made lodging arrangements for them."

❀ ❀ ❀

Immediately after Shabbos, my father began working feverishly to set up the guest room on the third floor. He installed a phone next to the bed, brought up a small empty bookcase, a desk, a chair — all for a man he had never met, wouldn't recognize, and wasn't even sure would stay in his home. Yet somehow, at the time it didn't seem unusual, just exciting.

The excitement in the house mounted as though my father was preparing for a long-lost friend.

On Tuesday afternoon, my father, grandfather, two brothers and I went to the airport to greet R' Schwadron. The first thing on R' Sholom's mind was to *daven Minchah* before it was too late. We were the first Jews he met and, after a quick hello, he asked if there was still time to *daven.* Assured that there was, he promptly took a compass from his pocket to determine which direction was east, and prayed, oblivious to the din of the world's busiest airport behind him. He had not yet spoken twenty words and already we were enamored of him.

True to his word, Rafi was at the airport and we found him in animated conversation with Rabbi Porush. We learned later that the lodgings arranged for R' Sholom had become unavailable at the last moment. Rafi explained that we had offered our home to R' Sholom, and assured Rabbi Porush, "I was just there this past *Shabbos!* It will be fine."

On the short ride home from the airport my father told R' Sholom, "Undoubtedly you have many customs and standards. Let me assure you that we will not inconvenience you in any way. To the contrary, our home is yours, and we are here to serve you."

Adjusting to America

After R' Sholom settled in his room, he came downstairs and said to my father, "R' Avrohom, I have traveled to many places but never have I had a delegation greet me as your family did today. We are not related. We don't know one another. Why have you gone to all this trouble?"

"We have never met," replied my father, "but I know you very well." He played a tape of one of R' Sholom's Jerusalem *drashos,* and explained, "My nephew, Chaim Dovid Ackerman, brought me that tape. He has told us much about you. I have learned some of your *sefarim.* I *do* know you, I just haven't met you until today. Now that we've met, I want this house to be your home whenever you are in America."

And it was.

But R' Sholom insisted that he would remain in our home only on the condition that he be allowed to pay rent. At first my father wouldn't hear of it, but R' Sholom insisted he would move out. My father had no choice, and reluctantly agreed.

Recently, R' Sholom told me, "Your father made his calculations and presented me with a figure that seemed quite high. I knew there was nowhere else where I would feel so comfortable, so I just accepted it."

After several days, R' Yisrael Grossman (who had first stayed with relatives) joined R' Sholom in our home. When he first came, R' Sholom said, "Come, I will show you something." He led R' Yisrael into a large room that my father had added to the house. The walls were lined with shelves of *sefarim*. "This room was built as a private *beis midrash*", R' Sholom said. "Here R' Avrohom Zelig learns Torah himself and with his children."

R' Yisrael looked around with delight. "A room just to learn in?" he remarked. "In America there is such a *Yid? Nu Nu,* I think I'll stay."

I was studying tractate *Kesubos* at the time, and many a night I would come home to find a *shiur* that R' Yisrael had recorded for me that afternoon in this very room that he came to love.

Night after night we sat around the dining-room table listening to R' Sholom and R' Yisrael exchanging stories about the *tzaddikim,* explaining *Midrashim,* citing teachings of the Sages and giving their perspectives on the issues of the day. Always a tape recorder was on the table, salvaging their every word and thought. We watched, observed and learned much from the two Torah sages whom we grew to admire and love.

R' Yisrael stayed for three months, R' Sholom for five, and an intense bond of friendship and admiration was formed between my father and the two *rabbonim.* Indeed the three families remain close to this very day.

A few days after Pesach, 1965, R' Sholom announced that he would be going home, explaining that he would go home by boat, to "thaw out" slowly from the *galus* of America to the sanctity of *Eretz Yisrael.* Our whole family, together with our *rav,* R' Yaakov Teitelbaum (1899-1968), accompanied R' Sholom to his boat.

In the privacy of R' Sholom's cabin, my father handed him a large envelope. "This is your rent money of the last five months." Before R' Sholom could utter a startled word, my father continued, "I never even *considered* that I would take a penny for your being at our home. If anything, we should have been paying you and R' Yisrael. These are the exact bills you gave me. I never used them, they went straight into this envelope."

R' Sholom was taken aback by this sudden revelation. "Tell me," he laughed, "if this was your intent all along, why did you quote such a high price for the rent?"

My father smiled and said, "I wanted you to feel as free as possible in our home. If you felt you weren't paying enough, you might have hesitated to take advantage of the phones, the electricity, and the food. But if you were paying a good price, you would feel free to do as you pleased."

With tears in their eyes, the two men embraced as they bid each other farewell.

◆§ *Rendezvous*

A few days later, my father began talking about how he missed his treasured guests. Suddenly it occurred to him, that if he would fly to *Eretz Yisrael* within a few days, he would be able to greet R' Sholom at the port in Haifa. The idea sounded implausible, yet it excited us so much that we put it into action immediately. In a frantic rush, my parents got passports, booked a flight and arrived in *Eretz Yisrael* two days before R' Sholom's boat. At the Lod Airport my parents were met by my cousin Chaim Dovid Ackerman, who had returned to Chevron to continue his studies.

After a joyful introduction to R' Sholom's family in Jerusalem, my parents, Chaim Dovid, and a number of the Schwadrons traveled to Haifa to greet R' Sholom. A spirited and lively group, the Schwadrons anticipated with relish the excitement and warmth with which R' Sholom would greet my parents. My father, however, did not want to interfere with the family reunion. With typical sensitivity, he said that he and my mother would wait out of sight until after the family had greeted R' Sholom.

After a separation of nearly half a year, the Schwadron family's reunion was very warm and emotional, but after several minutes,

Rebbetzin Schwadron said to her husband, "There are some people over there to see you." R' Sholom was flabbergasted when he saw my parents. He spread out his arms and his eyes widened with disbelief, as he exclaimed with unabashed gusto "הוֹדוּ לַה׳ כִּי טוֹב כִּי לְעוֹלָם חַסְדּוֹ — Give thanks to Hashem, for He is good, His kindness endures forever." And the two men embraced. That moment remains etched forever in the memories of those who witnessed it.

For the next ten days, the Schwadrons and Grossmans could not do enough for my parents. When the time came to bid farewell, none of them knew that this was the last time that my father would see his two treasured friends, for shortly after his return to America he learned that he had a fatal illness. For a year we lived with the terror of the inevitable. And then there was darkness ...

Together with my mother we struggled to overcome the obstacles of each new day and, with a mere semblance of normalcy, life went on.

Six months later, we received a letter from R' Sholom saying that he was planning to come to America again. Could he stay at our home?

People shattered by the death of a beloved family member, especially a relatively young one, feel not only grief, but also humiliation (real or imagined), a loss of pride and a partial loss of self.

With the knowledge that R' Sholom was coming, we felt an emergence of pride and confidence again. Our home would be a place of significance, activity and pleasurable excitement once more. We answered that we would be overjoyed to serve once again as his hosts.

He would be arriving by ship, and we counted the days to his arrival.

The morning of his arrival none of us went to school. We all went to the pier with our mother to greet him, to regain a link with the recent past.

Perhaps we were too young to comprehend the concept of us "appearing before him." After six months of bereavement, we looked to him for consolation. What would he say? What *could* he say?

After waiting a long while, we recognized him among the mass of people leaving the ship, walking slowly, cane over his wrist, and carrying his valise. My two brothers and I started running towards him. In the distance, he saw us, and stopped in his tracks.

He resumed walking at a slower pace, moving forward slowly, his head down. We waited for my mother, and then together walked quietly towards him. When he saw her, the widow of his friend, and mother of seven orphaned children, he nodded his head in greeting, shook his head to and fro, sat down on a bench — and wept.

Tearfully we inched closer to him and after a long few moments, he looked up, tried to say something and motioned helplessly that he could not talk. The man of a million words had none. The tears on his saddened face spoke instead, and his silence touched us. He knew our pain and he shared it. There could be no greater consolation.

His visit was therapeutic. His presence and encouragement gave us strength and direction throughout the next few months, through the bleakest period in our lives. Indeed the course of our lives has been changed by the foresight that my father had in bringing R' Sholom and R' Yisrael to our home twenty years ago.

May the good that comes from this *sefer* be a blessing to the memory of my father, R' Avrohom Zelig ben R' Chanoch Henoch Krohn ז״ל; and may it bring strength to, יבדל לחיים טובים, R' Sholom to continue in his sacred work of inspiring people and bringing them closer to Hashem.

Part A: Care and Concern

☙ The Tenth Man

One Friday night, after R' Sholom had spoken on the topic of "calculating the eternal reward one might lose by failing to do a *mitzvah*" (see *Avos* 2:1), a gentleman came over to him and said, "I have an outstanding story on the topic you were discussing tonight."

A crowd quickly gathered around and the man began his tale. R' Sholom and the others stood and listened, spellbound.

The Mensheviks in Russia took over the government after the first World War. For the first time in decades the Jews enjoyed freedom. Everyone was happy; people were making money, especially those Jews who were fortunate enough to be in the diamond and jewelry business. I, myself, was in diamonds and things were going very well indeed.

Every morning I was at my office in the diamond exchange at eight o'clock, and I was busy all day. One morning I happened to get up early and decided to go to my office to get some paper work done. I had my valise of diamonds and jewelry with me as usual. As I was walking, I heard someone yell out, "A *tzenter*, a *tzenter!*" I turned and saw a man standing outside the small doorway of a tiny synagogue. He was looking for a tenth man to complete a *minyan* (quorum of ten males over thirteen). When he saw me turn towards him, he shouted to me, "Come in, come in, we need you for a *minyan!*"

Realizing that I had some time to spare, I went in to be the tenth man. But, when I got inside, I saw that there were only three other men besides myself and the man at the door, who by now had resumed his searching for a *"tzenter."*

"What's this?" I said . "I'm not the tenth, I'm the fifth! It'll take all morning to get ten men in here!"

"Now don't worry!" he called back. "Lots of Jewish people walk these streets every morning. We'll have a tenth man in no time."

Frustrated that he had trapped me, I began reciting *Tehillim* (Psalms) for the next ten minutes. By that time all he had managed to find was one more person. I began to leave, but he started pleading with me. "Listen, it's my father's *yahrzeit;* I have to say *Kaddish.* Please stay. I'm trying to get the *minyan* together as fast as I can."

"I can't stay any longer," I protested. "I must be in my office at eight o'clock. And that's right now!"

At that point the man became nasty. "Listen," he said, "I'm not letting you out! I have *yahrzeit;* I have to say *Kaddish!* As soon as I get ten men together, we'll get it over with and you'll be able to go."

I didn't want to agitate him any more, so I reluctantly went back to saying some *Tehillim.* Another ten minutes passed and he had corralled only two more men. I began making my way towards the door again. This time he turned around from the doorway just as I was making my way past him. He pointed a finger at me. "Now listen here, if *you* were the one who had *yahrzeit* for *your* father, then *you* would want *me* to stay! Right? And I would stay! Now I want you to do the same for me!"

His pointing out to me how I would feel if I were in his shoes suddenly made me feel different about the situation. I resigned myself to losing part of the morning and decided, come what may, I would remain. About 8:30 he finally got his ten people together. I thought he would say a *mishnah* and then *Kaddish.* But no, he started near the beginning of the *davening,* right after *Korbanos,* with the first *Kaddish D'Rabanan.* Impatient and exasperated, I looked at my watch and calculated at this rate I would not get to my office until well after nine o'clock.

A number of times I looked around to see if an eleventh man

had wandered in, so that I could leave and there would still be a *minyan*. No such luck. I was stuck there until they finished *davening*.

Once we finished, the man who had *yahrzeit* thanked all of us profusely, served some cake and whiskey and then let us leave.

I began making my way to the office, still carrying my valise full of jewelry. When I came within two blocks of my building, a man I knew ran over to me, frantically waving his hands.

"Quick, get away!" he yelled at me wildly. "The Bolsheviks took over the government today and some of them came in and killed the Jews in the diamond exchange. They're now busy looting as much as they can. Run for your life!"

I did run for my life. I remained hidden for a few days and eventually, as you can see, I was able to get out of Russia.

The storyteller looked around at his captivated audience in the Zichron Moshe *shul*. Then he added, "That was my reward for the *mitzvah* of being part of a *minyan*. You can well imagine what would have happened to me had I left the *minyan* early!"

The people who had gathered around waited for R' Sholom to make the statement that would crystallize everyone's thoughts. He paused a moment and then, in a voice that bounded off the rafters of the ancient synagogue, he exclaimed in his own inimitable way, "*Pilay ployim* (wonders of wonders)! *Hafleh vofelah* (miracle upon miracles)! *Noyroh noyro'oys* (awesome of awesome)!"

The children poured out of the *shul*, into the cool Jerusalem night. They danced and skipped down the streets and alleys, imitating R' Sholom's very special voice, "*Pilay ployim! Noyroh noyro'oys! Hafleh vofelah!*"

The Forgotten Loan

Quite often we judge an individual with the smug self-assurance that we know the "whole story." However, there are many instances and incidents that are not as obvious or as simple as they appear. Often a hurried judgment leads to embarrassing retractions and deeply hurt feelings. Consider the following episode.

The *Rashash* (R' Shmuel Shtrashun of Vilna 1819-1885) was known for his great Torah erudition and great wealth. He spent many hours immersed in Torah study (his commentary on virtually the entire Talmud is printed in most editions of the Talmud) and took off time from his role as merchant banker to administer a free-loan fund.

One day, a tailor named R' Zalman came to borrow money. He explained his desperate needs to the *Rashash*, who granted him a loan of three hundred rubles to be repaid in one year. The transaction was recorded in the *Rashash's* ledger.

One year later, to the day, R' Zalman appeared with the money at the home of the *Rashash*. Deeply involved in a *sugya* (talmudic discourse), the *Rashash* did not wish to be disturbed. R' Zalman, who knew that the loan was due that day, came into the room where the *Rashash* was learning, excused his interruption and returned the three hundred rubles.

Wishing to minimize the interruption, the *Rashash* took the money, and tucked it into the back cover flap of the volume he was using, with the intention of removing it later on. He continued with his studies and was deeply engrossed for the rest of the afternoon. When he finished, he returned each of his *sefarim* to its proper shelf, including the volume which now held the money tucked away in the cover flap.

A few weeks later at his office, the *Rashash* reviewed his ledger and saw that the loan to R' Zalman had not been crossed out and was apparently overdue. He summoned R' Zalman to inquire about the money.

Naturally, R' Zalman claimed that not only had he returned the loan but that he had returned it on the very day it had been due. Yet, there were no witnesses to the event, nothing had been recorded and the *Rashash* had no recollection of the matter. A discussion ensued and it was decided that both parties would go to a *din Torah* (rabbinic litigation) where the matter would be decided.

The news spread around the town like wildfire that the plain, simple tailor, R' Zalman, was involved in a *din Torah* with the revered *Rashash.* People were outraged that anyone had the audacity to contradict the scholarly and saintly *Rashash,* and the tarnishing of R' Zalman's character and reputation had begun.

The *beis din* (rabbinical tribunal) ruled that since there had once been a debt and it was now the word of one man against the other, R' Zalman would have to swear that he had indeed repaid the loan and then he would be absolved of further debt. The *Rashash* however did not want to take a chance of having a fellow Jew possibly swear falsely, and so he relented and dropped the case.

Anger and bitterness were cast upon the hapless tailor. People stopped doing business with him, and the tailor and his family became the objects of mockery and degradation. Soon, unable to cope with the constant abuse, R' Zalman gave up his business and moved to a hamlet out of town, a broken and sorrowful man.

A year later the Rashash once again was involved with the same subject as he had been studying on that fateful day. Once more, he pulled out the rare volume he had used then. As he leafed through the pages he noticed a large number of bills in the back flap. At first he was puzzled, but then it struck him! R' Zalman! This was the money that R' Zalman had claimed he had paid.

Immediately he sought R' Zalman to make amends. He went to R' Zalman's place of business and couldn't find him. He went to his old house and was told that he had moved.

The *Rashash* didn't rest until he found R' Zalman living in a dilapidated shanty in a desolate area far from the city. "Please forgive me," pleaded the *Rashash,* "I just found the money in the *sefer* and I realized that it was you who was right, not I."

"What good is forgiveness?" said R' Zalman bitterly. "My business is gone, my money is lost, I have nothing, I am the laughing stock of the community."

"Not only will I return your money," said the *Rashash,* "but I will go to every synagogue, and announce from the *bimah* (center platform) that it was my mistake and that people should restore their proper respect towards you."

"No," said R' Zalman sadly. "People will only say that the *Rashash* is a *tzaddik,* and it is his compassion that compels him to act in this manner. They will never believe that I was really right."

The *Rashash* was perplexed, for he understood human nature and knew that R' Zalman was right. People wouldn't believe him after such a long period of doubt and rebuke. The *Rashash* thought a moment about how to rectify the situation and then said, "I have a daughter ... now if I take your son as a son-in-law, which means that you would become my *mechutan* (relative through marriage), then no one would doubt that you are indeed a respectable man."

R' Zalman agreed to this proposal. The prospective bride and groom agreed as well, and a marriage was arranged between R' Zalman's son and the *Rashash's* daughter, and R' Zalman regained his former status in the community.

Although the story ends here, R' Sholom always adds an interesting insight. The Talmud *(Sotah* 2a) teaches: "*Forty days before a child is born a heavenly voice proclaims, 'The daughter of this person (will be married) to this one.'*" Therefore, it must have been decreed in Heaven that the daughter of the *Rashash* would be married to the son of this simple tailor. But under normal circumstances it wouldn't seem even remotely possible that the daughter of such a prominent person as the *Rashash* would marry the son of so simple a man.

Hashem made a whole sequence of events occur — the *Rashash* becoming very wealthy, lending the money to the simple tailor, forgetting about the return of the loan, the lapsed time, the obstinacy of the tailor — all for what? So that the *shidduch* that was proclaimed in Heaven so many years earlier should indeed come to fruition.

The Prized Possession

The following narrative points out once again the importance of not jumping to conclusions. More than that, however, it displays the concern and sensitivity of a rare individual for the feelings of a fellow human being. Allowing another person to enjoy "his moment in the sun" is an act of compassion equal to helping a man when he is down.

The intimate circle of friends of the *Ksav Sofer* (1815-1871; *Rav* of Pressburg) were among the elite of the Torah world. This distinguished group of rabbis and friends had gathered for a *seudas mitzvah* at which various rabbis addressed the assembled guests. When the *Ksav Sofer's* turn to speak came, he told his audience that he had with him a treasured possession that he was ready to reveal for the first time.

Everyone watched in awe as the *Ksav Sofer* took from his pocket an authentic *machatzis hashekel* (a half shekel coin) that was used in the time of the *Beis Hamikdash.* The coin was over two thousand years old!

The discussion soon changed to the various ancient laws regarding the *machatzis hashekel.* The coin was passed from hand to hand, each person examining, fingering and caressing it gently with a nostalgic longing to be in contact even for a moment with the glorious bygone era of Jewish history.

The evening wore on and after a while the *Ksav Sofer,* not having seen the coin for what suddenly seemed a very long time, asked that it be returned to him. He asked the people on his right, but they didn't have it. He asked the people on his left and they didn't have it either. Everyone began searching for it, and soon it became obvious that it was nowhere to be found. A stony silence fell on the room.

One of the rabbis present rose and said, "*Rabbosi* (honored rabbis), we simply cannot leave this room before this precious coin is found. Perhaps everyone should empty his pockets. Who knows, maybe someone inadvertently put the *machatzis hashekel* in his pocket with some of his other coins."

A nervous stillness pervaded the room. No one was ready to accuse any of the distinguished guests of theft — nonetheless, the coin had to be somewhere.

Among the distinguished rabbis around the table sat an elderly *rav,* R' Yehudah Asad (1794-1866; *Rav* of Aszód, Hungary), who was a good bit older than the others present. He became very pale and slowly rose from his seat, as all eyes turned to him. "Honored rabbis," he began, "It is true, the suggestion of checking everyone is a good idea, but I must ask you that we wait before we check any pockets or take any action. Let us wait twenty minutes." The eyes that had turned to him with respect now betrayed surprise. He caught the others' reaction and calmly added, "I cannot explain just yet, but please be patient, wait just twenty minutes."

In deference to his seniority they agreed. It was the last thing they had expected him to say, but they had no choice but to abide by his wishes.

The time passed with quiet conversation and speculation as to why R' Yehudah had made such an unusual request. As the twenty minutes came to an end, the saintly R' Yehudah got up again and addressed the now apprehensive guests. "I beg your indulgence. Perhaps you consider this strange, maybe you even suspect me of taking the coin, but please let us wait just ten more minutes. I beg you. I will not ask for any more time."

The rabbis and guests were perplexed and impatient. Not only was it late, but they wished to resolve the matter. Yet, once again, because of their respect for R' Yehudah, they agreed to wait ten more minutes.

Time passed slowly but after just a few minutes, the door of the room swung open and in ran the waiter wildly shouting that he had found the *machatzis hashekel* among the dishes and silverware while he was cleaning the kitchen. Obviously the coin had been placed momentarily on the table and was swept off by mistake with the soiled dishes and silverware. Laughter and joy erupted, as everyone thanked the heroic waiter profusely. The *Ksav Sofer* was ecstatic as he beamed in relief.

In the bedlam, someone went over to R' Yehudah, and soon a crowd gathered around him. "How did you know?" someone asked. "What was your reason for waiting?"

R' Yehudah smiled softly and said in an apologetic voice, "My friends, it was surely not my intention to reveal to you what I now must, but under the circumstances I know you will understand." And from his pocket he took out an authentic *machatzis hashekel.*

After the collective gasps had subsided he continued, "As you see, I too have a *machatzis hashekel* of my own. However, when I saw the joy that the Pressburger *Rav* had in displaying his *machatzis hashekel,* I didn't want to show my own, for that might, Heaven forbid, diminish the pleasure he had felt in possessing such a coin. However, once the coin was missing and the suggestion was made that everyone empty his pockets, my own *machatzis hashekel* would have been found, and it would have been almost impossible to try and explain that I had one before I came here. Thus, I asked for the delay and prayed that somehow the lost one would be found and that Hashem would spare me the agony and embarrassment of trying to explain something that would be so difficult to believe."

◆§ *Seventeen Soldiers ... Lives on the Line*

During the First World War, a Russian army camp was stationed outside the city of Stutchin, Poland. In Stutchin, the atmosphere was tense as hundreds of people fled, fearing that their city would be overrun. The yeshivah *bochurim* in the local yeshivah, led by R' Leib (Stutchiner) Chasman, the future *mashgiach* of the Chevron Yeshivah in *Eretz Yisrael,* had all returned to their homes and the yeshivah was closed. The only *bochurim* around were those who lived in Stutchin.

It was *erev Yom Kippur* and one of the Stutchiner boys, fifteen-year-old Chezkel* was walking in the street. Suddenly a soldier approached him. "You look like a yeshivah *bochur,*" the soldier whispered in Yiddish. "I need someone I can trust."

"What do you want from me?" asked the startled Chezkel.

"Listen, please," said the soldier, whispering quickly as he took Chezkel aside, out of earshot of any passerby.

"A number of my Jewish friends and myself have been forcibly inducted into the Russian army. The officers forbid us from performing any *mitzvos,* do not allow us kosher food, and will do anything to tear us away from Judaism. We are stationed in the army camp outside of Stutchin. We just heard that tomorrow our whole battalion will be on the move. We'll be leaving early in the

* At the family's request, the name has been fictionalized. See the story "Yitzchak the Shikker" in this volume.

morning. The security in the camp right now is very lax because they are preoccupied with other things. We think that now is the time for us to escape. But we need two things. We need a place to stay overnight until the battalion leaves, and we need seventeen sets of civilian clothes. We must be able to change into civilian clothes so that we won't be recognized after the other soldiers are gone. If we can only hide tonight, then tomorrow, after the battalion has left, each of us will be free to return home. Today it would be all but impossible for a soldier to get on a train without arousing suspicion."

Chezkel, who was sharp of mind and swift of foot, realized that this was a situation of *pidyon shevuyim* (redemption of the captured) that had to be acted upon at once. Yom Kippur was approaching and there was much to do. After a quick discussion concerning information and tactics, he agreed to help the seventeen Jewish soldiers in any way he could. Chezkel and the soldier shook hands warmly.

It was decided between them that the seventeen soldiers would come that evening, one by one, under the cover of darkness to avoid arousing attention. They would all gather at the *Halvoyas Hames Shul,* and hide in the *ezras nashim* (women's section).

The *Halvoyas Hames Shul* was hardly ever used except for funerals. It was located just outside the city limits on the way to the cemetery. Those attending a funeral would gather there and listen to the eulogies. From the *shul,* they would accompany the deceased to his final resting place — thus the name *Halvoyas Hames,* which means accompanying the deceased.

Other than for funerals, the only time the *shul* was used was on an accasional Thursday night when a group of yeshivah *bochurim* would hold an all-night study session there.

Chezkel's first task was to locate clothing for each of the soldiers, who came in various shapes and sizes. Acting as quickly as he could, he borrowed pants and shoes from this friend, shirts from another and hats from a third. All afternoon he raced from place to place, picking up as many pieces of clothing as he could and bringing them up to the decrepit, dust-filled balcony of the *ezras nashim,* where no one had been for years. There, he piled the clothes on a large bench.

He spent the entire afternoon trying to get clothes for those seventeen soldiers. He could not stop, so desperate was his urge to fulfill his self-imposed obligation. There was no time to eat anything, and when the time for the *seudas hamafsekes* (final meal before the fast) came and went, Chezkel still had not eaten a thing. He was already hungry even before *Yom Kippur* had begun.

A few of the soldiers were able to get away in the afternoon and filter into the *shul*, where they changed into the civilian clothes that Chezkel had provided, and tried to make themselves comfortable for the perilous overnight stay. The others arrived after nightfall. Chezkel hoped that the boys would all get there soon so that he could return to his own *shul* before *Maariv* was over. But it took a while until they all came. Sixteen were in the *shul* and the seventeenth, a Stutchiner boy, decided that he would try and make it to his home instead.

Now all who were going to come had come and changed their clothes. They were afraid to light candles before evening, lest they be detected, so they milled around in almost total darkness. Only the eerie light from the moon sifted in through the open windows.

Chezkel got up to bid the boys goodbye, and wish them luck on their escape the next day, but they would not let him leave. "You are the only one from Stutchin," they pleaded with him. "If, Heaven forbid, we have to escape during the night, you are the only one who knows the area. Please stay with us."

The boys may have been soldiers, but they were afraid to be left alone. Chezkel was their only link with safety. He could not refuse them.

And so they sat. The boys coughed sporadically from the stench and dust that had accumulated over the years. Together they tried to *daven* whatever they remembered by heart. Murmuring softly, they tried *Kol Nidre*, then whatever they could remember of the remainder of the *Maariv* service of *Yom Kippur*. Eventually most of them dozed off.

An hour later, the still of the night was pierced by the voices of a screaming woman and other people. Then more yelling and shouting. Each cry was like a stab of pain. The boys shivered with fear and lay motionless, frozen by the terrifying fact that the sounds were getting closer.

As a Stutchiner, Chezkel was the most logical one to be chosen to go downstairs and try to find out what was going on. From his vantage point at the doorway of the *shul,* he could see a family in the distance, following two soldiers dragging a young boy with them. It was the family of the seventeenth boy.

He had been spotted and followed into the city. While he was hiding in the cellar of his home, soldiers were alerted and stormed his home. They found him and threatened to shoot him for desertion. His mother's pleas went unheeded as the soldiers yelled back at her that they would kill her too, if she and her family did not stop following them.

Chezkel was frightened. If the authorities knew that one soldier was missing, they would surely check to see if any others had escaped as well. He had been trying to save some boys and do a *mitzvah,* and now the whole city of Stutchin was in mortal danger, for if it was discovered that deserters were being protected and hidden by the people of Stutchin, the city would be burned and its people killed. He was so terror stricken that he wished he could die that very moment, rather than face the horror that could conceivably lay ahead. He staggered up the steps to the balcony and reported what he had seen.

Surely they were in more danger now than they had been before. Certainly they could not take the chance of running away, but it was absolutely imperative to get rid of the army uniforms just in case they were caught. But how? Where?

Chezkel remembered a custom that some people in Stutchin followed as a *segulah* (omen) for *arichas yamim* (long life). It was to purchase a *kever* (burial plot) and leave it open. He remembered that he had seen numerous open plots in the cemetery which was not far away. He could take the sixteen army uniforms and toss them into the open graves, but it would take more than one trip. For not only were the Russian army uniforms bulky and heavy, but there were so many of them. But he understood that he really had no choice but to dispose of them. He bunched up as many as he thought he could carry and slowly made his way down the stairs and into the night in search of an open grave. It wasn't long before he found one, for the cemetery was set up so that the new graves were all in one area.

He dumped his burden into the first open grave he found and returned for a second batch. He saw that there was no way he could manage the rest in one trip; he would have to make a third one. Reluctantly, he went out again, dropped the uniforms into the grave, returned and immediately set out again, carrying the last of the uniforms. He quickly shoved all the clothes into the grave and began his trip back to the *shul.* He walked quickly, thrilled that he had accomplished what he had thought would be impossible. No one had seen him. The rest of the night would be easy compared to his burial work. Suddenly he heard hoofbeats. It had to be the Cossacks.

Chezkel feared that he would be seen. His heart sank and fright paralyzed him, stopping him in his tracks. He didn't actually see anyone, but he could see flashing lights that were definitely being carried by soldiers on horses.

He thought to himself, "It is *Yom Kippur,* the holiest day of the year. I am not yet twenty years old and thus not a *bar onshin* (one considered mature enough to be punished by the Heavenly Tribunal). If I have to die, *Yom Kippur* is the best day to go. I'm ready."

If he was going to die, though, he wanted to say *viduy* (confession) first. He didn't think he had been seen, but he couldn't take a chance. In the cemetery he was as good as dead. Off to the side there was a forest. Swiftly and as quietly as he could, he ran to the nearby trees and stood quietly among them as he started to say *Viduy.*

"*Modeh Ani* (I acknowledge before You, Hashem) ... *Misasi beyadecha* (My death is in Your hands) ..." Suddenly he heard a yell in Russian, "*Stoy!*" (stop). He fell down and lay under some shrubbery next to a tree. "*Tehay misasi kaparah* (May my death be an atonement) ..." Again the piercing scream of "*Stoy!*"

Chezkel was determined he was going to finish his *Viduy.* "*Vezakaini ... Leolam Haba* (And privilege me to the World to Come) ..." And then the shooting started. Chezkel continued, "*Ashamnu ... bagadnu* (We have become guilty, we have betrayed) ..." A barrage of bullets flew screaming into the night, smacking branches, whistling by his head, landing near him, for a full five minutes. Miraculously, not one hit him. He could tell by the gunfire that he was completely surrounded. When the shooting stopped, the soldiers branched off into groups of two and started their search, shining their flashlights in all directions with the beams reflecting eerily against the trees and grass.

The footsteps came closer, and then, Chezkel thought his heart would burst as two soldiers flashed a light in his face. He was ready to be shot. He would die while performing his *mitzvah*. It was the best way to go. But the soldiers didn't shoot him. "Get up!" they barked in Russian. "Follow us!" and he was marched out of the forest to the Commandant, who was sitting on a big horse, with a look that froze the blood.

"You spy!" he screamed at Chezkel. "You dirty scoundrel! You pig of the earth!" he cursed, among other expletives. "What in the world are you doing out here? I'm going to kill you right here and now!"

Chezkel knew his end was near, but he decided to try to postpone it. He remembered the Talmudic teaching that "No one lies concerning something that can be openly revealed" *(Yevamos* 93b), and he decided to approach his desperate situation from that angle.

"Your honor," he said to the Commandant, in the little Russian that he knew, "I am in your hands. Why not listen to what I have to tell you? I am not a spy, nor a bandit. I was here for a reason." Again the Commandant started reviling him with Russian curses. After he had subsided, Chezkel said quietly, "Look, I can take you to where I was going. Let me tell you what happened."

"Okay" yelled the Commandant, "but if you are not telling me the truth I will cut you into little pieces."

Chezkel continued, "Tonight is the holiest night of the year, it is *Yom Kippur*. I would not lie about it, it's easy enough for you to check. Tonight a young boy died. He was an only child and when his mother saw her dead son, she fell on him wailing and carrying on so terribly that people thought she herself would die from the agony and the tragedy of the death of her only son. It is our holiest day and no one would take him and bury him. I had compassion for the mother, so I took the child from her and told the family that I would bury him. And that is where I was going, to bury this young boy and try to save the mother even more grief. You can come with me to his grave."

"Fine. Let's go and see," said the Commandant. They started walking in the direction Chezkel pointed out, Chezkel in front of the horse, walking calmly, with the Commandant right behind him, high on his horse. "Stop!" The Commandant pulled alongside Chezkel. He took out his flashlight and shone it in the boy's eyes. Then he took his sword from its sheath and shone the light on the tip of the sword, "You see this point. I will thrust it into you to cut you to pieces if you are lying."

Chezkel looked at the Commandant calmly; he was resigned to his fate. He shaded his eyes from the glare of the light and said softly, "Come with me, I will show you where the body lies."

They walked another twenty meters in silence. Suddenly the Commandant pulled up alongside Chezkel once again and stared at him. "You know, young boy, you're a *maladyetz* (a courageous person, a good soldier). I too have a mother and she too sits home and cries for the welfare of her son. If you had the courage to take a dead child, to spare a crying mother more agony, then you are a *maladyetz*." He blew his whistle and at once two soldiers came to him.

Chezkel was lifted up onto a horse and in two minutes he was back in the city of Stutchin. He ran back home and that Yom Kippur morning at seven o'clock everyone heard the bugles that indicated that the Russian troops were on the march.

By nine o'clock, the camp was cleared and shortly afterwards, Chezkel ran back to the *Halvoyas Hames Shul* where he was embraced by the sixteen soldiers who had feared the worst. Together they ran off to *shuls* where they spent the rest of the day in grateful prayer. That night all sixteen soldiers went back to their homes, safe and sound, all because of the epic heroism of a fifteen-year-old *maladyetz!*

◆§ *Secret Schemes*

The Mishnah (*Avos* 4:1) describes the man of true power as one who has complete control over his personal inclinations.

For example, the power to contain the ravishing hunger for revenge is a sign of character that befits a man of real strength. Although the Torah demands this dimension of behavior in all of us (see *Leviticus* 19:18), it is the rare person who can rise to these heights especially in times of stress.

This incident tells how R' Chizkiyahu Medini (1835-1908), a Sephardic Torah great, rose to the level of supreme self-control and the reward bestowed upon him because of it. Later in his life he was known as the *S'dei Chemed,* the name of his brilliant, monumental, multi-volumed compendium on countless Talmudic and halachic topics.

This story was related by R' Yosef Rotman, a brother-in-law of R' Elya Lopian, a noted *talmid chacham* who would often travel to Chevron to engage in Talmudic discussions with the *S'dei Chemed.*

One afternoon R' Yosef knocked on the open door of the *S'dei Chemed's* room. There was no reply. Obviously, the *S'dei Chemed* was deeply involved in a *sugya* (Torah topic) and didn't hear the knock. R' Yosef stood at the open door, quietly observing the *S'dei Chemed.* Suddenly the *S'dei Chemed* smiled to himself, and then he looked up and noticed R' Yosef.

"Oh, I apologize. I didn't realize you were here or I would have greeted you properly," the *S'dei Chemed* said. He thought for a moment then added, "Because I made you wait at the door let me make it up to you by telling you a story. You may have noticed that I was smiling to myself. Well, it's because I remembered an incident that happened a long time ago."

This is the story the *S'dei Chemed* told R' Yosef.

❀ ❀ ❀

Shortly after he was married, R' Chizkiyahu was accepted into an exclusive *kollel* (yeshivah for advanced studies, the student body consisting of married men). A wealthy philanthropist, R' Zorach, had undertaken to support most handsomely a select group of exemplary Torah scholars. He provided them with funds so that they could study Torah in comfort, with the assurance that they and their families would be cared for. All the scholars learned together in the same *beis midrash* (synagogue/study hall).

A young man who lived in the neighborhood of the *kollel* had a deep hatred for those who studied Torah. He was a vicious man of evil intent and so he devised a malicious scheme to humiliate and disgrace the most prominent scholar of the group, R' Chizkiyahu.

The wealthy philanthropist, R' Zorach, had a maid who did his household chores. As part of her duties she was required to tidy up the synagogue where the *kollel* studied. She cleaned up very early in the morning, before anyone was due to arrive, so as not to disrupt the men's learning. Only R' Chizkiyahu, who seemed to be learning all the time, was in the synagogue when the maid arrived.

The malicious schemer planned that one morning, as men entered the synagogue for *Shacharis* (morning) prayers, the maid would run out screaming that she'd been physically abused by R' Chizkiyahu. For this shameful hoax she was promised a goodly sum of money by the devious schemer.

On the chosen morning, as they had arranged, the maid came shrieking out of the synagogue much to the surprise and shock of the people about to enter. She claimed that while no one else was around, she was abused by the "vulgar" *kollel* student now sitting by himself in the synagogue.

A commotion started, and as she continued her tirade the young schemer began shouting that R' Chizkiyahu should be thrown out of the *kollel* for not only was he a disgrace to the *kollel*, but to the community as well. He further demanded that R' Chizkiyahu be expelled immediately and never be allowed to come back. People joined the battle cry and soon there was a mob marching to the home of R' Zorach to let him know what had transpired.

R' Zorach was not home, but his wife assured the group that he would come to the synagogue as soon as he could. When R' Zorach came home, he was told of the morning's events and he rushed over to the *kollel*. When he arrived he found no evidence of the earlier uproar; the students were learning diligently. He quietly walked up to the *bimah* (central platform) and looked around without saying a word.

For half an hour he observed R' Chizkiyahu sitting and

studying peacefully, totally oblivious to anything else but his learning. By now a small crowd of townspeople had gathered, muttering to each other while they waited and wondered what R' Zorach would do. After a while R' Zorach announced, "The man R' Chizkiyahu is a holy human being. I don't for a moment believe one word of the maid's vicious accusation. He stays in the *kollel,* if he will so honor us, and from this moment onward, my maid is fired! And anyone who discusses this matter shall not put a foot into my *beis midrash."*

For days afterwards, it was all anyone thought about — but hardly spoke about openly. The maid was paid in secret for her role and it did seem unusual to many that within a week of the incident, the leader of the march to R' Zorach's house suddenly died. After a while things quieted down, and people resumed their normal routine, everyone having drawn his own conclusions about the event.

Although she no longer had a job, the maid lived well from the money she had been paid. In a few months, however, her money ran out and she needed a job. While she had worked for R' Zorach she had been well paid, but now she couldn't find employment. One early morning she came to the synagogue to talk to R' Chizkiyahu.

"I need your help," she pleaded. "I have no more money and I need a job. You know that what I said about you was a lie. I am truly sorry that I accused you falsely. In truth, I did it because I was offered a large sum of money by the young man who died shortly afterwards, and I couldn't resist the temptation. The money is gone now, and I'm willing to go to R' Zorach to admit the truth. But I need you to intervene for me to get my job back. I am ashamed to have to come to you for help, but I am desperate. Please help me."

R' Chizkiyahu was so shocked that he could hardly believe what he was hearing. With a clear mind he curbed his turbulent emotions and considered his options. On the one hand there had to be some people who believed that he was guilty of the crime he had been accused of. Thus it was a *chillul Hashem* (desecration of G-d's Name) for it to be known that a person learning in a *kollel* would behave in such an immoral manner. If he now revealed the maid's admission, that would certainly clear his name, but once again there would be a *chillul Hashem* for it to be known that one Jew could perpetrate such an act against another. And so, the *S'dei Chemed* thought, what would Hashem gain? Either way there was a desecration of His Name, so why do something that would only bring everlasting shame and humiliation for the dead young man who had planned the hoax?

Therefore, R' Chizkiyahu told the maid that he would try to help her but in a different way. He had a scheme of his own. He knew of another wealthy individual who might need a maid for his home. If he could convince this man to hire her, she could have a job and the whole malicious plan of the past would not have to be revealed. And so R' Chizkiyahu approached the affluent man and convinced him to hire the maid.

After he completed the story, the *S'dei Chemed* added, " ... and when I walked out of that man's home, after he had agreed to hire the maid, I felt as if my mind had opened wide and Hashem had rewarded me with knowledge of *kol haTorah kulah* — the entire Torah, all because I was concerned only with Hashem's honor, and not with my own.

◆§ *Charitable Judgment*

Charity is a noble *mitzvah* with which Jews have sustained each other for thousands of years. Can there be anything wrong with the act of giving charity? Yes! That's why there are many laws governing how to give and how not to give (see *Yoreh Deah* 249-251). In the following episode we learn that one must also use good judgment when fulfilling the *mitzvah* of charity.

G-d said in praise of Abraham, "... he will command his children to keep My ways of charity and judgment" (see *Genesis* 18:19). Charity and judgment should not be separate entities; on occasion they must be fused.

This incident took place in the eighteenth century, when the great R' Yonasan Eybeschuetz (also known as R' Yonasan

Prager, c.1690-1764; author of *Yaaros Devash* and *Urim V'Tumim)* was but recently married. In those days, when a young man exhibited brilliance as a Torah scholar, he was much sought after as a *chasan* even at an early age. R' Yonasan was married in his late teens to a young girl, whose wealthy father gave him three thousand *gulden* as a wedding present. The generous gift was meant to enable the outstanding scholar to study Torah undisturbed and realize his fullest potential.

The gentiles of R' Yonasan's town had very little tolerance for Jews and their customs. They decided to build a huge church right across the street from the synagogue that would overshadow and dwarf the Jews' place of worship and study. The Jews were enraged at having to face a church the moment they stepped out of their *shul,* but being a minority in both numbers and power, they resigned themselves to this plan. That is, all the Jews except Aryeh Leib, R' Yonasan's hot-headed, temperamental young *chavrusa* (study partner). While the church was being built, Aryeh Leib seethed with anger at the audacity of the church officials. The constant flow of priests and nuns who looked at the Jews with contempt evoked a terrible fury in him. He promised himself that someday he would avenge the insult.

R' Yonasan couldn't calm his hot-headed friend. Even R' Yonasan's insistence that any attempt at reprisal would jeopardize other Jews went unheeded. Aryeh Leib was adamant.

When the building was finally completed, ceremonies were held for the inauguration of the church, and services began. Many gentiles moved into the neighborhood to be closer to the new church, and Aryeh Leib decided that he'd had enough. Late one night he entered the church and climbed the winding stairs to the steeple top, where there was a huge cross. Equipped with a hammer and chisel, he managed to break off and shatter the cross. The noise woke up the resident priest, who raced up the stairs to investigate what had happened. Another priest joined him and when they caught sight of an "accursed Jew" in their church, they ran after him in hot pursuit. In his blind rush to get away from the scene of the crime, Aryeh Leib lost his way in the dimly lit halls of the church. The priests caught him and beat him mercilessly. They then decided to lock him up until the morning when they would decide how to deal with him further.

In the morning, at a conclave with other church officials, it was decided to burn Aryeh Leib at the stake for desecrating their church.

When Aryeh Leib did not appear for learning the next day, R' Yonasan was surprised but not particularly worried, but when he did not come the next day either, his friends began to worry.

On the second night, as R' Yonasan and a few others were learning in *shul,* they heard a knock on the door. It was the priest in charge of security at the church across the street. He knew that Jews are charitable, and had devised a plan that would net him a large amount of money.

He told the small group that if they would agree to give three thousand *gulden,* he would see to it that Aryeh Leib was set free, as long as he agreed to leave town forever.

The sum was a very large one, but *pidyon shevuyim* (redemption of the captured) is a great *mitzvah.* R' Yonasan and his friends reluctantly agreed to the priest's price. The priest's intention was to run off with the money as soon as he had freed Aryeh Leib. A date and time was set for the exchange; one Jew's priceless life for three thousand *gulden.*

That evening Yonasan went home and spent many long hours deep in thought. There was only a small chance that the Jews could raise such a large sum of money before Aryeh Leib would be killed. The priest might change his mind about the deal if the ransom was not paid on time. He decided that he would use the three thousand *gulden* that he had received from his father-in-law to redeem Aryeh Leib.

The next morning he went to the church and met with the priest. "I have the money," R' Yonasan told him, "but first let me see Aryeh Leib."

"How did you get the money so quickly?" asked the incredulous priest.

"It's my own money," said R' Yonasan. "My father-in-law gave it to me as a wedding gift, but I'm glad to give it up to save my friend." The priest could not help but be in awe at the selflessness of the young scholar. He brought Aryeh Leib to a back door. R' Yonasan embraced his friend and gave the priest the money. Aryeh Leib was set free and told to leave town immediately.

That evening a group of men came to the synagogue and told R' Yonasan that they had collected a large sum of money for the release of Aryeh Leib. R' Yonasan told them that it wasn't needed anymore because he had already paid the ransom and Aryeh Leib was safely out of town. The men tried to convince R' Yonasan to keep part of the money, but he refused. "But we too would like to share in the *mitzvah,*" they argued.

"Save the money for a future emergency," answered R' Yonasan, and he refused to take a single *gulden* of their funds.

R' Yonasan did not think his wife would understand why he had given away such a fortune. He was afraid to face her. Instead he told her that he had to leave town for a few days. He knew that she would find it difficult to understand how he had sacrificed their future for the sake of a young man who had been repeatedly warned about his rash behavior. During his absence he would figure out how to explain the whole affair to her.

Meanwhile, at the church, the other priests found out that Aryeh Leib was missing. They were infuriated and tried to find out how he had escaped. They confronted the priest in charge of security who claimed that he had found the cell open and the boy gone. The others didn't believe him, for he had not reported the escape to them. They unanimously decided to put the scheming priest to death, for they suspected that he might have arranged for ransom money which he kept for himself.

The priest overheard their conversation and the death sentence they had pronounced on him. Now he would have to escape before his colleagues would be able to execute their sentence. He quickly took R' Yonasan's money together with other money and jewelry that he had amassed over the years and made his way to R' Yonasan's house. There he told the young wife how her husband had given his own money to free his friend, and then said to her, "I have no one to trust. I must get away quickly. Here, you hold the money and my gold and silver items. If I come back, I know you will return everything to me. I never saw such integrity as your husband showed. I'm sure you are the same. If I don't come back, it's all yours."

Later that day the priest's body was found in the river, under the town's bridge.

Three days later R' Yonasan returned home, somewhat uneasy about the reception he would receive. To his pleasant surprise, his wife greeted him with smiles, praise and warmth. "What a *tzaddik* you are. I know the whole story. I'm proud of your willingness to fulfill the great *mitzvah* of *pidyon shevuyim*, even at such great cost to yourself! But look how wonderful Hashem has been to you. He has returned all your money and even given us a great fortune."

R' Yonasan couldn't believe what he was hearing. "What are you talking about? How do you know about the *mitzvah?*" His wife told him how the priest had had to flee for his life, how he'd given her the three thousand *gulden* plus other things, with instructions to hold everything until he returned. "He said that if he doesn't return, everything belongs to you. Today I found out that he'd drowned under the town bridge. Everything belongs to you, now," said R' Yonasan's wife.

R' Yonasan's face fell, and he began to cry. His wife understood that these weren't tears of joy. "Why are you so unhappy," she asked, "when the whole incident has ended so well? Aryeh Leib is saved, we have our money back ... " R' Yonasan couldn't be consoled. "G-d has thrown the *mitzvah* back in my face," he wept. "For some reason he doesn't want me to have my reward in the World to Come, where righteous people enjoy their true reward (see *Avos* 2:21). That is why He gave me my reward here and now."

For three days R' Yonasan fasted. After the third day he beseeched G-d to reveal to him in a dream why his *mitzvah* hadn't been accepted.

That night he was told the answer in a dream. Because he had refused to share the *mitzvah* of *pidyon shevuyim* with others and had kept it for himself, it was not acceptable. He should not have refused his friends' money.

By "giving" all the money on his own, R' Yonasan had been "taking" — that is taking the whole *mitzvah* for himself when others wanted a share in it.

He had not used proper judgment in fulfilling the *mitzvah*, and therefore Hashem rejected his seemingly selfless act of charity.

‹§ *The Strength of a Tzaddik*

It is said that when one of our *gedolei hador* (greatest Torah scholars of the generation), R' Moshe Feinstein (1895-1986), was breathing his last, he said weakly, "I have no more strength ..."

Aside from the great scope of his Torah knowledge, a *gadol hador* is one who bears the burdens of his nation, and who feels the pains and frustrations of its individual members. The strength that the beloved R' Moshe felt ebbing from him was not only his own personal vitality, but his ability to continue carrying the accumulated burdens of his people.

The following episode and its dramatic climax reveal the care and concern that a *gadol hador* has for an individual. The *gadol hador,* the *tzaddik,* knows that he is a conduit to Hashem, whose involvement on our behalf can deflect a harsh heavenly decree. Thus, when someone approaches a *tzaddik* for a blessing, and he acquiesces, it is not merely an external expression of good wishes but an internal absorption of the problem, adding weight to his enormous spiritual burden.

A student who had been diagnosed as having a life-threatening illness came before his *rebbi,* the famous *Chofetz Chaim* (R' Yisrael Meir HaKohen, 1838-1933) in Radin, to ask for a blessing. The physicians had already told the student and his family that they knew of no cure for his illness, and with each passing day those concerned with his welfare were losing hope.

The *Chofetz Chaim* listened to the young man and told him that he would give him advice, provided that he never revealed it to anyone. The student readily agreed. The *Chofetz Chaim* then instructed him to go to a certain *talmid chacham* who lived in a small town. "Tell him your situation and ask for a blessing," said the *Chofetz Chaim.* "He will give you a *brachah* and with G-d's help you will recover."

Immediately the young man did so, and in an incredibly short time he became well. He continued his studies at the yeshivah, eventually married, moved from Radin, raised a family and, as he had been instructed, never told anyone about these events.

More than twenty years later, long after his yeshivah days, the man's sister-in-law became ill with a mysterious illness. It soon became apparent to the man that she was suffering from the same illness with which he'd been ill so long ago, but he did not say anything. His wife, though, remembered that he had once spoken of a mysterious illness from which he had suffered many years ago. Every time she spoke about it, he became evasive and refused to talk about it. The more vague he tried to be, the more she pressed him in order to save her sister's life.

Soon, both wife and sister-in-law were pleading with him to reveal what had happened and how he had been cured. Daily and incessantly he told them that he was bound to secrecy, but they kept insisting.

Finally, his resistance was worn down, and he rationalized that after so many years, perhaps he had already fulfilled the *Chofetz Chaim's* admonition.

And so he told his wife what had happened. He revealed the facts of his appearance before the *Chofetz Chaim* and the *tzaddik's* advice to go to a certain *talmid chacham* in a small town, far away from Radin. His wife and sister-in-law became hopeful. Maybe this would be their salvation.

But a short time later the man himself began feeling ill. He became extremely frightened, for his worst fears were being realized. He told his wife that he had to travel to the *Chofetz Chaim* at once.

He made the long journey back to Radin and made his way to the *Chofetz Chaim* who was by then old and frail. The *Chofetz Chaim* remembered their old encounter and listened quietly to the man's story. Then he spoke slowly. "I wish I could help you, but what can I do? When you first had the illness I was young myself and I fasted forty days on your behalf so that you would be healed. Today I am already too old and I cannot fast like that anymore ..."

What is incredible here is not only that the *Chofetz Chaim* fasted forty days on behalf of one of his students, but that he used the subterfuge of telling the *bachur* to go to a *talmid chacham* in another town to get a blessing for himself so that when the student did indeed become well, the *Chofetz Chaim* would not get any credit for it.

◆§ *Salty Conversation*

R' Sholom heard the following story from R' Yaakov Kaminetzky (1892-1986).

The *Chofetz Chaim* and another *rav* once set out together on a three-day journey to do a *d'var mitzvah* (a matter of religious significance) in a town somewhere in Poland.

Along the way they stopped at an inn known for its high standards of *kashrus.* They were seated at a special table, for the woman who owned the restaurant recognized them to be prestigious rabbis.

She had them served promptly, and when they finished the meal she approached them and asked, "So, how did you like my food?"

"Very good," said the *Chofetz Chaim.* "It was excellent."

"And how did you like my food?" she asked the other rabbi. "Oh, it was quite good," he replied, "but it could have used more salt."

As the woman left, the *Chofetz Chaim* turned white. "I can't believe it!" he exclaimed. "All my life I have avoided speaking or listening to *lashon hara* (evil talk; or simply saying bad things about a person) and now Hashem made me come with you, and I have to suffer by hearing you speak *lashon hara!* I regret that I came here with you and I am convinced that the purpose of our trip is not a true *d'var mitzvah* after all. Otherwise this would not have happened to me."

Seeing the *Chofetz Chaim's* reaction, his companion became flustered and frightened. "What did I say that was so wrong?" he stammered. "I said that the food was good — I only added that it needed some salt!"

"You simply don't realize the power of words!" cried the

Chofetz Chaim. "Our hostess probably doesn't do her own cooking. Her cook could well be a poor widow who needs this job to support her family. Now, because of what you said, the owner will go back to the kitchen and complain to the cook that the food didn't have enough salt. In self defense the poor widow will deny it and will say, 'Of course I put enough salt in the food. I even tasted it before you served it.'

"The owner will then accuse her of lying and say, 'Do you think that the rabbis out there are liars? *You* are the one who is lying!' They will argue, strong words will lead to even stronger words and the owner will get so angry that she will fire the poor cook. The woman will then be out of a job. Look how many *aveiros* (sins) you caused: (1) You spoke *lashon hara;* (2) you caused the owner and myself to listen to *lashon hara;* (3) you caused the owner to repeat the *lashon hara* and that is the sin of *rechilus;* (4) you caused the cook to lie; (5) because of you the owner caused pain to a widow, and (6) you caused an argument, another Torah violation."

The rabbi smiled at the *Chofetz Chaim* and said softly and respectfully, "R' Yisrael Meir, please, you are exaggerating. You're carrying this just a bit too far. A few simple words cannot possibly have done all that."

"If that is what you think," replied the *Chofetz Chaim* as he stood up, "let's go to the kitchen and see for ourselves."

As they opened the door to the kitchen, they saw that the owner was indeed berating the cook as the poor woman stood wiping the tears from her eyes. When the rabbi saw what was happening he became pale and ran over to the cook, begged forgiveness and apologized profusely for any harm or distress he may have caused her. He pleaded with the owner to forgive and forget the incident and begged her to let the woman stay on the job. He even offered to pay her to keep the cook.

The innkeeper was really a kindly woman and she also wanted to fulfill the rabbi's request.

"Of course, of course," she said hastily. "I only wanted to impress on her the need to be more careful. She is really a fine cook and she will remain here at her job."

◆§ *The Maid's Music*

An extraordinary act of caring was once performed by the *gaon* R' Isser Zalman Meltzer (1870-1953), who was a *rosh yeshivah* for almost sixty years, first at the Yeshivah of Slutzk and then at Yeshivas Etz Chaim in Jerusalem. [He was the father-in-law of R' Aharon Kotler (1891-1962).]

One afternoon, as R' Isser Zalman was about to enter his home, he suddenly walked down the stairs and began strolling back and forth on the sidewalk in front of his home. His nephew, R' Dovid Finkel (1917-1957), who was quite often at his side, was puzzled that his uncle should be walking around aimlessly. He knew that R' Isser Zalman considered every moment precious.

"Uncle," he began, "why are you just walking around? Are you expecting to meet someone?"

"No, no," replied R' Isser Zalman, "I'll go into the house shortly."

R' Dovid knew that everything that R' Isser Zalman did had a distinct purpose and so he persisted with his questions. "Tell me, for what or whom are you waiting? Why haven't you gone into the house?"

Knowing that his nephew would not relent until he got an answer, R' Isser Zalman Meltzer said, "As I walked up the steps I realized that the maid who was cleaning the house was singing to herself as she worked. Now since a woman may not sing in front of a man [who is not of her immediate family], had I entered she would have been embarrassed and she would have immediately stopped her music. I did not want to either embarrass her or deny her the joy of her song, so I'm waiting until she finishes cleaning, then I'll go in."

◆§ *May You All be Blessed*

When R' Yitzchak Elchonon Spektor (1817-1896), the Kovner *Rav* and author of the classic responsa *Be'er Yitzchak*, passed away, he was mourned by all Russian and European Jewry. Thousands of Jews who had been touched by his kindness and affected by his halachic rulings were deeply saddened by his death.

There was one particular *rav* who was almost beside himself with grief, R' Elya Boruch Kamai (1840-1917), one of the *gaonim* of his generation and the *rav* in the city of Mir. Long after the eulogies for R' Yitzchak Elchonon were over, and the standard period of mourning had passed, R' Elya Boruch could be found walking aimlessly, in a daze of depression, repeating over and over again that he could not accept the loss of his friend and colleague, R' Yitzchok Elchonon.

R' Elya Boruch would retell countless anecdotes about R' Yitzchak Elchonon's warmth and personal concern for the honor and dignity of a fellow Jew, young and old alike. The following story was one that he particularly cherished.

Kovno, where R' Yitzchak Elchonon was *rav*, was under Russian rule. By law all young men were obliged to enlist in the army. Not only did army service involve the ever present threat of loss of life, but to maintain religious observance in the army was almost impossible. Many yeshivah boys therefore applied for exemption from army service.

One such applicant was a young student, Yaakov, who was much beloved by his *rebbi,* R' Yitzchak Elchonon. Each day the *rebbi* and Yaakov's friends waited impatiently to hear news of his army status.

One afternoon, R' Yitzchak Elchonon was engrossed in a *din Torah* (rabbinic litigation). With him on the *beis din* (rabbinic tribunal) was R' Elya Boruch Kamai. The two litigants involved were wealthy businessmen who were arguing bitterly over a huge sum of money. The atmosphere was tense. Neither side was willing to compromise, and for hours R' Yitzchak Elchonon, R' Kamai, and a third *rav* tried to resolve the controversy.

Suddenly, the door opened and a young man stuck his head into the room. When he saw R' Yitzchak Elchonon he excitedly addressed him, "*Rebbi,* we just got the news, Yaakov is exempt!" R' Yitzchak Elchonon breathed a sigh of relief and said with a radiant smile, "May G-d bless you for bringing this wonderful news. Thank you so much for telling me! May you have long years and good health. Thank you ever so much!" The boy left smiling, glad that he had made his *rebbi* so happy.

The rabbis resumed deliberations in an attempt to resolve the *din Torah.*

A few minutes later another student opened the door. Not knowing that his *rebbi* already knew the news, he first apologized for interrupting and then announced with joy, "*Rebbi,* we've gotten word that Yaakov is exempt!"

"Oh," replied R' Yitzchak Elchonon with just as much enthusiasm as he had the first time. "How wonderful! Thank you so much for coming to tell me. May Hashem bless you with years and good health. Thank you, thank you!" The boy closed the door and left, beaming with joy that he had made his *rebbi* so happy.

Five minutes later, yet a third boy entered the room. "*Rebbi,* did you hear? Yaakov is exempt!" Once again R' Yitzchak Elchonon smiled broadly and blessed the boy for the "wonderful news." He thanked him profusely for thinking of him and sharing the good news with him.

Six times, different boys came in with the same news, each one anticipating the happiness their *rebbi* would feel at the news, each one not aware that others had preceded him. R' Yitzchok Elchonon smiled at each boy, expressed his gratitude and made him feel as important as the first one.

In retelling this incident, R' Elya Boruch would sigh, "Where can we find another with such *ahavas Yisrael* (love of a fellow Jew)?"

☙ *The Telegram Told All*

When R' Isser Zalman Meltzer told the following story his eyes would fill with tears, for he was always deeply moved by the episode. He would shake his head in disbelief and say, "Imagine to what great lengths a person went to save another

Jew from embarrassment. The ingenuity involved was incredible!"

The episode to which he referred involved R' Yitzchak Elchonon Spektor, the beloved *rav* of Kovno, who was known for his great love and concern for fellow Jews.

In a small town far away from Kovno, a local *rav* had erred in a ruling he had made on a religious question posed to him. Though not everyone realized his mistake, two devious and mischievous individuals knew that their *rav* had blundered badly. He had forgotten that the very same situation on which he had ruled was discussed in the *Shach,* one of the primary commentaries of the *Shulchan Aruch* (Code of Jewish Law).

Seeking to humiliate their *rav,* the two miscreants sent a letter to R' Yitzchak Elchonon, in which they posed the same question. They knew that R' Yitzchak Elchonon's answer would be in accordance with the *Shach's* ruling as opposed to their *rav's* opinion. Once armed with R' Yitzchak Elchonon's letter of reply they would show it around to the community at large and this would shame and disgrace the *rav.*

When R' Yitzchak Elchonon received the letter, his first reaction was one of surprise. For although he had received queries from people in this particular town before, he remembered that he had never received any from either of these men. Why would they be writing now, he wondered, and why would they be sending a question with which any *rav,* including their local *rav,* would surely be familiar?

Therefore, he investigated and learned that these men were exceptionally argumentative and had a history of causing trouble in the community.

R' Yitzchak Elchonon suspected at once that the two men were contemplating a plot to embarrass their *rav,* and he sought to foil their plot. First he sent a letter to the two men with the wrong answer to the question, ruling exactly as their *rav* had ruled. Then, the very next day, he sent them a telegram which would arrive before the letter, saying that he had erred in his written ruling, and that they should disregard the letter with the wrong ruling that would soon be coming.

Thus the mischievous twosome would not be able to use either the letter or the telegram to defame their *rav*, for the letter agreed with the *rav* and the telegram clearly indicated that even the great and sainted R' Yitzchak Elchonon had erred in this matter — just as their *rav* had.

◆§ *A Sense of Justice*

One *Shabbos* afternoon, shortly after a noted *talmid chacham* (according to some sources of this story it was R' Yitzchak Ze'ev Soloveitchik, 1887-1959) had been appointed *Rav* of Brisk, in Lithuania, a police official appeared at his home. He informed the *Rav* that one of the Jews being held in the local jail had been sentenced to death and that as the new official clergyman for the Jews in Brisk, he was obliged to come and say confession with the man. He went on to explain that official rules dictated that every man, regardless of his religion, be given the opportunity to speak with a clergyman of his faith one last time before his execution.

The *Rav* told the officer that he was sorry but he could not comply nor go along with him. The officer was surprised by the refusal. "What do you mean you won't come?" snapped the officer. "Every clergyman always goes for the sake of the people of his faith. Why won't you go?"

The *Rav* explained. "You say that the law states that a man cannot be executed until he meets with his clergyman, thus, as long as I don't go he can't be put to death. I don't want to be a cause *(gorem)* in his death, for once I go, I have, in essence, removed the last barrier to his execution."

The officer was at first intrigued by the *Rav's* reasoning, but he soon became outraged. But the more he argued, the more he realized that it was an exercise in futility. The *Rav* wouldn't budge from his position, so the officer went back to his headquarters.

Word of the *Rav's* refusal quickly spread through the town and soon a crowd gathered at his home. They wondered if he wasn't putting the Jews of the town in jeopardy, because his refusal to cooperate with the authorities would only antagonize them and add to the hatred they already had for the Jews. Some even criticized him for a lack of compassion, noting that he was merely a young and inexperienced man himself.

Later, a police lieutenant and a few underlings arrived at the *Rav's* home. He came straight to the point. "I demand that you come with me at once," he ordered. "We have business to take care of and we can't be bothered with your nonsensical reasoning. You are to return with me immediately."

Not impressed by the lieutenant's bluster, the *Rav* explained calmly once again that according to his understanding, he could not go to say the confession, for as he had stated previously, he would not be even an indirect cause of a fellow Jew's death.

The lieutenant threatened to drag the rabbi to the jail and put him in the same cell with the prisoner. Shaken but firm, the *Rav* stood his ground and would not go. Some people tried to send the *shul shammash* (attendant) to take the *Rav's* place, but the lieutenant was adamant. He would settle for nothing less than the *Rav.*

When he came back to headquarters the lieutenant ordered that the death of the criminal be delayed until he received further instructions from higher authorities.

That night an envoy came from a higher court with an order stating that the Jewish "criminal" had been pardoned. Thus a man's life was saved only because the new Brisker *Rav* refused to have any part, no matter how slight or indirect, in bringing about the death of a fellow Jew.

☙ *Orchard for Sale*

He walks in perfect innocence and does what is right, he speaks truth from the heart and has no slander on his tongue, he does his friend no evil (Psalms 15:2).

These are among the admirable traits that King David extols as belonging to the most noble people in Israel. They are simple, elementary traits, the foundation of the ideal Jewish character.

Yet, as children grow into adolescence and then eventually into mature adults, many of these traits seem to disappear. With age, many people feel they have earned the right to bend the truth a little, be less than honest in business dealings, and to disregard the feelings of others.

How rare and exceptional, then, is the man who lives his daily life by the standards set forth by King David. One such exemplary person was R' Elya Hacohen Dushnitzer, the *mashgiach* (supervisor) of the Lomzer Yeshivah that R' Sholom attended as a youth in Petach Tikvah. (Many years earlier R' Elya had been a *mashgiach* at the *Chofetz Chaim's* yeshivah in Radin.)

R' Chaim Kanievsky (the son of the late Steipler *Gaon)* wrote that at R' Elya's funeral, the *Chazon Ish* had called R' Elya one of the *lamed-vov tzaddikim* (thirty-six exceptional *tzaddikim* of every generation).* His character and traits displayed in this story illustrate why he was held in such reverence.

R' Elya owned a small orange *pardes* (orchard) outside Tel Aviv. The *pardes,* however, proved to be quite costly to maintain and the expenses far exceeded the income. Crops didn't grow well, but the workers had to be paid nevertheless. R' Elya found himself falling more and more into debt every month. Finally he decided to sell the *pardes.*

He asked the *bochurim* in the yeshivah to please recite *Tehillim* three times a week that he be successful in selling the *pardes.* If he knew someone who was going to speak to a *gadol* (a great *tzaddik),* he would ask the person to seek a *brachah* for him, that he successfully sell the *pardes.* R' Elya kept repeating that he had to sell the *pardes* quickly because he was getting older, and to leave this world as a *baal chov* (one who owed debts) would be tantamount to *gezeilah* (stealing).

Actually, the *pardes* had not been his originally. He had taken over its ownership as a favor to his son R' Asher, who had been given the *pardes* as a *nadan* (dowry). It was hoped that it would

* The Talmud *(Sanhedrin* 97b) notes Abaye said there are thirty-six *tzaddikim* in every generation who welcome the *Shechinah* (Divine Presence). The Talmud *(Chullin* 92a) also says that there are forty-five *tzaddikim* in every generation on whose merits the world rests.

bring in enough income so that R' Asher could remain in his yeshivah and continue his Torah studies. However, since the *pardes* did not produce enough, R' Elya, who had some money, bought it from his son. Soon things had deteriorated so badly that even R' Elya had to sell it. However, many years passed and the *pardes* was not sold.

Meanwhile, in Jerusalem, one of R' Elya's former *talmidim* of the yeshivah in Petach Tikvah, Michel Rosenblitz, had married and gone into business. One day a wealthy Jew from America came into Michel's office and said that he wanted to buy an orchard in Israel. Michel was ecstatic. Here was an opportunity to help his *rebbi*, help the Jew from America, and even make a little money, simultaneously.

He told the man that he had just the right orchard for him and contacted his *rebbi*, R' Elya, at once. He arranged a meeting between R' Elya, the American and himself in his office in Jerusalem. From there they would all travel together to the *pardes* which was located in the *moshav* (settlement) Ir Shalom, outside of Tel Aviv.

As the three were sitting in the bus from Jerusalem, the conversation naturally turned towards the *pardes*. "You know," R' Elya said to the American, "the Talmud *(Bava Metzia* 29b) states that if someone wishes to lose his money, he should hire workers and not watch over them. If you expect to live in America and won't be here to oversee your workers, I don't recommend that you buy the *pardes*. It would be what the Talmud *(Kesubos* 107b) calls putting money on *keren hatzvi* (the horns of a running deer); you would lose it very quickly."

Michel looked at R' Elya in disbelief. He knew very well that the American wouldn't be coming to Israel often and so he might just listen to R' Elya's sound advice and the whole deal would fall through. The American, however, just listened, nodded his head and didn't say anything.

R' Elya continued. "I think you should know," he said to the American, "there are quite a few trees in the orchard which bear no fruit at all. They are mostly in the northwest corner. I just wanted you to know that."

Michel was beside himself, and yet at the same time marveled at his *rebbi's* honesty. He began to understand why the *pardes* hadn't been sold for so many years. He listened with relief as the American said, "*Rebbi,* it's no problem. I want to buy the orchard anyway."

"But that's only because you don't know its faults," R' Elya retorted. A little while later, R' Elya said, "There is also a small section of trees surrounded by rocks and stones that have stunted the growth of the oranges." Michel was afraid that the American would surely get off at the next stop and return to Jerusalem. But he didn't say a word. He just listened and nodded his head.

Finally they came to Ir Shalom and made their way to the *pardes*. "Here," said R' Elya, taking the man by the hand, "let me show you where those bad trees are. The *Mechilta* says you cannot compare seeing something to merely hearing about it." And they began walking through the *pardes.*

Suddenly the American looked at his watch, stopped, took out a small bottle of pills from his pocket, took one and swallowed it. "What's that?" asked R' Elya curiously. "Is everything all right?"

"Oh, it's nothing, nothing," said the American, brushing away the question. "Nothing to worry about."

'No, tell me," insisted R' Elya. "What did you take from that little bottle?"

"It's nothing," repeated the American. "I have a minor heart problem and my doctor in America gave me these pills that I have to take every few hours. It's really all right."

"Oy!" exclaimed R' Elya. *"Zolst du zein gezunt* (May you be well). *Der Aibishter zoll dir helfen* (May G-d help you)." Then R' Elya shook his head and said, 'I'm afraid that this *pardes* will be too much of a strain on you. With your condition, I certainly would not recommend that you buy it. For one thing, you certainly won't be able to travel to Israel too often to oversee it, and besides I know how much aggravation this *pardes* can be. There is simply no way I can sell it to you. With your delicate heart, you would be throwing out your money and hurting your health at the same time." Taking the American's hand in both of his, he said most fervently, *"Zolst du zein gezunt* (May you be well)."

Despite the American's protests, R' Elya refused to sell him the *pardes.* Instead he wished him a *refuah shelaimah* (complete recovery), thanked him for his interest, and that was the end of their association.

> When telling this story, R' Sholom interjects a question at this point. If indeed it was not meant for the American to buy this *pardes,* why did Hashem lead him to meet R' Elya in the first place?
>
> "The answer, it would seem to me," says R' Sholom, "is that Hashem wanted to give this Jew the opportunity of receiving a *brachah* for good health from a great *tzaddik.*"

Another year passed and now R' Sholom himself was married and learning in Jerusalem. One day, as he was waiting at the central bus station in Tel Aviv to board a bus to Jerusalem, he saw R' Elya, his *rebbi,* in the distance. He ran over to him and they greeted each other warmly. *"Sholom aleichem." "Aleichem sholom."*

After some small talk, R' Elya said to R' Sholom, wistfully, "You remember the *pardes* ..." Having heard from Michel about the American Jew, R' Shalom was not exactly shocked that the *pardes* had not been sold. But now R' Elya was saying, "You remember we had a *talmid* in our yeshivah, R' Yaakov Kriliansky?" Yes, R' Sholom did indeed remember him and he knew that R' Yaakov together with another friend had recently opened a *cheder* for small children in Jerusalem. "If you happen to see him in Jerusalem," R' Elya said, "please remind him once again to have the children in his *cheder* say *Tehillim* for me that I might be able to sell the *pardes.* It is a great *zechus* (merit) to have pure and holy children pray for you." R' Elya went on to assure R' Sholom that he had insisted to R' Yaakov that the children do not, Heaven forbid, take away one moment of time from their learning to say *Tehillim.* Rather, only after they had completed their designated time for study and before they went home for lunch, should they spend a few moments saying *Tehillim.* Then, not wishing to cast aspersions on R' Yaakov Kriliansky, R' Elya added, "I know that R' Yaakov is occupied with so many *mitzvah* matters — which is the only reason he might have forgotten — so please remind him again for me."

R' Sholom, who stood in awe of his *rebbi* and always sought to gain an insight into his way of thinking, replied respectfully, "And how does the *rebbi* know that R' Yaakov indeed forgot to have the children say *Tehillim?*"

R' Elya answered matter-of-factly, with pure and simple faith, "Because I haven't sold the *pardes* yet!"

R' Sholom said he would remind R' Yaakov immediately. Sure enough, when he got off the bus in Jerusalem, he headed straight for *Cheder Yavneh,* in the Me'ah Shearim section of Jerusalem. As he was walking down the main street of Meah Shearim, nearing the post office, he saw R' Yaakov Kriliansky running in his direction. "Wait! Stop, R' Yaakov!" called R' Sholom. "I must talk to you."

"I can't," R' Yaakov called back, "I have an important matter to take care of; I must get to the bank."

"But this is a matter concerning the *rebbi,*" protested R' Sholom, "Come back here!"

R' Yaakov, who had already passed him, stopped and made his way back to R' Sholom.

R' Sholom explained that he had met R' Elya in Tel Aviv and the *rebbi* had asked to remind R' Yaakov that his *talmidim* should recite *Tehillim.*

"Oy vay! Oy vay!" said R' Yaakov, "The *rebbi* is right. I completely forgot! I've been so busy with so many different things for the *cheder!* It's already ten minutes to twelve, but I can still get back to the children before they leave for lunch. I'll take care of it at once!" And with that he ran back to the school.

The next week the *pardes* was sold.

Part B:
The Gift of Giving

◆§ *Confession at Sea*

R' Sholom heard this story and the next one from R' Yisrael Grossman, a *dayan* in Jerusalem (see Introduction).

Ten years after the death of the Vilna Gaon, many of his *talmidim* (disciples) decided to leave Europe and to settle in *Eretz Yisrael*. Thus began the Ashkenazic *yishuv* (settlement) in Jerusalem. The long trip across the Mediterranean was fraught with danger. One of the most hazardous of the voyages was the one led by R' Yisrael of Shklov, one of the Gaon's greatest *talmidim* (author of *Taklin Chadatin* and *Pe'as HaShulchan*).

The year was 1809. R' Yisrael Shklover and one hundred and fifty of his followers packed their belongings, bade their families and friends farewell. They traveled over hill and dale until they reached the seaport. There they boarded a frail-looking vessel for the final leg of their trip to *Eretz Yisrael.*

After a month at sea, torrential rains started to fall. For hours the rain pounded the ship as gale-force winds rattled the vessel and its passengers to their very core. Wave after wave slammed against the ship's sides and spilled over onto the deck. Children huddled against parents who were themselves overcome with fear. The ship floundered helplessly, reeling from each blow of the storm.

After two days of unremitting wind and rain it became obvious that the trip was in danger of ending right there on the high seas. People were ordered to lighten the ship's load and they began throwing their belongings overboard. Only a few, highly prized possessions could be kept, but most baggage had to be thrown into the water.

The captain called for R' Yisrael. Bracing themselves against the wind, the two men huddled together. The captain said, "As the leader of your group, I feel that I must tell you that we are in very grave danger. I don't know how much you want to tell your people, but this is the worst weather I have encountered in thirty years at sea. I will do everything that I can to save the ship and its passengers, but I can tell you that I believe our end is near." The *rav* was pale with fear as he went back to talk to his people, many of whom were sick, exhausted by the rigors of the voyage, and afraid for their lives.

R' Yisrael was filled with anguish at the realization that the voyage to which his followers had been looking forward for years, the dream that they had dared to dream, would soon come to a terrible end. Their aspirations, their years of spiritual preparation to live in the Holy Land would soon be dashed. What could he say? Could he hold out any hope — or just prepare them to meet their end?

He gathered his people together and in earnest began, "I tremble as I say this, but the captain has informed me that we are in danger of sinking. He says that this is the worst weather he has ever encountered, and fears that at any moment the ship will split apart and we will all be lost." He could hardly bear to look at the shocked faces before him, but he continued, almost choking on his next words. Holding back his tears, he said, "Soon we will be in the *Olam HaElyon* (the World Above). It is the custom that before one dies, he recites *viduy* (confession). The Talmud *(Sotah* 7b) tells us that it is wrong for someone to reveal his sins in public [lest others learn to follow them], but that is true only if those hearing the sin will remain alive. However, since we will all be going together to the *Olam HaElyon,* if we openly confess our sins, the embarrassment we feel as a result of their being made public will in itself be an atonement for us. In its merit we will go directly to *Gan Eden* (Paradise), and not to *Gehinnom."*

The *talmidim* of the Gaon, many of them great Torah scholars themselves, agreed to R' Yisrael's suggestion. Despite their terror, they decided they would begin a public *Viduy,* one by one, starting with the youngest of them all. The one chosen to be first was a young man who had lived in Vilna. The winds roared and the rain battered the people as they battled to stand upright while trying to hear the young man speak.

He was so overcome with emotion that he burst into tears. "For two years I violated the *mitzvah* of honoring my father and mother. I lied and deceived my mother day after day, and I am sorry that I did so, but I wish to explain the circumstances."

"When I was thirteen years old my parents moved to Vilna. We were fortunate that our new home was right next door to that of the Vilna Gaon. When the Gaon learned, it was like music to our ears and his sweet voice enraptured us. One night my father who had come home from a hard day's work at his grocery store heard the Gaon repeat the Talmudic phrase, "מַנִּיחִין חַיֵּי עוֹלָם וְעוֹסְקִין בְּחַיֵּי שָׁעָה — They leave the eternal life, and are involved with temporary life" (see *Shabbos* 10a), a number of times. The repetition and the intensity with which the Gaon repeated the phrase (which is a criticism of those who pursue the materialistic aspects of life at the expense of the spiritual aspects) over and over made such an indelible impression on my father that the very next morning he told my mother he felt that he had to leave his job and study Torah exclusively. He locked himself in a room and no one was allowed to disturb him. He felt that he was fulfilling his life's mission.

"My mother was left with the responsibility of caring and providing for her nine children. She couldn't take care of the store and so we had to sell it. The only way she could support the family was by selling some bread and cleaning people's houses.

"One day my mother gathered all of us around her and said, 'My dear children, I can no longer afford to feed you twice a day. We'll have to manage with just one main meal, *mittag* (the afternoon meal).' It became unbearable. The little that she brought home had to be divided eleven ways. I realized that if I didn't take my portion there would be a little more to be divided among my brothers and sisters. And so I made up a story and told my mother that in my *cheder* (day school) *mittag* was now being given to all the boys in the school.

"For two years I lied every time she asked me if I had gotten my meal and eaten that day. In reality all I ate were some of the scraps that the other boys had left over. I now beg Hashem for forgiveness for having lied to my mother all those times."

The young man finished his story and the others stared in sympathetic silence. They hadn't known of this quiet *talmid's* travail, and were awed by his story. R' Yisrael was visibly touched by the tale, particularly because the young man had developed into a great *talmid chacham,* despite his hardships.

The *rav* turned his face towards the crying heavens and with imploring, outstretched hands called out, "Hashem in Heaven! In the first *selichos* (penitential prayers) before *Rosh Hashanah,* we say: 'פְּנֵה נָא אֶל הַתְּלָאוֹת וְאַל לַחֲטָאוֹת' — Turn to our travails and not to our sins. We plead with You to see the travails that we have endured through the past year, so that they may atone for us, but not to see our sins. Now I plead with You, Hashem, 'Look at the sins!' Look at what this young man calls his eternal sin! These are the 'sins' of Your children! In his merit, have mercy on us."

R' Yisrael had barely finished his plea when the rains stopped. Moments later there was a break in the thickly clouded sky, and between the clouds a shaft of sunlight shone through.

The winds swept the clouds away and the group began to relax, the tension easing for the first time in days. R' Yisrael instructed them to recite together psalm 100, מִזְמוֹר לְתוֹדָה, *A Song of Thanks,* for the great miracle which had occurred. The captain and the sailors, all gentiles, stood by respectfully as they marveled at the *rav* and his very special people. It was a *kiddush Hashem* (sanctification of Hashem's Name) in the truest sense.

The rest of the trip was uneventful, and the entire group arrived safely at the shores of the Holy Land.

❧ ❧ ❧

When the Satmar *Rav,* R' Yoel Teitelbaum (1887-1979), heard this story, he remarked cryptically, "This is what Moshe *Rabbeinu* (Moses) did."*

* The *Yerushalmi (Shevuos* 1:5) notes that when Hashem informed Moshe that confession on Yom Kippur would atone for the nation's sins, Moshe responded by reciting psalm 100 in gratitude that the confession would be accepted. Moshe's gratitude is alluded to in the word וְהִתְוַדָּה, *and he shall confess,* which contains the word תּוֹדָה, *thanks.* Thus, when R' Yisrael realized that the confession on the boat was accepted by Hashem, he led his people in reciting the hundreth psalm — just as Moshe had done.

◆§ *The Priest's Garments*

Shortly after the first World War, the municipality of a small Polish town decided to build a major highway to a neighboring city. The roadway was to cut through a large Jewish cemetery. Although the Jews protested bitterly, the town fathers went ahead with their plans. Thus, the Jews had no choice but to dig up the graves, and rebury the deceased in a newly designated cemetery.

The job was a gruesome one, but it had a positive aspect since it brought to light an amazing incident that had happened many years before. When they uncovered the remains of a certain R' Naftali, the *chevra kadisha* (burial society) was shocked to find that he had been buried in the garments of a priest! Even more amazing was the fact that R' Naftali's body had not decomposed at all — it was in perfect condition, as if it had been buried that day!

Traditionally, it is known that only the bodies of the greatest *tzaddikim* remain complete until the time of *techias hamaisim* (revival of the dead in the time of *Mashiach).* R' Naftali must have been such a *tzaddik,* but who was he, and why had he been buried in such a strange shroud?

News of this finding spread quickly through the town and it remained a puzzle until some older people revealed a series of events that had occurred many years before.

R' Naftali had been the town's *gabbai tzedakah* (collector of charity). He went about his duties nobly, collecting funds from the townsfolk and then disbursing the money fairly and with integrity.

One afternoon, R' Naftali had just come home after collecting throughout the town for a dire emergency. Almost everyone to whom he had spoken that day had responded handsomely and warmly. Indeed, he had collected at least something from almost everyone in town.

As R' Naftali was relaxing at home with a glass of tea, a poor man knocked on his door. "Please help me," he begged. "I just moved here and I don't know anyone at all. I have a large family and one of my children is sick. Please take up a collection for me. I know that you are the one who does these things."

R' Naftali sympathized with the man, but said, "How can I ask people for money twice in one day? They will refuse me and tell me to come back some other time!"

The poor man pleaded that his family had not had a decent meal in days, and so R' Naftali finally gave in. Embarrassed and exhausted, he went out to make his rounds again. As he had expected, people looked at him with narrowed, critical eyes. But they knew he was sincere, so they contributed again. After two hours, he came back home where his visitor thanked him profusely for his efforts.

About half an hour later, another downtrodden man came to R' Naftali. He, too, had a very sad story and he, too, pleaded with the *gabbai tzedakah* to raise some money for him.

R' Naftali was at his wit's end. How in the world could he collect from the same people three times in one day! People would ridicule him; they would curse him. But the pleas and the persistence of the poor man wore R' Naftali down, and he consented. With a heavy heart he went out slowly and hesitatingly to someone whom he had always tried to avoid, but under the circumstances he felt he had no choice.

The "customer," who had more money than he knew what to do with, happened to be the son of a wealthy man, and he was carrying on boisterously with his friends in a local tavern. He had helped R' Naftali before, and the *gabbai tzedakah* hoped that he might do so again. R' Naftali entered the tavern where the young man was hooting and hollering, while playing checkers with some of his drunken cronies, and walked up to him.

"Don't tell me you are here collecting again?" shouted the fellow with derision.

"Yes," said R' Naftali softly. "I hate to bother you, but there is a poor family that needs money immediately. I need your help."

After a short discussion with his laughing friends, the young man told R' Naftali he had a plan for him. "How much do you need all together?"

"Twenty rubles," answered R' Naftali.

The young drunkard howled, "I'll give you the whole amount — but on one condition."

A crowd gathered to listen to what they knew would be an

outrageous plan. "I've got a set of priest's clothing back home. I'll run home and get them, and you put them on and march through the town leading us as the Pied Piper would lead his followers. We will play music behind you and liven up this sleepy town. When we get back, I will give you all the money you need and you won't have to go begging to anyone else today."

R' Naftali turned red, and then white with embarrassment. Here was a way for him to get all the money he needed, but how could he pay such a heavy price of humiliation and degradation? On the other hand he thought, the whole matter would take only twenty or thirty minutes, and then the ordeal would be over. He would be spared the burden of going from person to person all over again, and perhaps being refused by many who had already donated twice before. Reluctantly, he agreed.

R' Naftali marched through the main street of town dressed as a priest with a band of half-drunk, rowdy youths marching behind him, singing with a raucousness that attracted everyone's attention. R' Naftali's face was beet red with shame as people peered out of their windows and thought that he had gone insane. People showered him with insults for degrading the position of *gabbai tzedakah* and others pelted him and his followers with eggs.

Eventually, though, the deed was done. When the "priest" and his unholy band of followers returned to the tavern, the wealthy rowdy gave R' Naftali his money and told him he could keep the priest's clothing. He even gave the *gabbai* an "extra" contribution for being a "good sport."

His head hanging in shame, R' Naftali came back home and gave the money to the grateful man anxiously waiting there. "How can I ever thank you?" asked the man, little knowing at what great cost to R' Naftali the money had been raised. R' Naftali threw his uniform into a back corner of a closet and threw himself onto his bed, a broken and exhausted man.

Months later the great R' Chaim Sanzer (1793-1876), author of *Divrei Chaim*, came to the town. As the Sanzer *Rav* walked through the streets, he said to his *gabbai* that he smelled the fragrance of *Gan Eden*. He said, "There is something exceptionally holy in this town." As they walked past the house of R' Naftali, the *rav* told his *shammosh* to knock on the door and see who lived there. The *shammosh* knocked and R' Naftali came out to greet them warmly.

The Sanzer *Rav* told him that the fragrance of *Gan Eden* was coming from his house, but R' Naftali could not understand what his great visitor meant. R' Chaim Sanzer entered the home and sat in the dining area. Then he rose and pointed to the closet. "This is the source of the fragrance," he said.

R' Naftali walked to the closet and opened it. The *rav* peered in. He picked up the wrinkled priest's clothes from the floor and said, "It is coming from here. Tell me the story behind these clothes."

R' Naftali remembered his ordeal wearing those garments and he felt the shame again, but he told the story. At its conclusion R' Chaim Sanzer said, "Because of this incident you will go directly to *Gan Eden*. Leave instructions to your family that when you die, you are to be buried in these clothes. The *malachei chavalah* (angels of destruction) will not dare touch you."

And thus it was when the *chevra kadisha* was reburying its dead, they found R' Naftali dressed in priest's garments, and the body had not decayed at all, for R' Naftali was truly a great *tzaddik*.

◆§ *For Boots and a Sweater*

It was Tishah B'Av night, 1974 (5734), and thousands of people sat huddled together in small clusters all across the stone floor of the plaza in front of the *Kosel Hamaaravi* in Jerusalem. Under the glaring yellow lights atop the *Kosel*, each group somberly recited *Kinnos*, the lamentations recounting the destruction of both Holy Temples which had stood not far from where they were presently sitting.

Hundreds of people milled around observing the diversity of the people: the Sefardic groups in their colorful robes, the Chassidic groups in their long black frocks, and the tourists from abroad with their brightly colored shirts. Each following his own tradition in mourning and grieving for the loss of the Temple and the centuries of pain and exile.

Suddenly, two men started shouting at each other with happy excitement. Laughter followed, mixed with tears of joy as they hugged each other spontaneously. The somber mood of the moment was shattered and those who witnessed it could hardly believe their eyes or understand the sudden explosion of exuberance. If they had known this story, they would have understood.

When Chaim Shia was a twelve-year-old boy in Russia in the early 1900's, his parents hired a *melamed* (teacher) to teach him *Chumash* and *Mishnayos.* As an incentive to do well in his studies, Chaim Shia's grandfather promised him a gift if he learned a certain number of *mishnayos* by heart. Chaim Shia's friend, Pinchas Sholom, studied with the same *melamed.* When Pinchas Sholom's grandfather heard of the offer that had been made to his grandson's friend, he too agreed to give a reward to his grandson if he learned an equal number of *mishnayos* by heart.

For weeks the boys studied together. Finally, they came to their grandfathers who listened with pride to their achievements and kept their promises. Chaim Shia received a shiny new pair of boots for the damp, frozen Russian winters, and Pinchas Sholom was given a warm woolen sweater. The proud boys went out into the frigid streets to display their prizes. As they walked together, they saw Shaika, a poor orphan boy, walking dejectedly towards them. Shaika lived alone with his mother in a dilapidated apartment, and had been wearing the same ragged clothing for months.

Chaim Shia and Pinchas Sholom quickly consulted with each other and decided to give their new gifts to Shaika. Chaim Shia took off his boots and Pinchas Sholom took off his sweater as Shaika approached. They gave him their own new treasures and explained that they had bought him these gifts for the bitter winter. Amazed at his sudden good fortune, Shaika couldn't thank the two friends enough and ran home to tell his mother. Shaika was totally oblivious to the fact that Chaim Shia had been left standing in the freezing snow in his socks. Chaim Shia trudged home to get his old pair of boots, but by the time he got home he was shivering violently and his toes were frostbitten and blue with cold. His mother was furious that he had walked home practically barefoot in the snow. She was even further incensed when she realized that he had given away the expensive gift he had just received from her father. Chaim Shia didn't help matters any by coming down with pneumonia.

A few weeks later, when Chaim Shia was able to go outside again, he and Pinchas Sholom asked their *melamed* to let Shaika join them in their studies. Although there was no one to pay for Shaika's learning, the *melamed* agreed to let the orphan boy join them gratis.

A short month later Shaika's mother died suddenly. The poor lad, left with no parents and little family, was destitute. Once again Chaim Shia's compassion was aroused. Although he and his parents and five siblings lived in a small apartment, Chaim Shia begged his parents to take in his unfortunate friend. He was flatly refused. After much pleading, begging and crying, the maximum to which Chaim Shia's father would agree was to provide money for Shaika's food and shelter. He absolutely wouldn't agree to allow Shaika to move in with them. There simply was no room.

Chaim Shia couldn't accept his father's decision and became even more insistent. Finally, in exasperation, Chaim Shia's father shouted, "If you're so eager to live with Shaika, you move in with him to the *ezras nashim* (women's section) in the big synagogue." The *ezras nashim* of the largest synagogue in town was where beggars and vagabonds slept every night and shared the food they had managed to scrape together during the day. Chaim Shia hadn't even thought of that idea as a possible alternative. But, once his father brought up the idea, his heart said, "Why not?" And so, with courage tinged with fright, he said, "That's exactly what I will do!"

Shaika was speechless when he heard about Chaim Shia's plans. How could anyone give up a comfortable home and readily available food to live in the squalor of the *ezras nashim* with the beggars and lost souls who had no other place to go? Utterly bewildered but grateful, he welcomed the thought of having his friend with him, especially at night. In the darkness they huddled together, talking until all hours of the night about the events of the day. They fantasized about their future, finally dozing off when exhaustion brought sleep to their weary bodies.

At that time the world situation was extremely volatile and many countries were on the brink of war. Shortly after Chaim Shia sacrificed home and family for his friend, World War I erupted in all its fury. Thousands of people fled their homes and their countries to seek safer havens.

The boys were compelled to return to their families, Chaim Shia to his parents and Shaika to some distant relative, for no one was permitted to live in the synagogue any longer. The two fast friends became separated, losing sight of each other for many long years.

Shaika's relatives eventually settled in South America where he went into business, married, raised a family and became a very wealthy man.

Chaim Shia, on the other hand, made his way to *Eretz Yisrael* with his family, where he too worked, married and had a large family. But, unlike his childhood friend, he could never make ends meet. The poverty in Israel was excruciating. Chaim Shia and his family lived through the most difficult times in the history of the land and he struggled daily to make ends meet.

Tonight was Tishah B'Av and Chaim Shia had come to the *Kosel,* as he often did, to pray and cry over the destruction of both Holy Temples. Shaika too had come to the *Kosel,* on his first trip to *Eretz Yisrael* from South America. He stood bemused, listening to the cacophony of voices while gazing at the panorama of people from all parts of the world. It was amazing how all these diverse people were united in their fervent prayers to Hashem for the coming of the *Mashiach* and the rebuilding of the Temple.

Suddenly Shaika heard a familiar voice. He had heard *Maariv* (evening prayer) recited just that way somewhere else, but not in South America. It had to be earlier than that. He looked around. There were so many people near him that he couldn't tell where the voice was coming from. It was maddening. The voice was so distinctive, there was no mistaking it. His heart was pounding so wildly, he was afraid it would burst. And then he pinpointed the source of the voice. As recognition dawned on him, he couldn't believe what he was seeing and hearing!

Shaika listened intently to the man reciting the *Kinnos*. He faced the man and looked into his eyes. The man seemed perturbed and looked away. He seemed embarrassed by the scrutiny.

But Shaika kept staring. The man couldn't *daven* any longer. Shaika kept examining him from head to toe, and then still afraid to believe his eyes and ears he said, "*Slichah* (excuse me), is your name Chaim Shia?" The man looked up from his *Kinnos*, surprised. How did this stranger know his name? Shaika knew that the man's name had to be Chaim Shia. "Chaim Shia?" he said, tentatively at first. Then, "Chaim Shia!" he shouted. The lump in his throat was making it difficult to talk.

"I'm Chaim Shia. But, who are you?"

"I'm Shaika, from Moscow, the boy to whom you gave your boots ... the *ezras nashim* ..." They began to shout in their excitement, crying and laughing at the same time. The people around them couldn't help shedding their own tears of joy at the intense emotion felt by the reunited friends.

That night, neither Chaim Shia nor Shaika slept. The spent hours recollecting events of the many years of separation.

Today, Chaim Shia is no longer poor. The *chessed* (charity) he had once shown, from the selflessness of his innocent heart, bore fruit. Today his needs are met and his children and grandchildren are well fed. Every month he receives a check in the mail from South America.

The warmth of a pair of boots on a frozen afternoon thousands of miles away had lasted for decades. A cherished friendship, interrupted by time and distance, remains intact to this very day.

☙ *The Face of Self Control*

R' Yisrael Salanter said that it is harder to break a single *middah* (personality trait) than to learn the entire *Shas* (Talmud). He writes that our purpose in this world is to refine our character traits — and that can take a lifetime.

Yet, every once in a while, the act of an individual is so

outstanding that it can serve as a sterling example of what man can be. A man should be in control of his traits and not let his traits control him. In this story, we meet that sort of man.

In Jerusalem, long ago, an incredible incident took place in the office of a *gemach. Gemach,* an acrostic for the word *gemilas chessed* (literally, granting kindness), is the generally used term for an interest-free loan fund. Customarily, the various *gemachs* in Jerusalem were all open on Thursdays, to be available to people who needed to borrow money for food for *Shabbos.* By Thursday night, all the *gemach* offices would be closed, mainly because money that had been available for the week was already gone. Most people knew from experience to come early in the day, while there was still money available.

If a few *gemachs* happened to be open Thursday night, none would be open Friday, except for one. The compassionate and sympathetic R' Reuven kept his *gemach* open, just in case someone needed him at the last minute. True, there was not much money left by Friday, but he felt that one never knew who might be in desperate need.

One Friday, when all the *gemachs* except for R' Reuven's were closed, a *kollel* fellow (married scholar) came in and asked to borrow money for his family's Shabbos food. R' Reuven recognized the young man for he had just been at the *gemach* the day before, and said, "If I'm correct, I recall that you were here yesterday."

"Yes," chimed in R' Reuven's attendant who was standing by. "How can we lend you money two days in a row?"

The young man's face flushed with anger. "Are you trying to tell me that I don't need the money?" he fumed.

"No, we are not saying that at all ..." started R' Reuven.

"Well, then lend me the money that I need! I already have cosigners for surety," interrupted the young man.

R' Reuven looked at the young man compassionately and said, "I'm truly sorry, but the policy of the *gemach* is not to lend an individual twice within such a short period, and besides you have already borrowed the limit that we allow someone to borrow."

The young man was enraged. Yelling, he stormed towards R'

Reuven and slapped him across the face!

The gentle R' Reuven stood there in shock and disbelief. No one had ever had the audacity to scream at him, let alone slap him. The attendant started towards the young man, but R' Reuven held him back.

"Wait a moment," R' Reuven said to the young man. "I'll be back with the money right away." R' Reuven went downstairs and hurried directly to some people on whom he knew he could rely for funds in an emergency, and came back shortly with the money.

He gave the bills to the young man and wished him well. The young man thanked him and left.

Because of the noise and commotion a few neighbors had gathered in the office to see what had happened. They stood by respectfully and quiet as R' Reuven handed over the money, but when the young man left they all began to talk at once, asking R' Reuven why in the world he had gone to get the money after such a humiliating experience with this disrespectful man. "If I were in your shoes," one man shouted, "I would have demanded that he give back the money you had lent him yesterday and maybe even have pushed him down the stairs for good measure!"

R' Reuven, whose face still stung from the slap, explained. "I know this fellow. Under normal circumstances he never would have acted this way. He must be having such terrible problems that he lost himself completely. It's because he did behave in such an unnatural way that I realized how desperate his position is. Now, more than ever, is the time to help him. So I went out and got the money for him. May Hashem help him."

◆§ *Challah Sweeter than Wine*

When R' Sholom tells the following story he prefaces it by saying, "To my mind this is one of the nicest stories I know. It shows what a Jew can be." In fact, it is a story that leaves one with tender feelings of *ahavas Yisrael* (love for a fellow Jew).

R' Sholom relates that he heard this story from R' Zaidel

Shapiro, the father of the *shammosh* (attendant) of the Shaarei Chessed *shul* in Jerusalem. R' Zaidel himself was involved in the incident.

The story centers around R' Yudel Holtzman, who was one of an exceptional breed of *Yerushalmi* (Jerusalemite) Jew. A kind, loving, and deeply sensitive man, R' Yudel was also a noted *talmid chacham* who, with some of his friends, comprised the *baalei halachah,* a small group known for the exceptional diligence and attentiveness they showed in the performance of every *mitzvah.*

R' Yudel was very poor and had no children, but had a deeply caring heart that would break for another man's troubles. He was a soft touch for any cause and at his insistence, the *gabbaei tzedakah* (collectors of charity) were always at his home.

It happened that a simple tailor, beloved by many, known in Jerusalem as the "Parisian tailor," required an operation in the old Hadassah Hospital. He had very little money himself, and still had to raise the considerable sum of sixty pounds for the operation.

The *gabbai tzedakah,* R' Zaidel, came to R' Yudel's home and explained the tailor's plight. R' Yudel sat dejected as he listened. "Oh, that's terrible," he interjected when R' Zaidel paused for a moment, "*nebach* (how unfortunate), how awful," he kept on repeating.

When R' Zaidel finished, R' Yudel sighed and said, "I wish so much that I could help. But what can I do, you know how little money I have. Everything that I do is from my *maaser* (tithe) money. And in case you want to know how I can give as much as I do — and *nebach* the needs of *Klal Yisrael* are so many — I'll tell you. I borrow against my future *maaser* account. But what should I do?" he continued with anguish, "My policy is that I don't borrow against the *maaser* money if I'm a year overdrawn against that account. And I've already reached that point.

"I feel so bad for that tailor," R' Yudel continued, "May Hashem grant him a *refuah shelaimah* (complete recovery)."

R' Zaidel nodded and said he fully understood and left R' Yudel's home. He had walked only a half block when R' Yudel came running after him. "Wait a minute! Wait a minute, R' Zaidel, come back. The *Ribbono Shel Olam* (Master of the world; G-d) suddenly inspired me with a great idea!"

R' Zaidel turned back with a puzzled look and returned to R' Yudel's home. He sat down in the dining area that consisted of some dilapidated furniture, on a chair that looked as if it would barely hold him up.

R' Yudel began excitedly, "The *Ribbono Shel Olam* put into my mind a plan which would allow me to help the tailor. Yes, it can work out! Listen, R' Zaidel, you go to one of the larger *gemachs* in Jerusalem and tell them to lend you twenty pounds in my name and I'll pay it back. You see, it occurred to me that every week I spend a half shilling on the wine that I need for *Kiddush* for Shabbos. But the *halachah* is that a person can make *Kiddush* on *challah* as well as on wine, and if I make *Kiddush* on *challah* every week, I'll have the extra money to repay the loan."

At that rate it would take more than fifteen years for R' Yudel to repay the loan. And for over fifteen years that is exactly what R' Yudel did!

Many, many years later, on a Friday night, R' Sholom retold this story at his weekly *drashah* in the Zichron Moshe *shul* in Jerusalem. Afterwards, a young man came to him and said, "I'm R' Yudel's nephew. I was at my uncle's home many times for Shabbos and it always seemed strange to me that he recited *kiddush* on *challah*. I never knew why, until tonight." Then the young man added, "Incidentally, this week is my uncle's *yahrzeit*."

◆§ *Two Baked Apples*

One of Avraham *Avinu's* (the Patriarch Abraham) remarkable characteristics was his *hachnosas orchim* (hospitality to guests). The Torah *(Bereishis* 18:1-8) details how, though recovering from his *bris milah* (circumcision; Abraham was circumcised at age ninety-nine), he ran enthusiastically in the heat of the day to invite wayfarers into his tent and then provided them with a lavish meal. The following episode which took place just a few years ago also involved the *mitzvah* of *hachnosas orchim,* and incidentally happened to a person named Avraham.

Perhaps the word incidentally is the wrong word to use, for if this story proves anything, it is that nothing happens incidentally. Everything is guided by Divine Providence. It only takes slight effort on the part of an individual to study an event in its entirety to see how the hands of Hashem shaped and formulated the entire sequence. The juxtaposition of events in this story is truly remarkable.

R' Avraham is a congenial man who greets everyone with a friendly smile and a warm hello, and is always ready to help a fellow Jew. One afternoon he was in the Crown Heights section of Brooklyn, going into a restaurant for lunch. In the distance he noticed a well-known Jewish vagabond, a bearded individual who was a familiar figure in all the yeshivos in Metropolitan New York.

It was said that he had been an important *talmid chacham* in Europe and that he possessed a sweet melodious voice with which he could sing hauntingly beautiful melodies. But after the shattering experience of the war he became very quiet, almost a recluse. No one seemed to know where he lived or how he survived from day to day. With his crushed hat and ragged clothes, he was known simply as R' Berel.

R' Avraham saw an opportunity to do another Jew a favor. "Sholom Aleichem, R' Berel," he said, as he walked to greet the vagabond. "Please come and eat with me. I don't like to eat alone."

A pleasant sort of fellow, R' Berel agreed to sit down but insisted he was not in the mood to eat. R' Avraham was sure that R' Berel hadn't had a decent meal in days and offered to buy him anything he wanted. But all R' Berel would accept were two baked apples and a glass of hot tea.

The two ate together, chatting amiably, R' Berel eating his apples while R' Avraham ate his lunch.

After lunch, R' Avraham left to attend to some business matters and to prepare for a trip he was to take later that evening to Binghamton, New York. When he came home, his wife tried to convince him not to start on the four-hour drive to Binghamton. Rain was predicted, and she felt it would be better for him to wait for the morning rather than drive late at night in bad weather.

But R' Avraham, who had made the trip many times and was familiar with the roads, preferred to drive through the night and, if the weather worsened, he could always check into a motel on the way. The rain began soon after he left the city and intensified as the night wore on. He drove over the Tappan Zee Bridge, past Harriman and onto Route 17. The rains became torrential and before he realized what was happening, his car skidded on the slick road across the highway into the path of oncoming traffic. Everything was a blur, and the car was out of control. R' Avraham heard a thud and the shatter of glass. The impact knocked him senseless. When he came to, he tried to get out of his car, but could barely push the door open. He finally squeezed himself out and saw his car had plunged deep into a ditch. People appeared from nowhere, trying to help him, and eventually lifted him to safety.

It took two tow trucks to get his car out of the ditch and R' Avraham went to the service station in one of the trucks. It was suggested that he stay in a motel nearby but he remembered that a friend of his owned a hotel nearby. It was only two weeks after Pesach and often the owner and his wife remained in their hotel until the summer season began.

He dialed their number and fortunately they were in. It was late, almost midnight, but they said they would wait up until he arrived. The tow company called a taxi for him and it was after midnight when the cab pulled up to the Friedmans' hotel in the Catskills.

Knowing what had happened, the Friedmans greeted him warmly and expressed their thanks to Hashem that he was alive. Then Mrs. Friedman said to him, "You must be so tired; here let me give you something to eat. I just made these."

And she set two baked apples and a glass of hot tea before R' Avraham.

The mishnah in *Pe'ah* says that *hachnosas orchim* is one of the rare *mitzvos* for which a person is rewarded in this world as well as in the World to Come. R' Avraham is sure that the baked apples and the hot tea symbolized why his life had been saved.

After all, Shlomo *Hamelech* said in *Mishlei (Proverbs* 10:2): "צְדָקָה תַּצִּיל מִמָּוֶת, *Charity saves from death."*

No More than a Sniff

In the town of Zhitomir, near Berditchev, there lived a man known as Hirsch Ber. His business ventures always seemed to fail, the community accorded him no respect, and even at home, his wife pestered him mercilessly.

It was *erev Yom Kippur* and Jews throughout Zhitomir were eating their *seudah hamafsekes* (last meal before the fast). But in Hirsch Ber's house there was very little food for the *seudah.* In frustration his wife berated him as a poor provider and sent him off to face the long fast on a nearly empty stomach.

He made his way to the synagogue dejected, despondent and hungry. In the synagogue everything was gleaming. The curtain of the *Aron hakodesh* (Holy Ark) was a radiant white, and each man sat in his freshly ironed white *kittel* and *tallis,* reciting the earnest, personal prayer of penitence known as *Tefillah Zakah.* Hirsch Ber took his seat at the very back of the synagogue.

Sitting there, hungry and miserable, he knew it was too late to get anything to eat, but he thought perhaps he could still ask R' Boruch, the wealthy industrialist who sat up front at the *mizrach* (eastern) wall, for a *shmek tabak* (a sniff of strong, sharp snuff) from the elegant silver snuffbox that R' Boruch always kept with him in *shul.*

Hirsch Ber made his way slowly to the front of the synagogue and hesitantly approached R' Boruch from behind. He placed his hand on R' Boruch's back. "Perhaps a *shmek tabak,* R' Boruch?" he asked softly.

R' Boruch was annoyed. Who could be bothering him in the middle of this important prayer? What earthshaking matter could justify the interruption of *Tefillah Zakah?* As he peeked out from under his *tallis* and saw that it was merely Hirsch Ber, he turned to him with disgust and said, "Hirsch Ber, in the middle of *Tefillah Zakah?*"

Hirsch Ber was embarrassed and humiliated. Red faced, he turned and walked back to his seat muttering to himself, "*Ribbono Shel Olam,* am I not even worth a *shmek tabak?*"

The heavenly angels were in an uproar at R' Boruch's lack of sensitivity. It was decreed that in the new year the tables would be turned. R' Boruch would lose his money and become poor, while Hirsch Ber would become wealthy.

The day after Yom Kippur, a cousin of Hirsch Ber's came to Zhitomir and offered to lend him some money. Hirsch Ber started a new business venture and the profits skyrocketed. Slowly but surely he paid off his debts, gained much esteem and went on to become a prominent member of the community.

On the other hand, R' Boruch made one bad business decision after another and soon he began to lose his fortune. Realizing that his wealth was fading fast, he went immediately to his *rebbe,* R' Levi Yitzchak of Berditchev, for advice. They sat and analyzed all of R' Boruch's actions and couldn't find any reason for his downfall. However, when R' Boruch told R' Levi Yitzchak that at the same time of his financial setbacks, Hirsch Ber, who until now had been in abject poverty, had suddenly become wealthy, R' Levi Yitzchak asked, "Can you think of any incident that involved both you and him?" When R' Hirsch Ber recalled the incident with the *shmek tabak* at the start of Yom Kippur, R' Levi Yitzchak said, "That's it. It is the humiliation that you caused Hirsch Ber on the holiest day of the year that is at the root of your downfall."

"But what can I do?" cried R' Boruch. "There's no simple answer," replied Reb Levi Yitzchak, "only you can help yourself. If a time comes when you ask the now wealthy R' Hirsch Ber for a *shmek tabak* and he refuses you, then you will have a justifiable claim to G-d to once again reverse the situation. Until then, there is no advice I can offer."

Years went by and people forgot that R' Boruch had once been affluent. Now it was he who was mired in poverty. Every day he waited for an opportunity to reclaim his wealth. Since R' Hirsch Ber was now highly regarded in Zhitomir, when his daughter came of age, he received a marriage proposal from the son of the *rav* of Zhitomir. Father and daughter accepted the proposal and a lavish wedding was prepared.

All the Jews of Zhitomir were invited to the wedding, and festivity and happiness reigned everywhere. At the wedding, R' Hirsch Ber stood under the *chuppah* holding the *kesubah* (marriage contract). The rabbi, who was the father of the groom, asked for the *kesubah* so that it could be read aloud. As R' Hirsch Ber was about to give the *kesubah* to the rabbi the bedraggled R' Boruch rushed forward, stood under the *chuppah* along with the *chasan* and *kallah* (bride and groom), and said softly, "A *shmek tabak,* R' Hirsch Ber?"

R' Hirsch Ber immediately put the *kesubah* back in his pocket, took out his snuffbox and said, "Of course! Of course! Here, have a whiff." Upon hearing these words, R' Boruch fainted right under the *chuppah,* in front of all the assembled guests.

A tremendous commotion ensued. People ran up to revive the fallen R' Boruch, a hundred voices spoke at once, and confusion reigned. When R' Boruch came to himself, R' Hirsch Ber asked him, "What happened? What did I say to make you faint?"

"I can't talk now," stammered R' Boruch. "Let's go into a private room after the *chuppah* and I'll explain."

After the *chuppah,* the two men went off together. R' Boruch revealed to R' Hirsch Ber the entire sequence of events that had led up to this moment, and the advice of Reb Levi Yitzchak. "And when I thought I finally had a chance to catch you off guard, I approached you in order to bring about your decline. You were so nice to me that I guess I was just overcome."

R' Boruch and R' Hirsch Ber agreed to go to Reb Levi Yitzchak to ask for his advice. The very next week they traveled to Berditchev where they told Reb Levi Yitzchak what had happened. Reb Levi Yitzchak listened to the whole story and then asked R' Hirsch Ber if he would give a percentage of his wealth to R' Boruch — for it was obvious that his fortune had been transferred from R' Boruch to him.

R' Hirsch Ber decided to give half of his wealth to R' Boruch and both of them lived out the rest of their lives as prosperous Jews in Zhitomir.

☙ *Spoonful for Spoonful*

As a boy of thirteen, R' Dovid Finkel traveled alone throughout Europe to visit the *gedolei hador* (most prominent Torah scholars of that generation). A prodigy in learning, he was also the scion of a very distinguished family. His father was R' Moshe Finkel (d. 1925), a *rosh yeshivah* in Chevron, and his uncles were R' Lazer Yehudah Finkel (1878-1965), *rosh yeshivah* of Mir, and R' Isser Zalman Meltzer, *rosh yeshivah* of Yeshivah Eitz Chaim. Thus, the young lad was welcomed heartily by the Torah luminaries he visited.

In the city of Dvinsk, R' Dovid visited R' Yosef Rosen (1858-1936), better known as the Rogatchover *Gaon*. The Rogatchover was known throughout the Torah world for his unmatched *bekius* (broad scope of knowledge), his phenomenal recall, and for his tremendous *hasmadah* (diligence and constant involvement with Torah learning). It is said that when the Rogatchover suffered agonizing pain after unsuccessful surgery in Vienna, he could find solace and comfort only when young men stood and discussed topics of Torah with him.

As young Dovid sat with the *Gaon*, the *rebbetzin* brought her husband a plate of soup and some *smetena* (cream) to eat. The *Gaon*, who ate very little and then only the most simple foods, protested that he couldn't eat *smetena*. But then, looking at the young lad, he said, "But if Dovid'l here will eat, then I'll eat as well. We need two spoons."

He said to the boy, "You take a spoonful and then I'll take a spoonful." There they sat, the Torah giant and the fledgling *talmid*; only when the boy took a spoonful did the Rogatchover follow suit. So it went until the cream was finished.

Years later, R' Dovid would say, "The Rogatchover knew that I would be too embarrassed to eat in his presence. Yet he also knew that I was going from place to place and probably had not eaten much that day. In order to fulfill the *mitzvah* of *hachnosas orchim* (hospitality), he ate, so I too would eat. He understood that I couldn't refuse the *smetena* when his nourishment depended on it."

◆§ *Wedding Plans*

The Rebbe R' Zisha of Anipoli (d. 1800) was a happy man who never worried, because he felt that he had no problems. Though he was burdened with ailments, beset by such extreme poverty that he never knew from where his next meal would come, he lived with the credo that everything that happened was ordained by G-d. Therefore, he accepted his lot in life with unbounded happiness.

R' Zisha's *rebbe* was the *Maggid* of Mezritch (1704-1772), whom he would often visit. One day, as R' Zisha was about to travel to his *rebbe,* his wife reminded him, "You know that we have a daughter to marry off. I've asked you many times to get a blessing and some advice from the *Maggid* concerning our daughter, but you always forget. Please remember this time."

"I'll try to remember," he said as he left the house.

R' Zisha went to the *Maggid* and expressed concern for all problems except his own — and once again forgot to mention his daughter. As he was about to leave, the Mezritcher *Maggid* said to him, "Zisha, don't you have a daughter to marry off?"

"Oh, yes, yes. I forgot to mention it," said R' Zisha.

"Here are three hundred rubles," said the *Maggid,* "and may you have *hatzlachah* (success)."

"Thank you, thank you!" said R' Zisha, as he left for home. On the way, he passed an inn and saw that it was full of people. Curious, he went inside to investigate. There was a wedding in progress, but although the people on the outskirts of the crowd were celebrating, the people in the main hall were in a different mood. There was no joy, only unhappiness, frustration, and confusion.

R' Zisha learned that the mother of the bride had promised the groom three hundred rubles as dowry and somehow had lost the money. She was frantically trying to figure out where the money could have gone. In the meanwhile, while everyone was giving her advice on where to look for the money, the family of the groom was becoming very impatient.

R' Zisha stepped into the middle of the banquet hall and asked for quiet. "I understand," he began, "that there is a problem of some lost money. It just so happens that I found some money today." He was interrupted by bursts of joyful clapping as everyone cheered the news.

"Wait!" said R' Zisha, "I need the mother of the bride to tell me exactly how much money there was and in what denominations."

The woman came forward and gave, to the best of her recollection, the number of tens, twenties and fifties that she had had in the packet. R' Zisha announced that he would have to go back to his room and check whether the money he had found fit her description. Some people began dancing as joy returned to the scene,while others stood around waiting with apprehension for him to return.

R' Zisha went to a moneychanger, changed the *Maggid's* three hundred rubles into the denominations that the woman had described, and came back triumphantly to the inn.

He walked in with a broad smile, went straight to the middle of the hall and announced, "Yes, the money that I have is exactly the way the woman described it!" The guests cheered in relief and happiness, but once again R' Zisha called for quiet. He held up his hand and said, "It's true the money goes to the mother of the bride, but I feel that I deserve some reward for my efforts."

Stunned, the people stood numbly, not knowing how to react. They couldn't believe the audacity of the man. It was obviously the woman's money, and now, on the night of her daughter's wedding, how could he be so cruel? The guests started shoving and pushing as they made their way to have a word or two with this impudent stranger.

A family member called for quiet and said to R' Zisha, for all to hear, "Nu, nu, tell us already how much you want for your efforts?" The people waited as R' Zisha thought for a moment. Then he answered, "Twenty-five rubles!"

"Twenty-five rubles!" the crowd shouted in unison. "It's unfair, it's absurd!" They pushed forward and started to beat him, dragging him out of the hall. Pandemonium reigned, with everyone screaming at once, as R' Zisha held tightly onto the money. Every few moments he reeled from another shove or punch. He held up his hands and shouted, "There is a *rav* in this town, let's go to him and get his ruling."

The crowd muttered its consent and R' Zisha was led out with the strong grip of several of the guests on his arms, preventing his escape. A crowd followed as they made their way to the *rav's* house. The *rav* listened carefully to both sides, first to the hysterical mother and then to the *chassid* who claimed that he was a disciple of the Mezritcher *Maggid*. As the story began to unfold the *rav* became infuriated at the lack of sensitivity of this Zisha, and ordered that he give the entire sum to the woman.

R' Zisha did so and left the city as people showered him with ridicule and abuse.

A few months later, the Mezritcher *Maggid* happened to be passing through this town. He stopped to visit with the local *rav*, unaware that his disciple R' Zisha had had a confrontation with him. As the two spoke, the *rav* related the incident, and expressed his surprise that a disciple of the *Maggid's* should have acted in a way so unbecoming of any Jew, especially a *chassid*. The *Maggid* smiled and assured the *rav* that he would look into the matter. He knew that if anyone was concerned for others it was R' Zisha. There had to be an explanation.

When the *Maggid* returned home he sent for R' Zisha. When R' Zisha stood before him, the *Maggid* said, "I can understand why you wanted to give away the money in the first place. But when you returned to the inn a second time, why did you make such a ridiculous demand?"

R' Zisha, somewhat embarrassed that his ploy had been discovered, smiled sheepishly and explained his feelings. "When I went to the moneychanger, my *yetzer hara* said to me, 'Zisha, you are a *tzaddik!* No one but you would do such a thing! This *mitzvah* is the best thing you have ever done.' He was trying to trap me to succumb to haughtiness. I realized that if I fell into his snare and began to feel conceited, the *mitzvah* would be tarnished and incomplete. Thus I decided on a plan which would earn me abuse and insult and would assure me that I couldn't possibly feel important, even to myself. As a result, I hope the *mitzvah* was a true one, undiminished by any unworthy thoughts on my part."

◆§ *Reversed, Revealed, Revered*

Quite often people think they know their neighbors well. They believe that because they are somewhat familiar with their neighbors' sources of income and socialize with them a bit, they are able to make judgments, criticize, and evaluate the other people's lifestyle. Often, their impressions are wrong. Every person has his own private life and there is much that even close friends don't know. Quite often, circumstances make a person act and react in ways that seem inappropriate. Since it is easier to pass judgment than to search for the truth, people tend to be hasty in their opinions. The following incident might make people think twice before they speak once.

The Berditchever *Rebbe,* R' Levi Yitzchak, once called his *shammosh* and told him that a man called Naftoli Hertz was near death, and that if indeed he did pass away, R' Levi Yitzchak wanted to be notified about the funeral arrangements.

The *shammosh* was quite surprised, since Naftoli Hertz had a reputation as a selfish miser, never giving charity or showing concern for others. The faithful *shammosh,* however, did not question the *rebbe* and when Naftoli Hertz passed away, the *rebbe* was informed and made plans to attend the funeral.

Word quickly spread around the town that R' Levi Yitzchak was going to Naftoli Hertz's funeral. No one could believe it, but they reasoned if the *rebbe* went, they should go as well.

As the *chassidim* followed behind the *rebbe,* they couldn't contain their curiosity. One of them asked him, "Naftoli Hertz's reputation is not a secret. Why would the *rebbe* give him the honor of participating in his funeral?"

The Berditchever *Rebbe* explained that he knew much that they didn't know. "I was involved with three *dinei Torah* (religious arbitrations) with Naftoli Hertz and they, more than anything else, revealed his true character."

The *rebbe* then told them the following three episodes:

❧ ❧ ❧

A number of years ago a businessman in town lost an enormous amount of money. As an agent for other merchants, he had been carrying the huge sum of a hundred rubles with him and had misplaced it. He became frantic and searched all over, trying to retrace his steps, asking everyone he saw if he knew where he had left the money. As he went from synagogue to synagogue making his frenzied announcements, Naftoli Hertz went up to him and quietly said that *he* had found the hundred rubles. Hardly believing his sudden change of fortune, the businessman was ecstatic and followed Naftoli home, where the money was returned.

A few days later it suddenly dawned on the businessman where he had probably left the money. He had made an unexpected stop and had hidden the money there for the moment, and had forgotten about it. He ran back to that place, and sure enough, the money was there, hidden in a small sack exactly where he had left it.

He searched from *shul* to *shul* looking for Naftoli Hertz and when he located him, thanked him profusely for his kindness and tried to give back the hundred rubles.

"It was noble of you to give me the money," said the businessman, "I realize that you gave it to me out of the goodness of your heart. Here, please take your money. I found my own."

"No," said Naftoli Hertz. "You keep it. I gave it to you with no thought of getting it back."

"But it's not my money," protested the businessman, "I can't keep it."

"Now it's yours," answered Naftoli Hertz.

Realizing that he could not persuade him, the businessman brought the kindhearted Naftoli Hertz to me for a *din Torah* (rabbinic litigation) to settle the matter.

That was the first case.

⁂

The second *din Torah* involved a husband and wife who were having financial problems. The husband decided to go overseas to make some money and then come back to support his wife and children properly. The wife was distraught at the thought that her husband would leave her alone with the children, with no means of support while he was away.

When she threatened to divorce him he told her that the "rich Naftoli Hertz" had agreed to give her a weekly stipend every Thursday. Actually, no such arrangement had been made, but the woman, being a simple trusting soul, believed her husband's fabrication.

The first Thursday after her husband was away, the woman went to Naftoli Hertz's place of business. "I'm here to collect my money," she said, not believing for a moment that it might be a hoax.

At first Naftoli Hertz didn't understand what the woman wanted. "What money?" he asked.

The woman became frightened and pale. She said, "My husband told me that you and he had agreed that you would give me money every week until he returned." She told him the story of her husband's departure and how he had made an arrangement with Naftoli Hertz to support her and the children until he returned.

"Yes, yes!" said Naftoli Hertz, realizing what must have happened. "Excuse me, I had forgotten all about it. I've been so busy." And then he gave her a goodly sum of money and continued doing so, week after week until the man returned — almost two years later.

When the husband finally returned, he expected to find his home in worse condition than when he had left. Instead, he noticed some improvement. His wife didn't seem to be lacking for anything and his children were happy, well fed and clothed. Surprised, the husband asked his wife how she had managed while he was away.

"Oh," said the wife, "maybe you forgot, but the arrangement you made with Naftoli Hertz was wonderful. He has been so good to us! He gave me money every Thursday, just as the two of you had agreed. He didn't miss even one week."

At his first chance, the husband ran to Naftoli Hertz and begged forgiveness. He thanked him from the bottom of his heart and said that he would spare no effort to repay every cent.

Naftoli Hertz wouldn't hear of it. "I gave it to a family that was in need and I never dreamed of getting the money back." Here again, the man tried in vain to convince Naftoli Hertz to accept payment, but it was hopeless. In desperation, he summoned Naftoli Hertz before a *din Torah,* to get a ruling on whether he should be forced to take back any money.

That was the second case.

The third *din Torah* involved a very poor man who sought to borrow money from Naftoli Hertz. He approached him for the loan and Naftoli Hertz said to him, "Who will be your guarantor? I can't take a chance lending you money. I must be assured that someone will repay me if you can't."

The poor fellow knew that no human being would back his loan. His poverty was obvious and his poor credit was common knowledge.

"Hashem will be my guarantor," the poor man answered. Naftoli Hertz said, "Good – Him I trust!" He lent the poor man money for six months. When the six months were up, the poor fellow couldn't repay the loan. Being embarrassed, he didn't even contact Naftoli Hertz.

Months went by and the poor man still couldn't repay the money. Since Naftoli Hertz didn't contact him the poor man did nothing except hope that his fortunes would change. Finally, after two years, he came into some money and with much embarrassment approached Naftoli Hertz to repay his loan.

"That won't be necessary," said Naftoli Hertz. "Your Guarantor has already paid back the loan."

"How is that?" wondered the startled fellow. "The day that you were supposed to pay me," explained Naftoli Hertz, "my business started becoming more profitable than ever. That was Hashem's payment for your loan. It has more than covered the amount."

Naftoli Hertz steadfastly refused to take any money from the poor man. The poor man brought him for a *din Torah.*

❦ ❦ ❦

"This," continued the Berditchever *Rebbe*, "was the kind of man Naftoli Hertz was; extremely discreet, but committed to *tzedakah* and *chessed* in their truest forms."

The funeral continued with reverence and appropriate tributes for the hidden *tzaddik*.

Part C: Parents and Children

◆§ *A Little Girl's Promise*

This story is a story within a story, connected with yet another story. It wouldn't have come to light except for the probing curiosity of one R' Boruch Yadler, a tireless volunteer for the *Yad L'Achim* organization in Israel. Singlehandedly, he rescued hundreds of children from the clutches of missionaries, irreligious schools and non-observant *moshavim* (settlements) throughout Israel. Having dealt with innumerable families in myriad circumstances, he knew countless stories and always loved to hear new ones.

Unfortunately, he was a very sick man and spent much time during the last years of his life in and out of hospitals. The people who visited him would sit on his bed and exchange stories. His room became more of a social club than an impersonal place of medical charts, intravenous bottles, dangling tubes and small paper cups filled with pale-colored pills.

During one of his hospital stays, R' Boruch noticed that the man in the bed next to him, Yechiel Kruger,* was regularly visited by his children, who were exceptionally well bred, respectful, attentive to his needs, and religiously observant.

One evening, when the room was quiet and the last of the day's visitors had gone, R' Boruch remarked to Mr. Kruger, "I've been working with children of all ages for years, and I can tell that your children are very special. How did you raise them that way?"

---

* The names are fictitious, but the story is true.

Mr. Kruger was surprised and pleased at the sudden compliment, although it wasn't the first time he'd been so complimented. He smiled sheepishly. "I've been very fortunate. Hashem has been very good to me. Years ago I wouldn't have imagined that my children would grow up this way."

"Oh, really?" said R' Yadler, sensing a story.

"Yes," said Mr. Kruger. "I've noticed that you like stories, so you might find this one interesting."

Yechiel Kruger then told his story.

He had been living in an anti-religious, atheistic *kibbutz,* sponsored by *Shomer Hatzair,* in northern Israel. *Shabbos* had no sanctity there, except as a day off from work. One *Shabbos* afternoon Yechiel, or Chiki as he was called, took a leisurely drive to see the sights in Jerusalem. The ride was uneventful until he got into the heart of Jerusalem's Geulah neighborhood. Suddenly his jeep was pelted with stones, and youngsters were yelling, "*Shabbos! Shabbos!*" Chiki had no idea what they were yelling about. When another stone hit his car, he jumped out to chase the boy who had thrown that last rock. But as he got out of his jeep, a well-dressed man came over to him and calmly took him aside. "I see you're not from around here, so perhaps you don't understand what these people want from you," he said. "Leave your car here — they won't harm it — and come with me." The man was very gentle and courteous and he put his arm around the young driver as they walked.

The man, R' Shapira, the *rav* of a local *shul,* invited Chiki into his home. After the initial pleasantries of introduction, R' Shapira began explaining some of the laws of *Shabbos.* He tried as best he could to explain how strongly the rock throwers felt about violations of *Shabbos* in their midst.

And then the *rav* added, "It's almost nightfall, stay with us until after *Shabbos.*" Chiki agreed and in the course of the evening, the two became friends and exchanged addresses. R' Shapira assured Chiki that he would stay in contact with him.

Within six weeks, R' Shapira made his first visit to the *kibbutz,* looking up Chiki Kruger and his family. Chiki was surprised that the *rav* had made such a long trip just to see him and invited him to stay for a meal. R' Shapira explained that because of *kashrus* laws he couldn't eat there, although he agreed to have a cup of tea. Chiki and his wife and the *rav* chatted amiably for a while and then Chiki excused himself to go to work in the fields.

Mrs. Kruger was interested in continuing the conversation, for she was more religiously inclined than her husband. Although totally non-observant, she had an interest in *Yiddishkeit* and asked many questions about *halachah* and customs that she had not been taught in her irreligious upbringing.

R' Shapira realized that the woman was searching to bring meaning into her life. The more he spoke to Mrs. Kruger, the more he became convinced that there was a spark of *Yiddishkeit* that was waiting to be fanned into a fire of faith. His only question was whether he could kindle it. When he was about to leave and was invited to return, he knew that the spark would eventually ignite.

Within three weeks, R' Shapira came back. Once again he and the young couple spoke about the purpose of life, the basic tenets of Judaism, and the possibility of leaving this particular *kibbutz* for a religious one. "If you are a socialist," said R' Shapira, "be a *religious* socialist." The Krugers couldn't see themselves moving from their comfortable surroundings, especially since they lacked the funds for such a move.

However, just a day or two after one of R' Shapira's visits, Mrs. Kruger received a letter stating that her request for restitution from Germany would be granted. The *Wiedergutmachung* Agency had helped her file a claim for damage to her family's property and for valuables lost during the Holocaust years. Now that her claim had been processed she would be getting a stipend every month.

With their new-found fortune, the Krugers, who were becoming increasingly disenchanted with the emptiness of their life on the non-religious *kibbutz*, decided that indeed the time had come for a change. With the help of R' Shapira they resettled on a religious *kibbutz*. On the first *Shabbos* there, one of the Kruger children put on the light and caused an uproar, but they soon became accustomed to the religious rules and regulations and to their new and friendly surroundings.

They began to enjoy a happy and fulfilling life.

❦ ❦ ❦

Chiki, now sitting up in his hospital bed, ended by saying, "It was the pleasantness and diligence of R' Shapira that persuaded us in the end. Right from the first day we met in Jerusalem, R' Shapira never talked down to me. He understood my background and never held it against me. Instead, his warmth and genuine concern led our family back to the ways of our ancestors. Eventually we left *kibbutz* life and settled in Jerusalem, where my children attended wonderful schools."

R' Boruch Yadler who was now also sitting up in his bed shook his head to and fro. "It's a beautiful story," he said, "with a very nice ending. R' Shapira was exceptionally nice to you. But, in my experience, I have come to realize that not every non-religious person gets the opportunity to become religious and then go on to have such wonderful children. I get the feeling that there was something more, something unique that made you deserve this exceptional gift from Hashem."

Chiki knew that R' Yadler was right. At first, he had not planned to mention the other part of the story because it was a personal matter. But everyone seemed to tell R' Yadler everything, so he decided to tell him the rest. R' Yadler would probably find a way to make good use of the story.

Chiki smiled and told another story from an even earlier period in his life.

❦ ❦ ❦

Well, maybe Hashem was watching us for another reason, too. You see, I was one of the *Yaldei Teheran*, the refugee children gathered from the concentration camp survivors who were transported through the Balkans and Turkey on the way to Teheran, from where they were eventually brought to Israel. I was placed in a *kibbutz* and there I spent my days and nights, thinking that I would be there forever. I met a girl who had come from Germany and we became friendly. After a while our relationship became serious and I asked her to marry me. It was then that she told me she had a secret of great importance to tell me.

We walked out into a field, and there she told me of her last emotional moments with her mother. The Germans had burst into her home and the Jews knew they were going to be carted away. Rumors abounded about parents being separated from their children, never to be reunited again.

The desperate mother took her seven-year-old daughter, held her tightly, and said to her, "My dear child, they will soon take us away and who knows if we will ever be together again. I want you to promise me one thing. There is something called *taharas hamishpachah* (family purity). You're too young to understand what it is, and there is no way that I can explain it to you today. When you get older go to a *rav* and he will explain what it means. Promise me that you will abide by those laws." The little girl was bewildered but saw the seriousness in her mother's face and promised to obey her wishes.

Mother and daughter were torn apart and never saw each other again. But she remembered. Years later, after being freed from the torture of imprisonment in the valley of horror and death, she went to a *rav* and learned the significance of her promise. Although she was not an observant Jewess, she resolved to observe the laws of *taharas hamishpachah.*

As we walked in the field, she told me that she could only consent to marry me if I would agree to her commitment. The fact that we would be living on a *kibbutz* where no one else observed these laws would make matters very difficult. But the young woman was determined to uphold these laws. I told her I would need time to think about it and asked for three days.

After much thought I told her that I would agree to her condition. All the years that we lived on the *kibbutz,* we had to make extra efforts, usually in secret, and often go to the nearby town to use the *mikveh.* Nevertheless, we were very serious about the promise, and until we met Rabbi Shapira, that was the one *mitzvah* that we observed.

❦ ❦ ❦

Now R' Boruch Yadler smiled broadly. "I knew your children

were special. Indeed, they are truly holy children." And then he repeated it again softly. "Pure and holy children. It's no wonder Hashem gave you both the opportunity to become observant Jews."

◆§ *Forbidden Food*

For the first forty years of his life, R' Sholom Schwadron never left Israel. He had been to countless towns and villages throughout his own country, lecturing and teaching, but now for the first time he found himself in a foreign land — Belgium — on a mission to raise funds for the Chinuch Atzmai schools in Israel.

A strange language, Flemish, surrounded him wherever he went, making him feel isolated and lonely. If sometimes, in the street, he overheard a Yiddish or Hebrew word, his ears would perk up as he warmed to the comfort of the friendly music of a recognizable cadence and inflection.

After a few weeks in Belgium, he had to leave what had finally become 'familiar territory,' and journey to a new unknown country, Holland.

Reluctantly he boarded a train in Antwerp for the two-and-a-half-hour trip to Amsterdam. As he walked down the aisles, a man in the back of the car jumped up from his seat. His hair was white, fluffy and unkempt, sprouting from the sides of his head. "*Shalom!*" the man exclaimed. A relaxed, contented feeling spread through R' Sholom for he knew he was going to travel with at least one Jew aboard. R' Sholom walked straight to the seat next to this gentleman whom he had never seen before, and made himself comfortable. "*Shalom U'vrachah* (greetings and blessings)," R' Sholom replied, smiling broadly. No matter that the man had no *yarmulke* (head covering), he was a *Yid* (Jew) and that was wonderful.

After the usual courteous exchanges and introductions, the gentleman, in a mixture of Yiddish and German, told R' Sholom that he was an artist who also owned an art gallery and was traveling to Amsterdam on business. "I'm not religious," he said. "Nevertheless, I eat only kosher food. Non-kosher food is repulsive to me and the thought of eating pig's meat is revolting. When I saw you get on the train, I was very happy," he continued. "I realized that you'd certainly be staying in a hotel in Amsterdam where kosher food is served, so I could follow you."

The two new friends struck a deal. R' Sholom would take him along to his hotel if his new friend would show him how to get there and be his interpreter. For over one hour the train snaked through various cities on the way to Holland while the two passengers sat, quietly immersed in their own thoughts. The dealer was reading a book and R' Sholom, a *sefer,* when suddenly the artist turned to R' Sholom and broke the silence.

"My father was religious, very religious!" he said.

"Really?" said the surprised R' Sholom.

"Yes," the man answered rather proudly. "He was even willing to risk his life for what he believed."

"How is that?" R' Sholom asked, always interested in a good story.

The artist then told this incredible episode.

❧ ❧ ❧

My father was drafted into the German army as a young soldier. It was almost impossible to maintain any religious standards there, but he was determined that he would eat only kosher food regardless of the consequences. At first he lived on fruit, fresh vegetables and bread. Day in day out, he took great care to conceal his eating habits from his superiors, but it wasn't long before they became aware that the man was ignoring most of the food. The officers interrogated him and finally he had to tell them the truth. For religious reasons he was eating only food that he was sure to be kosher. The officers were totally intolerant and accused him of being a disloyal soldier. They whipped him cruelly, claiming that he was trying to make himself weak so that he would not have to fight for his country.

Every morning at line-up he was singled out for a humiliating tongue-lashing, but he held his ground. Finally, he could not stand it any longer and he did a desperate thing. He wrote to Kaiser Wilhelm complaining about his treatment in the army. I can imagine what the officers would have done to my father if they had learned that he had complained about them, but somehow the letter got through to the Kaiser himself.

Every day my father kept hoping that something would happen that would stop the constant abuse he received from his officers and fellow soldiers who by now had joined the effort to humiliate him. He realized that if the Kaiser was angered by his letter, things could get even worse and he might very well be court-martialed. But he had been willing to chance it.

One afternoon a call went out to the barracks that everyone was to line up at once. It was highly unusual and no one could imagine the reason for it. They took their positions, row upon row of soldiers, standing smartly at attention. The captain barked out orders and announced that their unit had received a personal letter from the Kaiser and that it would now be read aloud.

Before the reading began, the captain ordered my father to take three steps out of line and to stand by himself. since the letter concerned him. You can imagine how he trembled.

The captain roared out the contents of the letter for all to hear.

> With regard to Private Deutsch #657487 who has written to me concerning the hardships he has endured because of his religious commitment to eat only kosher food; I hereby order that one of these options must be followed:
>
> (a) Kosher food must be made available at the facilities where Private Deutsch is now serving;
>
> (b) If none is available, then a special effort must be made to procure these items from other sources;
>
> (c) If this is not feasible, then Private Deutsch shall be transferred to a different unit where he can get his required food.

❦ ❦ ❦

The artist ended the story with a proud contented smile.

> Now, years later, when R' Sholom recounts the incident he notes, "I have often wondered why the artist merited that he should not commit the sin of eating non-kosher meat. True, he claimed that he hated pig's meat, but in essence he was observing the law of *kashrus*. He had a *zechus* (merit) and it was

obviously the *zechus* of his father's *mesiras nefesh* (devotion) for the observance of *kashrus*. Hashem granted the son a repulsion for non-kosher food so that he would not transgress the religious precept that his father had held so dear. As the Talmud (*Yevamos* 121b) notes: "דָּבָר שֶׁהַצַּדִּיק מִתְעַסֵּק בּוֹ, יִכָּשֵׁל בּוֹ זַרְעוֹ? — If a righteous man occupies himself with a particular mitzvah, can it be that his children will stumble regarding it?"

◈§ *A Trolley Ride — Tailor Made*

On a trip to England on behalf of Chinuch Atzmai, R' Sholom delivered numerous lectures to yeshivah students. One time, after his *drashah* in the Agudath Israel of Stamford Hill, a young man came up to him and said proudly, "My father too was a *maggid*."

"Really?" said R' Sholom, "Where are you from?"

The young man replied that he came from Hungary. After a short conversation the fellow related an incident that had changed his life, only because his father had been a prominent *maggid*. This is the story.

The young man's name was Lazlo, or as his father called him, Ezra. His father was one of the most famous *maggidim* in Budapest and traveled throughout Hungary holding *drashos* in every Jewish community. One day, in the *maggid's* home town, the tailor died. He had been a simple but deeply religious man, yet his son Moshe, who worked alongside him, had no religious convictions at all. Nevertheless, out of respect for his father, Moshe sat *shivah* (the mourning period of seven days).

During the week of *shivah*, Ezra's father, the *maggid*, went to pay a condolence call on Moshe. Little nine-year-old Ezra tagged along. When the *maggid* walked into the room where Moshe was sitting alone, Moshe was stunned. Everyone knew that he was a rebellious lad and few in the community had much to do with him. That the esteemed *maggid* came and consoled him during his time of mourning, and then spent time chatting with him, was truly remarkable.

A day later the *maggid* came again. Moshe sat and listened

attentively as the *maggid* said softly, "I think, for your father's honor, it would be nice if you would come to *shul* to say *Kaddish.*" To everyone's surprise, Moshe agreed.

Throughout the months, as Moshe continued coming to *shul,* the *maggid* slowly began having a calming influence on the young man. At first they discussed Jewish concepts and attitudes and then they began to study together. By year's end Moshe had become a religious man.

With a rekindled spirit that burned enthusiastically, Moshe began performing *mitzvos* with a fervor that left very little tolerance for those less committed than himself. In *shul* it was he who would demand that others refrain from talking during the services, unlike past years, when people had silenced him constantly on the few occasions that he came to *shul* with his father. Eventually everyone got to know Moshe the *schneider* (tailor) as a man in whose presence one would dare not violate a *mitzvah.*

Two years later, the German barbarians overran this Hungarian town, and the Jews were taken to forced-labor camps. Moshe the tailor was swept off the streets as were the *maggid* and his son Ezra. Together with multitudes of other frightened Jews they were crammed into the tightest quarters imaginable. With calculated cruelty, the Nazis tore children from parents — and that was the last time little Ezra, now twelve years old, ever saw his father.

Ezra was placed in bunks together with other children his age, and soon began to pick up their bad habits and corrupt behavior, in the daily struggle for survival. Any religious commitment that he had made slowly began to ebb away as he battled to stay alive in any way he could, even if it meant cheating, lying, or stealing. Like everyone else he suffered from malnutrition and indecent living conditions, but together with a tight group of friends, managed to persist and survive.

When the horror finally ended, the feeble remnants of the Holocaust had to be taken to rehabilitation areas where they were slowly reacclimated to normal foods and regular living conditions. Many could not eat solid meat, and it had to be ground so that their bodies could slowly relearn the process of digesting heavy foods.

The facility in which Ezra found himself was located high on a hill overlooking the city. The only way to get to the downtown area was to take a trolley down the long hill.

One Friday night, Tomas, a friend from another camp, suggested to Ezra (now called Lazlo) that they go downtown to enjoy themselves.

They had begun to feel like human beings once again and Tomas said it would be interesting to see nightlife in the city. Ezra was in a dilemma, for in the rehabilitation camp he had begun to think about going back to the religious practices of his father. In the labor camps it had been impossible for him to be observant, but now that he was back in civilization, perhaps it was time.

He knew that the trolley was the only feasible way to town but that was an open violation of the Sabbath. True he had been very lax these last years, but now that he was on his own, he was trying to become observant again.

"Have a cigarette," Tomas said, offering one to Lazlo. In an automatic reflex Lazlo stuck out his hand to accept it. The cigarette trembled in his hand. He wondered if Tomas noticed it. He wanted to throw it away but he couldn't, not in front of his good friend Tomas. He thought that if he inhaled his first puff, he would surely choke on it. He was going to have to make a decision: would he make the break now, or never? Before he could organize his thoughts, Tomas lit a match and held it to Lazlo's cigarette.

Lazlo put the cigarette in his mouth, bent forward, squinted as the flame caught on the tip, and inhaled slowly. It felt good. He was going downtown. Laughing nervously, they both got onto the trolley and began planning their night out.

The trolley rolled into the brightly lit town, while Ezra stood away from the window, hoping that no one he knew would see him.

And then he saw him. It couldn't be! But it was, Moshe the *schneider,* walking alone! Ezra's stomach tightened.

He recalled the first visit he and his late father, the *maggid,* had made to Moshe's home on a *shivah* call. Then he remembered Moshe reprimanding people in *shul* to be more respectful during prayers, and he said to himself firmly, "I will never allow the man whom my father made religious see that his son has become irreligious." And with that newly formed resolution, he got off the trolley at the next stop, walked all the way back up the hill to the rehabilitation camp and remained an observant Jew to this very day.

Ezra never saw nor heard from Moshe the *schneider* again. At times he has wondered if he had really seen Moshe the *schneider* at all. And if it was truly Moshe, how did he survive when all the others did not? Yes, there had been miracles. Or perhaps it could have been *Eliyahu HaNavi* (Elijah the Prophet) disguised as Moshe, just so the boy should repent in honor of his father's having made another boy repent. We will never know.

Certainly he saw something, that is positive, and it brought him back to the ways of his father and his Father in Heaven.

☙§ *Tears for Torah*

It is a fact that most people do not fulfill their potential. For some this is because they have never been inspired or encouraged, but many others are too lazy or complacent to exert the necessary effort and make the sacrifices needed to accomplish their utmost.

It is sad enough when one wastes his talents, but it is even more grievous when he doesn't even realize that he *has* those talents. How wasted is such a life, how bare is such an existence!

R' Naftali Tzvi Yehudah Berlin (1817-1893), better known as the *Netziv* (the acronym of his name), *rosh yeshivah* of the Yeshivah of Volozhin in Lithuania, was not only one of the greatest Torah scholars of his time, but also one of the most prolific authors. He wrote a volume of responsa *(Maishiv Davar),* a commentary on *Chumash (Ha'amek Davar),* and a commentary on most tractates of the Talmud *(Meromei Hasadeh).* But it was when he finished his first work, *Hamek*

She'alah, the classic three-volume in-depth study of the *she'iltos* of R' Achai Gaon, that the following incident took place.

The *Netziv* had invited a group of friends and students to a *siyum,* a festive meal to commemorate the completion of *Hamek She'alah.* During the meal, the *Netziv* revealed a moving incident from his youth.

When I was a young child, I was once playing at home when I heard my father crying. He and my mother had been talking in the kitchen, not aware that I could hear them. Since I overheard them mention my name, I paid close attention to the rest of the conversation. My father said, "I don't know how to handle the situation. I've tried every possible way to get Hirsh Leib (Yiddish for Tzvi Yehudah, a nickname by which the *Netziv* was often called) interested in learning. I have offered him prizes, but nothing seems to work. It was my fervent dream that he should become a *talmid chacham.* I guess we'll just have to train him to be a *baal melachah* (craftsman)."

I was shaken by my father's pain and tears, and when he finished talking I ran in and promised him that from then on I would devote my time to learning Torah.

[Little Hirsh Leib went on to become such an incredible *masmid* (one exceedingly diligent in his studies) that he eventually attained a position of worldwide Torah leadership.]

Imagine for a moment where I would be today had I not heard my father's anguish. I would have grown up to be a shoemaker, a tailor, or a carpenter. Coming from the family that I do, I would have been honest in business, and each night when I would come home from work, I probably would have looked into a *Mishnayos,* studied some *Chumash,* maybe even some *Ein Yaakov* (compendium of Aggadic material in the Talmud), and that would have been the extent of my Torah learning. Every Yom Kippur I would have asked Hashem for forgiveness for my sins that I might have committed that year, and before my death I would have recited the *viduy* (confession).

But the Heavenly Court would have asked me why I hadn't written the *Hamek She'alah* — and that would be something that, as a craftsman, I would never have imagined I was capable of doing. Yet the Heavenly Court would have been right for indeed you see that I actually did write it. Therefore the reason for this *siyum* is twofold: first, to celebrate the completion of this work; and second, to express gratitude to Hashem that He led me on the path to fulfill the potential within me, which otherwise would have lain dormant forever.

Whenever R' Sholom recounts this story of the *Netziv,* he usually accompanies it with another one showing the *Netziv's* level of *hasmadah* (diligence in Torah study). He had heard this story from R' Velvel Soloveitchik (1887-1959), the Brisker *Rav,* a great-grandson of the *Netziv.*

The *Netziv* was known to have a great love for *Eretz Yisrael* and every year he would make sure to use only an *esrog* that had been grown in the Holy Land. His esrog was beautiful, perfect in its shape and without the slightest flaw. On Succos many of his family members would come to him to recite a *brachah* on his *esrog.*

One of the most notable among the family members to come every year was R' Chaim Soloveitchik, the Brisker Rav, who was married to the *Netziv's* granddaughter.

One Succos, a year after *Shmittah* (the sabbatical year during which many agricultural activities are forbidden in *Eretz Yisrael),* R' Chaim did not come to recite the *brachah* on the *Netziv's esrog.* His absence was noted and the *Netziv* suspected that R' Chaim was hesitant to use an *esrog* from *Eretz Yisrael,* because of the many halachic questions involved in using fruit grown during *Shmittah.*

One morning, during Succos, the *Netziv* spoke to R' Chaim after davening and said, "You can believe me, there is no problem about making a *brachah* on my *esrog* this year." He assumed that R' Chaim was using an *esrog* from a country other than *Eretz Yisrael.* "You may come and make a *brachah,* it is just as kosher as in previous years."

Out of respect, R' Chaim didn't reply, but the next morning he still did not use the *esrog.* Late that night, well after midnight, R' Chaim was awakened and told that the *Zaide* (grandfather) was calling him.

Afraid that something was wrong, R' Chaim summoned his children and together they ran to the *Netziv's* home. They saw a light burning in the *succah* and rushed in to see what was wrong. The *Zaide* was sitting at a table piled high with open *sefarim,* as fresh and vibrant as ever.

R' Chaim breathed a sigh of relief and said, "I was so worried. Are you all right?"

"Yes I am, I just wanted you to come here so that I could show you that I have gone through the whole *sugya* (topic) and your fears are unfounded with regard to using my *esrog* this year."

Much relieved that everything was fine, R' Chaim sent the children home and then turned to the *Netziv* and said, "Please allow me for a moment to say *birchas hatorah* (the blessing that must be recited each morning before one begins to learn Torah) and then we can discuss your findings."

Falling back in his chair, the *Netziv* clasped his hands in amazement and deep disappointment. "*Vei iz zu meir* (woe is me) that I should have lived to see that my own grandson has not yet said *birchas hatorah* at three o'clock in the morning!"

Such was the *hasmadah* of the *Netziv,* and all because of his father's tears.

When he retells this story, R' Sholom is careful to add that R' Chaim — who was also known for his *hasmadah* — had probably been up late into the night at his own Torah studies and had retired only a short while before.

Yahrzeit

In the last years of his life, the *Ridvaz,* R' Yaakov David Wilowsky (1845-1913), lived in the holy city of Tzefas in *Eretz Yisrael.* Prior to that, he had been *Rav* of Slutzk, Poland,and was considered one of the *gaonim* of his generation. He authored two classic commentaries on the *Talmud Yerushalmi,* the *Ridvaz* and *Tosfos HaRid* which today are published as part of almost every edition of *Talmud Yerushalmi.*

One winter afternoon in Tzefas, on the day of his father's *yahrzeit*, the *Ridvaz* came to *shul* earlier than usual for *Minchah*, before most of the people had arrived. He went to a *shtender* (lectern), rested his elbows on its surface, cupped his chin in his hands and became lost in thought. As he stood there for a few moments meditating, tears welled up in his eyes and slowly trickled down his cheeks. And then, he started to cry, softly, to himself.

The people in *shul* knew that the *rav* had *yahrzeit*, and so they respectfully kept their distance, assuming that he was lost in memories of the past.

However, a close friend went to him and said, "R' Yaakov Dovid, why are you so upset? Your father was eighty years old when he passed away, certainly not a youngster, and he died almost fifty years ago"

"I'll tell you," said the *Ridvaz*, composing himself. And this is the story he related.

❦ ❦ ❦

I was thinking of the time when I was a young boy and my father arranged for me to have the best *melamed* (teacher) in our town, a certain R' Chaim Sender, as a private tutor. He charged one ruble a month, which was a large sum of money in those days, especially for my father, who was very poor. It took quite an effort to put the money together every month.

My father made his living making furnaces for people. One winter, business was very bad because there was a shortage of cement and lime, and my father couldn't meet the payments to R' Chaim Sender. Three months went by and still he had not paid the *melamed*. Then one day, I came home with a note from the *melamed* which said that if he did not get money the next morning, he would be unable to continue teaching me.

When my parents read the note they were devastated. To them, my Torah study meant everything. They felt that nothing should stand in the way of my becoming a *talmid chacham*. When my father went to *shul* that evening he heard a wealthy man complain that the contractors building a house for his son and future daughter-in-law could not get a furnace because of the cement and lime shortage. He offered six rubles to anyone who would get him a furnace. In Russia, a furnace was a vital household item, for it was used to both heat the home and cook the food.

When he came home from *shul,* he discussed the matter with my mother and they agreed that my father should take apart our oven, brick by brick,and build a new one for the rich man. Then they would have the six rubles for my *melamed.*

My father did just that and received the six rubles which he immediately gave me to pay R' Chaim Sender. "Tell the *melamed,*" he said to me proudly, "three is for back pay, and the other three are for the next three months for my Yankel Dovid."

The winter was bitterly cold and we all froze and shivered. All that, so that I should have the best *melamed* and grow in Torah.

❧ ❧ ❧

The *Ridvaz* paused, took a breath and continued. "This afternoon it was cold outside and I thought that maybe I should arrange for a *minyan* in my home instead of coming to *shul.* Then I decided that in honor of my father, I should make the extra effort to go to *shul* instead.

"When I came to *shul* a little while ago, I thought about the *mesiras nefesh* (self-sacrifice) of my father and my whole family during that bitter cold winter, just for me and my learning. That's why I cried, because I remembered the boundless affection and devotion that only parents can have so that their child should learn our holy Torah."

◆§ *A Time to Cry*

R' Michoel Ber Weissmandl (1903-1957), the *rosh yeshivah* of the Nitra Yeshivah, was known throughout the world for his tireless efforts in the 1940's to save thousands of Jews from the Nazi barbarians. R' Weissmandl himself escaped from an Auschwitz death train and eventually made his way to America where he opened the Nitra Yeshivah in Mt. Kisco, New York. His brilliance and scholarship were recognized the world over. (See *Sefer Toras Chemed.*)

After the war, when R' Weissmandl was in America, two business partners came to him and told him of their terrible problem. Each of them had a son who was planning to marry a gentile girl. The fathers were devastated by this turn of events and were beside themselves with grief.

R' Weissmandl began asking them about the *chinuch* (religious education) they had given their children, which schools they had attended and how much time the fathers had studied with them, and so on. Both men told the same story. They had come from Europe, settled in cities where there were no yeshivos, and had sent their children to public schools. There, the children became part of the secular society and eventually lost their *Yiddishkeit.*

R' Weissmandl listened to their problem and told them that he would tell them a story. (R' Sholom is not sure if the following episode actually happened or if it was meant as a parable.)

After World War I, new territorial borders were drawn between Poland and Russia. The new boundaries cut through many regions that had previously been under one government. In one city where many Jews lived, the new lines separated the Jewish cemetery from the community, thus the Jews who lived in Poland now had to bury their dead in Russia.

Whenever Jews had to bury someone they had to get a special visa from the Russian consulate, granting permission to cross the border. At times the red tape would take days to complete. In the interim the deceased person would remain unburied, which was a transgression of Jewish law.

After a number of such occurrences, the Jews appealed to the Russian government to allow the *chevra kadisha* (burial society) special permission to bypass the border formalities. Permission was granted. Now, every time there was a burial, the *chevra kadisha* was waved through by the border guards.

Some unscrupulous gentile smugglers heard about this leniency and decided to take advantage of it. They filled a coffin with contraband and, posing as members of the Jewish *chevra kadisha,* smuggled goods into Russia. Once on the other side, they would meet their previously arranged contact, who would buy the goods from them and then sell it for a nice profit. Thus, a thriving black market was established.

This went on for months and these border runners enjoyed a lucrative business. One morning, as they walked across the border a young soldier called them over. "Where are you going?" he inquired.

"To bury a fellow Jew in the cemetery." they replied.

"You don't look very sad to me," the soldier said. "You've been laughing and joking the entire time. I've been watching you and I don't think you're going to bury anybody."

The impostors realized they were in trouble, so they tried to make excuses for themselves. However, they were unable to allay the young soldiers' suspicions. Finally he demanded, "Open the coffin and let me see what's inside!"

"We can't," the group insisted, "that would be a lack of respect for the deceased. We have a religious law that once a coffin is closed, it may not be opened."

The soldier would not let them proceed any further, and when they refused to obey his orders, he called for a higher official, a lieutenant, to pursue the matter further.

The lieutenant had little patience with these people and demanded that they open the casket at once, but once again the "pallbearers" claimed it would be a humiliation to the deceased and against their religious beliefs. When the lieutenant finally threatened them with jail, they realized that they had no choice but to open the coffin. They began to plead for forgiveness. Ignoring their pleas, the lieutenant had the casket opened and there to the utter humiliation of all in the group, was the merchandise, neatly packed, ready to be delivered. They had been caught red handed.

The culprits broke down and cried, pleading for mercy and promising they would never do it again.

The lieutenant turned slowly, looked at each one of them and said, "If you would have cried before, then you would not have to cry now."

❦ ❦ ❦

"And this is what I say to you," continued R' Weissmandl, looking at each of the two men in front of him, "If you would have cried years ago, and been concerned for your children's *chinuch* earlier, then you would not have to cry now!"

Part D: A Sixth Sense

◆§ *Yitzchak the Shikker*

Before R' Sholom tells a long story, he paints a verbal background of colorful information about the characters in the story and the era in which they lived, until the listener pictures the episode as vividly as if he were witnessing it first hand. Here we will record part of the background of the emotional tale of R' Chezkel. R' Sholom knew R' Chezkel personally, so the incident, told with every nuance and detail involved, becomes more meaningful. Add to this the fact that R' Chezkel had only one leg for the last thirteen years of his life, and it is a small wonder that those who hear the tale shudder.

R' Chezkel was a brilliant *talmid chacham*. He was a *talmid* of R' Leib Chasman (who later became the *mashgiach* in the Chevron Yeshivah) when R' Leib had his yeshivah in Stutchin, Poland. Eventually, R' Chezkel moved to *Eretz Yisrael* where he became a *melamed* in the Chayei Olam Yeshivah in Jerusalem and then opened the first yeshivah in Haifa.

After many years in Haifa, he died on a Friday night. Although he left a will in which he asked that there be no eulogies for him, the will was not found until after his well-attended funeral had taken place and lengthy eulogies had been delivered. It was taken to mean that G-d wanted the world to know of this man's great virtues despite his modesty. R' Chezkel had requested that his monument bear no titles, but rather read simply, "Here lies a man who suffered greatly, a man who did not attain everything he could have."

Indeed he suffered with ulcers and poor circulation in his legs for over two decades. Finally because gangrene had set in and doctors feared that it would spread to the rest of his body, his leg was amputated.

About the time that his son was married, the doctors feared that R' Chezkel's second leg might have to be amputated as well. It was then that he decided to reveal this story in the hope that a public recounting of it would serve as a *zechus* (merit) to save his second leg. Thus, at his son's *sheva berachos,* on Succos, he recounted the story in poetry.

This is R' Chezkel's story:

When Chezkel was fifteen years old, he studied in the Yeshivah of Stutchin, Poland. Once a week, Thursday evening, the *bochurim* in the yeshivah would trek to a certain synagogue known as the Halvoyas Hames *shul* where they would study all night. The synagogue was located on the outskirts of the town, not far from the Jewish cemetery. In this synagogue people from all surrounding areas would gather to pay final tribute to a Jew who had passed away. Psalms would be recited and eulogies delivered, then the people would slowly walk to the gravesite for the burial. Thus the synagogue's name — Halvoyas Hames ("escorting the dead".)*

The Polish winters are frigid and the biting wind can chill the marrow of the bones. One Thursday night the boys were studying in the *beis midrash* (synagogue / study hall) of the Halvoyas Hames *shul* huddled near the coal stove, warmed by the crackling of the oven and their own Torah study.

Behind the stove lay a tattered and ragged man, a constant victim of ridicule known only as "Yitzchak the *Shikker*" (drunkard). People claimed that all he did was drink whiskey or beer in the local tavern and then fall asleep in one of the *shuls.* Children jeered as they ran behind him, mimicking his uneven gait.

One freezing Thursday night, as the six boys sat around the warm stove of the Halvoyas Hames *shul,* a bedraggled wagon driver came in from the icy cold, almost frost bitten, the tears on his face turning into glistening icicles.

---

* See page 42, above, "Seventeen Soldiers' Lives on the Line".

"Boys, I need help," pleaded the man. "I was riding on my horse and wagon outside of town when the horse slipped on the ice. He must have hurt his leg because I can't get him to stand up. I need help to lift my horse. I have merchandise in my wagon to deliver by tomorrow. If I don't deliver it, I'll have no income. My horse is my livelihood. Please come and help me."

The young boys listened and turned to consult each other. They debated, rationalized, weighed and considered their obligation to help the unfortunate peddler, as measured against *bitul Torah* (the suspension of Torah study). Perhaps the warmth and comfort of the *beis midrash* made the young boys less objective than usual as to their moral obligations. After all, they thought, they were studying Torah, the most important of all *mitzvos*.

After their huddled discussion they announced, "We feel that you should go elsewhere to get help. We would like to help but we feel that we are obligated to stay here because we are in the midst of Torah study."

As the discussion went on, Yitzchak the Shikker lay behind the oven, observing what was happening. As the traveler left the synagogue dejectedly, Yitzchak called out from where he lay, "Is that how you treat a man in need?" He then cursed them, "Your feet won't carry you."

The boys were surprised that Yitzchak had even been paying attention to what had transpired. Chezkel laughed and snapped back at him, "Yitzchak, since when did you become a *paskunyak* (a derogatory term for one who sits in judgment)?"

Yitzchak turned over and shrugged his shoulders and answered, "*Nu, nu!*" — as if to say, just wait and see!

The boys were startled by Yitzchak's reaction, but nonetheless tried to resume their studies. They couldn't. A feeling of guilt at their lack of concern gnawed at them. After fifteen minutes, they discussed the matter again and decided, that, on second thought, perhaps they should go out and find the wagon driver. They walked out into the brisk wind and biting cold of the night. They huddled in their coats as they walked in the direction from which they thought the peddler had come. They began looking in homes and buildings where he might have gone for help. No luck.

Finally, they decided to go to the road outside the town. They had been walking for about twenty minutes when, in the still of the night, they heard soft, anguished cries. As they came closer to the sounds, they could see the peddler sitting on the road, leaning against his horse who had died in the frost. The boys were devastated. They tried to apologize and then made their way back to the yeshivah, embarrassed and saddened.

About a half year later, fifteen-year-old Chezkel was studying in the yeshivah one afternoon when Yitzchak the Shikker approached him. "Can I have a word with you?" "Yes, Yitzchak, what would you like?"

"Chezkel, I would like you to do me a favor. Tonight I am leaving this world and I'd like you to be in my room with me."

"Don't be ridiculous," retorted Chezkel. "You've had one drink too many."

Yitzchak looked Chezkel straight in the eye and said in a low, even voice, "Chezkel, this is not a laughing matter. I need you in my room tonight, for tonight is my last on this earth." Chezkel looked into Yitzchak's eyes. They were clear and serious, as was his demeanor.

"All right," Chezkel muttered. "I'll be there. What time and where do you live?"

"Eleven-thirty," said Yitzchak, and gave the young boy directions.

That evening, Chezkel went to the outskirts of the town where Yitzchak had told him he lived. The area was a slum and the house was dilapidated. It creaked in the wind, as Chezkel went up the stairs and into a back room. As he entered he realized that Yitzchak was already lying on his bed. The small room contained only the bed and one chair.

"Thank you for coming, Chezkel," said Yitzchak softly. "Please sit down."

"Yes, yes," stammered Chezkel, who suddenly realized that this was no joking matter.

"Chezkel, in a little while, I will leave this world and I have a favor to ask you."

"Yes, *Reb* Yitzchak," the frightened fifteen-year-old said. Now it was *Reb* Yitzchak.

"I would like to be buried next to the *tzaddik* in the town's old cemetery."

"But," Chezkel interrupted, "everyone knows that there is not a single spot in the old Jewish cemetery. For years, they've been using the new cemetery. Besides, be realistic, R' Yitzchak, they won't let you be buried there, you know your reputation."

"Don't worry, young man," said Yitzchak reassuringly. "There will be a place, and besides, this will help. I want you to bring the sheets of paper in this box to the *rav* of the town."

Chezkel then noticed the box filled with papers. On the papers was a magnificent pair of *tefillin* and a beautiful *tallis*. Chezkel was taken aback. Everyone had been used to seeing Yitzchak in a tattered and threadbare *tallis*, yet this *tallis* was immaculate and the *tefillin*, too, gleamed in the dimly lit room. It was becoming obvious to Chezkel that Yitzchak the Shikker was not the simpleton that everyone thought he was. They spoke for a few moments and when Chezkel assured Yitzchak that he would fulfill his wishes, Yitzchak recited softly, "*Shema Yisrael* ...," closed his eyes and expired.

Holding the papers tightly, Chezkel quickly left the room, hurried down the stairs and ran screaming in the streets, "A *tzaddik* was *niftar*, a *tzaddik* was *niftar*." He ran as fast as he could to the home of the *rav*, and told him everything that had happened. The *rav* leafed through the manuscripts and realized that the writings were of a kabbalistic nature. He was amazed. What they had had in their midst, scorned and often ridiculed, was one of the *lamed-vav tzaddikim* (the thirty-six exceptional *tzaddikim* in each generation, see above, p. 67).

The *chevra kadisha* was summoned and told of Yitzchak's request. They looked at the *rav* incredulously. There hadn't been room in the old cemetery for over thirty years. "Still," said the *rav*, "knowing what I know now, I thing we should check if there is indeed a space."

"It's impossible," said a member of the *chevra*.

Chezkel went along as the *chevra* went to the cemetery the next morning. To their utter astonishment, there was indeed a place right next to the old *tzaddik*, just as Yitzchak had said there would be. By midday, news of the previous night's events had spread around the town and a crowd of people appeared at the Halvoyas Hames *shul* to pay their final respects to R' Yitzchak. Everyone followed his bier, as each person begged his forgiveness for the abuse they had showered upon him all his life.

As R' Chezkel told this story to the stunned listeners in the *succah,* he continued in a quiet tone. "The words of a *tzaddik* are like the words of a prophet. I never forgot the words with which he scolded me that night when the wagon driver came into the *beis midrash,* and as you see they came to pass." R' Chezkel was referring to his having only one leg. The hush in the *succah* was almost tangible.

R' Chezkel never needed a second amputation. To the contrary, he made such a remarkable recovery that even his doctors were surprised. A short time after relating this incident, R' Chezkel passed away, but his incredible story lives on.

Yankele Moser and the Kelmer Maggid

The Kelemer *Maggid,* R' Moshe Yitzchok (the *Darshan*, 1828-1899), was known for his masterful oratory. He could depict a scene so vividly that people would listen entranced, and feel that they were actually witnessing the event he was describing. When the Kelemer *Maggid* came to town he would seek out the aspects of Jewish life that needed reinforcement and improvement. At the *bimah,* he minced no words and held back no fury, often singling out individuals who were known as notorious wrongdoers. Nevertheless, people flocked to hear him whenever he came. He was a man of unusual stamina. It is said that once, in the month of Elul, a month of introspection in preparation for the holy days of Rosh Hashanah and Yom Kippur, he delivered a staggering sixty *drashos!*

In Bialystok, where he would often speak, each trade had its own synagogue. There was the *Garber's Shul* for men in the leather trade, the *Stolyer's Shul* for carpenters, and the *Shneider's Shul* for tailors.

One night, in the *Shneider's Shul,* people from all walks of life gathered to hear a *drashah* from the Kelemer *Maggid.* That night, with great flamboyance, he depicted how the town of Bialystok appeared before *Hashem* on the final Day of Judgment. For over an hour he detailed the city's virtues and faults, describing the debates among members of the Heavenly Court of the fate of the townsfolk. Then the *Maggid* announced, "The moment of truth has arrived for the tailors of Bialystok, the people of the *Shneider's Shul.* Listen," he thundered, "the voices in the Heavenly Court call, 'Tailors of Bialystok, stand at attention'." And incredibly all the tailors in the audience actually got up and stood at attention!

The scenario had become so real to them that for a moment they forgot where they were and imagined themselves actually being judged.

The following extraordinary story which R' Sholom heard from the Chazon Ish's brother, R' Meir Karelitz (1877-1955), portrays the Kelemer perfectly. His charisma, charm, piety and relentless rage all blend in this delightful story. The story has become another of R' Sholom's classics.

The Kelemer *Maggid* never traveled anywhere after midday on Friday. Wherever he was at that point that is where he settled for Shabbos.

One Friday morning while riding with a coachman, the *maggid* looked at his watch and saw that it was getting close to noon. He called out for the coachman to stop, saying that he had to get off. "But, *Rebbe,*" the driver protested, "we're so far from a city, how can you get off the wagon right here in the middle of a forest?"

"I don't travel on Fridays after midday. That is my custom and I won't change it now," answered the Kelemer.

"Very well, have it your way," the driver said. "But let me give you some directions. Walk easterly for about an hour, and then at the crossroad, turn left, you will eventually come into a city."

"Fine," said the *maggid,* "that is exactly what I will do."

Slowly but surely the Kelemer made his way to the crossroad, turned left and made his way into a city. As he came to the perimeter of the city he saw a Jew walking along. "Tell me, *Reb Yid* (Mr. Jew, a title of respect for a stranger whose name is not known)," he said, "What is happening in this town of yours?"

"Oh, everything is just fine here," answered the man. "Why do you ask?"

"I am a *maggid,*" the Kelemer *Maggid* said, "and I usually speak before the townsfolk. I like to know if there is anything doing in the city that needs correcting so that I may address the people about it."

"Everything is fine here, really."

"How about *shmiras Shabbos* (Sabbath observance)?"

"Yes, that's good."

"*Hachnosas orchim* (hospitality)?"

"That's fine," came the reply.

"What about the *chevra kadisha?*"

"In perfect order."

"Is there nothing wrong in this city at all?" asked the Kelemer in amazement.

"Oh yes, we do have one terrible problem. We have a young fellow named Yankele who is a *moser* (informant) of the worst kind. He loves to give incriminating information to the authorities which gets people into all kinds of trouble. Besides that, he beats people."

The man suddenly turned to run away. "I see him coming down the mountain now, out there in the distance. I'm getting away from here."

"Wait, wait," cried the Kelemer, "isn't there anything good about him at all? He has to have at least one good trait."

"Oh yes," said the man as he rapidly walked away, "if he promises that he will ruin someone you can be sure that he will. He keeps his word."

"Fine, thank you. I'll find a way to use the information," said the Kelemer.

The *maggid* started walking towards the evil Yankele. As he came within hearing distance,the Kelemer stuck out his hand, smiled broadly, and said, "*Shalom Aleichem, Reb* Yankele."

The young man was taken aback. No one had ever called him "*Reb* Yankele" before. Most people ran from him or cursed at him. "What do you want from me?" asked Yankele.

"I'll tell you," said the Kelemer. "I am a *maggid* and I travel from place to place. Wherever I give *drashos,* people pass around a plate and put some money on it; that's how I make a living. But I'm getting old now, and very tired. So I have to make as much money as I can. If you would come to my *drashah* this Sunday night, that would be very helpful to me."

"Me? Go to the *drashah?* You have to be joking!" said Yankele angrily. "I wouldn't go there for anyone."

The charismatic Kelemer did not give up. "Yankele, you are a popular person. If I can tell people that you will come to the *drashah,* then it will lend importance to the event and surely many more people will show up. Please do it for an old Jew. I need the money."

Yankele was softened by the pleasant manner with which he had been addressed.

"All right, all right," he finally agreed. "I'll come." After a few minutes, Yankele caught himself and said, "It's ridiculous. Forget what I said before, I will *not* come. I never come to those kind of things."

"Now wait," said the Kelemer, "I was told that you are a truthful person and once you say something you don't go back on your word."

Yankele was snared. A hunter trapped in his own net. And so he said, "All right, all right, I'll come."

On Sunday night the Kelemer made his way to the *shul* where a huge crowd awaited him. A *maggid* coming to town was an event, not only a religious experience but an occasion of entertainment that brought out men, women and children. A *maggid* could speak for hours and people would be spellbound, especially by a *maggid* as famous as the Kelemer.

The people found their places in the large *shul* and waited for the *maggid* to make his way to the *bimah.* But the *maggid* just sat in the front row together with the *rabbonim* of the town and refused to go up to the *bimah* until Yankele the *moser* came into the *shul.* Ten minutes went by ... fifteen minutes ... still no sign of Yankele. The people were beginning to get impatient. After all, Yankele had never come to a *drashah* before, so why bother waiting for him now?

Finally, after an hour, from the back of the *shul* people began whispering nervously that Yankele was coming. All eyes turned toward the door. As he entered a path was cleared, forming two walls of people so that Yankele could walk through without touching anyone. The Kelemer stood up, ordered that Yankele be given a seat up front. He was given a seat in the very front row along with the rabbonim present. He sat down stiffly, uncomfortable in such lofty company.

The Kelemer made his way up to the *bimah,* put on a *tallis,* kissed the curtain on the *Aron Hakodesh* and began his *drashah* by citing the Mishnah (*Sanhedrin* 10:1) "כָּל יִשְׂרָאֵל יֵשׁ לָהֶם חֵלֶק לָעוֹלָם הַבָּא — Every Jew has a share in the World to Come." And for over an hour he expounded on the commendable virtues and traits of self-denial, morality, goodness, and exemplary behavior. The people loved it and were entranced as he wove parables and stories together to bring out his points.

After an hour he said, "For years I have been speaking in cities and towns throughout Poland and Russia. In many places people have rectified wrongs because of what I have said. Men have become more honest, people have started doing *mitzvos,* many have become repentant. Surely I have some reward waiting for me in the World to Come. But tonight I am going to give my reward to my friend Yankele, because he did me a great favor by coming to my *drashah* just as he promised he would. Yankele, come here, I am going to sign a contract, witnessed by the *rabbonim* of the city, that will give you the reward that I have earned all these years."

The Kelemer *Maggid* called up three rabbonim from the front row and sat down with them to write the contract. With much flair and pomp he signed over to Yankele all the reward he had earned in the World to Come. The *rabbonim* signed and then called up Yankele to accept it. Yankele looked around him as he felt the weight of a thousand eyes on him. Slowly he began to rise, and then hesitantly went up the steps to the *bimah* where he sat down, signed his name, and to the awe and shock of all who were gathered there, he accepted the contract. A hush pervaded the crowd. The Kelemer knew that he had Yankele exactly where he wanted him.

Then the Kelemer, with a song on his lips, took off on the

second part of the same Mishnah: "וְאֵלוּ שֶׁאֵין לָהֶם חֵלֶק לָעוֹלָם הַבָּא" — But these do *not* have a share in the World to Come ..."

He then went into a tirade about man's baser characteristics, his evil ploys and plans. He criticized those who sinned and in self-righteousness considered themselves worthy people when in reality, they were wicked. For another hour he stormed about the deplorable level to which a man can stoop through sinning. Then he pointed a finger at Yankele sitting in the front row and said, "Yankele, Yankele, you have the opportunity to do *teshuvah* (repentance) right now. Don't give up and lose all that reward you got tonight. Come back to the fold of *Yiddishkeit.* Come back to a society that will embrace you. Come back, come back. You will be fortunate, you will be lucky." Yankele could barely lift his head, so filled was he with fear and remorse.

The Kelemer finished his *drashah,* organized a *minyan* for *Maariv* (evening services) and left the *beis midrash.* The next day he was gone.

Some say it was twelve, some say it was seventeen years later, when the *maggid* made his way to the same small forsaken town again. While in the city he decided to look up his old friend, Yankele the *moser.* He inquired about him, but no one seemed to remember anyone by the name of Yankele the *moser.*

Finally, in the market place, he came upon an older gentleman who responded to the Kelemer's inquiry with a smile. "You must surely mean *Reb* Yankele."

"Who?" asked the *maggid.*

"Yes, Yes," said the old man. "A long time ago there was someone in town called Yankele the *moser.* At that time he was a troublemaker, but then something happened. A *maggid* came to town and gave him a powerful *drashah,* and it is said that Yankele went back to his house and cried all night. The next morning he came early to *shul,* prayed and then went up to the empty area of the *ezras nashim* (women's section) where he stayed for a long time. For years he lived there. The women provided him with food and clothing. And every day he would get people to teach him Torah. Eventually he became a big *tzaddik,* and today people know him as Yankele the *tzaddik.* Most don't even know he was ever Yankele the *moser.*"

"Tell everyone that the Kelemer *Maggid* is here," said the *maggid*, "and call them together for there will be a *drashah* in two nights." The word spread quickly around town as signs were posted and people went from door to door to announce that the famous Kelemer was going to give a *drashah* in the big *shul* where he had spoken many years ago.

Now once again everyone gathered and the Kelemer began his impassioned *drashah.*

After a few introductory remarks, the Kelemer said, "I am told that there is a man in town known as Yankele the *tzaddik.* Yankele, I am surprised at how you can allow yourself to be called that. You of all people should know the Mishnah *(Yoma* 85b) states: 'For sins between G-d and man, Yom Kippur provides atonement. But for sins between man and his fellow man, Yom Kippur does not provide atonement until he appeases his fellow man.' But what if a man dies before he has been appeased by someone who has wronged him? Then the wrongdoer must go to the gravesite of the deceased man together with a *minyan,* and recite a confession. (See *Rambam Hilchos Teshuvah* 2:11.)

"Yankele," continued the *maggid,* "you know in your heart what your past was and you know how many people you ruined with your terrible actions years ago. Have you begged forgiveness? How many widows and orphans did you create? Did you go to the graves of those husbands and fathers against whom you sinned and who are here no longer? Yankele, you have come so far, but you still have one more major step to go. Yankele, it is almost impossible for you to know where all those people from long ago are buried. But we, the community, can in absentia be their representatives and accept your confession for amongst us there are many of their descendants. Make your way up here and confess openly!"

The Kelemer instructed someone to open the *Aron Hakodesh* and called for Yankele to come forward. Yankele could hardly walk, for he was convulsed with weeping. He understood the deep truth of the maggid's words. "Come forward!" bellowed the *Maggid,* "so that you can finally obtain forgiveness properly."

Assisted by his friends, Yankele made his way forward but found that he could not utter a word. He was silent. The Kelemer then said, "Very well, I will say the words and you repeat after me," the Kelemer said, "*Chatasi,* I have sinned" — Yankele repeated, "*Chatasi,* I have sinned" — "to Hashem the G-d of Israel" — "to Hashem the G-d of Israel" — "and to the people of this town" — "and to the people of this town."

The shul was deathly quiet. Everyone listened with compassion and deep feelings of forgiveness for the man who had truly become repentant over the years. Then all together, led by the Kelemer they shouted loudly, "*Mochul loch* (you are forgiven); *mochul loch; mochul loch.*"

"Now," said the Kelemer maggid, embracing Yankele, "you are truly *Reb* Yankel the *tzaddik.*"

◆§ *A Treasure of "Glowing Letters"*

Rambam (Maimonides; *Hilchos Issurei Mizbayach* 7:11) writes that when one feeds or clothes the needy, he should give them his finest. And when one builds a synagogue it should be more beautiful then his own home. He cites as an example Abel, who presented Hashem with the choicest of his produce (see *Genesis* 4:4), which Hashem accepted, as opposed to the inferior offering that Cain presented, which Hashem rejected.

Rambam closes his thoughts by citing a verse in *Leviticus* 3:16, *kol chelev* ... (All of the choicest ...). This verse dictates that if one sanctifies something for use in the Temple, that too should be from his finest possessions. The next incident is an illustration of just these points.

In Europe it was known that the most sought-after pairs of *tefillin* were those that contained the *parshios* written by the renowned *sofer* (scribe), R' Moshe P'shevorsker, a disciple of the *Maggid* of Mezritsch. R' Moshe was not only a great *tzaddik,* he also took meticulous care in writing every letter in the *parshios,* embellishing each one with all the refinements contained in the *Shulchan Aruch.* Additionally, he wrote each word, especially the name of Hashem, with proper intent. It was not easy to find a pair of *tefillin* written by R' Moshe, and those that were for sale were extremely expensive.

The Gerer *Rebbe,* R' Avraham Mordechai Alter (1866-1948), who was *rebbe* for more than forty years, owned a pair of R' Moshe P'shevorsker's *tefillin.* He treasured them and used them only once a year, on *erev* Yom Kippur.

It happened once that a poor young boy came to the Gerer *Rebbe* and told him that he couldn't afford a pair of *tefillin.* The *Rebbe* thought for a moment, then told the boy to wait. He came back shortly with a pair of *tefillin* in his hands. It was his own treasured pair, the ones with the *parshios* of R' Moshe P'shevorsker. When the rebbe's family realized which pair the *rebbe* had given the boy, they were aghast. They protested and complained. But the *rebbe* exclaimed, "What's wrong? The Torah says *kol chelev* ..." For charity he had given his very best, in accordance with the *Rambam's* directive.

> When R' Sholom finishes telling this story he wistfully remarks that he has yet another story about the *parshios* of R' Moshe P'shevorsker. Master story-teller that he is, people around him smile knowingly, for it is obvious that his listeners will be rewarded.

R' Sholom lost his father at the tender age of seven. His mother, a deeply religious woman [she completed the sefer *Ein Yaakov* (on the Aggados of the Talmud) numerous times], was very poor and eked out a living selling bread to support her children. Every morning she would get up early to pick up the loaves, and spend the morning and afternoon delivering them. For a while the financial crisis was so bad that little Sholom'ke (his mother's nickname for him) had to be placed in an orphanage. For his *bar mitzvah,* his mother scraped together whatever money she could and bought him a pair of *tefillin.*

R' Sholom interrupts himself to explain something about the poverty of his mother. One day when he was much older, he came home and found his mother sick in bed. She seemed deeply despondent and on the verge of tears. "What's wrong, Momma?" asked the young Sholom'ke.

"Sholom'ke mit vus kumpt mehn oif yener velt (With what

merit will I come to the next world)?" his pious mother sighed.

"Momma, *lomir machen a cheshbon* (let us make a moral audit). How many breads did you sell every day? How many days of the year did you sell these breads? How many years did you go around the city? How many steps did you climb each day to deliver the breads? And all for what, Momma? So that your children should become *bnei Torah,* be good and *frum,* and do *mitzvos.* If so, then each step and each bread was a *mitzvah* and will surely outweigh, in the scales of Final Judgment, any *aveiros* (sins) you may have."

A smile began to spread over his mother's face, wiping away the wrinkled frown of sadness. She looked up at her Sholom'ke and said contentedly, "*Nechamtani b'ni, nechamtani* (you've consoled me, my son, you've consoled me)."

Getting back to the main story, R' Sholom tells how after his *bar mitzvah,* he went to learn in the Yeshivah of Petach Tikvah where the renowned *tzaddik* R' Elya Dushnitzer was the *mashgiach.* After being under his tutelage for two years, Sholom'ke developed a more heedful attitude in his performance of *mitzvos* and began paying more attention to the finer points of their observance. He became convinced that the inexpensive pair of *tefillin* his mother had been able to afford for his *bar mitzvah* could not possibly measure up to his new standards of what *tefillin* should be. Thus, when he came home for the next *yom tov* he told his mother that he felt he needed a new pair of *tefillin.*

His mother had no money to spend for a new pair, so she said to him, "You know, I still have your father's *tefillin* on a shelf. Take them down and see if they would be suitable."

He took them down and after *yom tov* recess took them back to the Yeshivah in Petach Tikvah where he showed them to R' Elya Dushnitzer. R' Elya opened the *tefillin* and began examining the *parshios.* Suddenly R' Elya exclaimed in astonishment, "These are *lichtige osios* (glowing letters), these are *lichtige osios.*" He was amazed at their beauty. R' Elya, however, told the young boy that the letters and the parchment on which they were written were extraordinarily large, and thus they were more suitable for *chassidim* who wore large *tefillin.* He suggested that Sholom'ke get another pair for himself and not wear these, even though they were his father's.

The young boy followed his *rebbi's* suggestion and somehow managed to get a new pair. When he went home for the summer vacation he told his mother how impressed the *rebbe* had been at his father's *tefillin,* but that he had been instructed to wear another pair.

He repeated again to his mother how the *rebbi* had said the *parshios* contained "glowing letters" and he suggested that perhaps his mother might take these *tefillin* to the local *sofer* and see if he could find a buyer for them. In that way she could make some desperately needed money.

She thought it a good idea since her son would not be wearing them anyway, and she took them to the *sofer.* The man told her that though he could not promise to find a buyer, he would try his best. Looking over the *parshios,* he told R' Sholom's mother that the parchments on which they were written were quite large and that not too many people wore such *tefillin.*

Years went by and R' Sholom was married. One Purim night he davened in the *chassidishe shul* in the Shaarei Chessed section of Jerusalem. After the *Megillah* reading one of the *gabboim,* an elderly Jew named R' Eliezer Yaakov, called R' Sholom over and said, "Come here, do you want to see something special?"

Curious, R' Sholom went over as R' Eliezer Yaakov began to unfold once again the *Megillah* he held in his hand. "What do you say to this handwriting?" inquired R' Eliezer Yaakov. "Tell me truthfully, have you ever seen a *Megillah* like this in your life?" R' Sholom observed that the calligraphy was indeed exceptional in neatness and in its form and shape. Before he got a chance to reply to the question, R' Eliezer Yaakov said, "This is a *Megillah* written by R' Moshe P'shevorsker! The Tshortkover *Rebbe* (1842-1933) offered me a hundred *gulden* for this *Megillah,* but I wouldn't part with it for anything."

Now R' Sholom looked at it with added interest for he had indeed heard of R' Moshe P'shevorsker. He examined each letter, noting how delicately every one was formed, and how ornamental and perfect each one was. Clearly, every word had been meticulously and reverently written.

R' Eliezer Yaakov saw how overwhelmed R' Sholom was by the

writing and he said to him, "What are you so amazed about? Your own father's *tefillin* contained the *parshios* of R' Moshe P'shevorsker."

R' Sholom's mouth fell open in disbelief. He suddenly remembered his *rebbi* R' Elya Dushnitzer, back in Petach Tikvah, gazing in astonishment at the letters of the *tefillin* he had brought to him as a fifteen-year-old. He remembered how R' Elya had exclaimed at how the *parshios* contained *lichtige osios.* But then he recalled that he had not used them but instead had advised his mother to give them to a *sofer* to try to sell them.

All night he was worried and impatient to find out what had happened with those *tefillin* and he fell asleep thinking about it. The next day when R' Sholom went to bring *shalach manos* to his mother he asked her about the *tefillin.* She told him that she had followed his advice long ago, and that she even remembered to which *sofer* she had given them, but that she had never heard from him again. R' Sholom told her why it was so important to find out where the *tefillin* might be and so immediately his mother went to the *sofer* to inquire about them.

The *sofer* told R' Sholom's mother that he had held on to them for a very long time, years, in fact, and when he saw that no one wanted them, his store being cluttered as it was, he buried them along with other *shaimos* (worn out or otherwise unusable *sefarim, tefillin,* etc.).

True, the story does not have a happy ending, but there is a lesson to be learned here. At times people possess a treasure, but unfortunately are unaware of the fact. How sad! The treasure can be a heirloom lost somewhere in one's attic, or it can be a fertile and brilliant mind that is wasted because it is not being used, or it may be an untapped talent hidden within a person. It behooves us to pray to Hashem not only for the good things in life, but for the ability to recognize and appreciate them when we do have them.

✥ The Lights that Returned

The Sassover *Rebbe*, R' Moshe Leib Sassover (1745-1807) was visited by thousands of people seeking his blessing. Some were in poor health, others sought advice in family matters, while still others discussed business or religious interests with him.

Once, when R' Moshe Leib visited the city of Brodt, a wealthy woman, known in the town as Riva'leh, asked him to pray for her desperately ill daughter. R' Moshe Leib had heard of the woman's philanthropy and knew that she was the daughter of a wealthy businessman, the late R' Nachum the *Parnes* (community leader).

Riva'le described her daughter's illness and the *rebbe* assured her that he would pray on the child's behalf. It was customary for a visitor to leave the *rebbe* a *pidyon* — a sum of money which the *rebbe* would disburse to the needy. The amount of money was left to the discretion of the giver.

As Riva'le was about to leave, she thanked the *rebbe* fervently for his concern and prayers on her daughter's behalf, and left a large envelope with money on the table. The *rebbe* returned the envelope to the woman saying, "It's not money that I want from you!"

"What do you want then?" asked the startled woman. "Please say what it is. I'll do anything for my daughter's sake."

"I believe that you have a very precious Chanukah *menorah*. I want that *menorah*."

"Yes, I do have a precious *menorah* and I treasure it dearly," Riva'le replied. "It's a family heirloom. But if you want it, it's yours."

"I understand the family tradition behind it," R' Moshe Leib said, nodding his head, "and that's why if you do give it to me, I must be sure that you're giving it with all your heart."

"Yes, *Rebbe*, it's yours," Riva'le said firmly. That very evening she returned with the *menorah* and presented it to R' Moshe Leib.

The followers of R' Moshe Leib were astounded. First of all, how had he known that Riva'le had the *menorah*? Secondly, the request for it seemed so out of character. Besides the fact that it was strange for their *rebbe* to ask for a gift, they could not imagine why he needed that *menorah* when everyone knew that he always used the *menorah* he'd received from his *rebbe,* R' Shmelke of Nikolsburg (1726-1778).

As the first night of Chanukah approached, the *rebbe* prepared the wicks and oil for Riva'le's *menorah* with elaborate care. He then sent one of his *chassidim* to bring R' Yechiel the *Tzoref* (silversmith).

The *chassidim* crowded around as R' Moshe Leib began to recite the introductory prayers to the candle lighting. The prayers seemed to be taking much longer than usual. R' Yechiel stood at the *rebbe's* side and wondered why he had been singled out for the honor of standing beside the *rebbe* on this first night of Chanukah.

The blessings were said, the wicks were lit and there was great joy that evening in Brodt. Then R' Moshe Leib asked R' Yechiel to come into his private study.

"I'd like to tell you a story about your late grandfather, after whom you were named. Like you, that R' Yechiel was a silversmith. I wouldn't be surprised if you yourself do not know this story."

❧ ❧ ❧

Your grandfather did not have the money to arrange for his daughter's marriage. He tried to borrow it, but few people would lend him money because he was poor and thus a bad risk. He was in debt and earned so little as a silversmith that he was always far behind in payments.

Your grandfather approached a very wealthy man, the late R' Nachum Parnes, for a loan. R' Nachum told him that he could not lend him the money because he feared that he would never be repaid, but R' Yechiel had a beautiful and precious Chanukah *menorah* that R' Nachum wanted. If R' Yechiel would give up the *menorah,* R' Nachum would give him 10,000 *gulden* — enough to marry off his daughter and have quite a bit left over for his family!

Your grandfather would not hear of it. You see, it was the custom of the *rebbe* R' Zisha of Anipoli to give out silver coins to many of his *chassidim.* These were valued very highly, and people would give large amounts to buy the coins from the *chassidim* who were fortunate enough to get them. Your grandfather had a collection of these coins and he would never sell them for any price. Instead, being a silversmith, he melted down all the coins he had amassed over the years and from the melted silver he made a beautiful *menorah*. Everyone admired it and it became his most treasured possession. It was this *menorah* that R' Nachum wanted.

When your grandfather refused R' Nachum's offer, he tried desperately to raise the money elsewhere, but in the end he had to consent to give R' Nachum the *menorah* in exchange for the money that he needed so desperately.

A few years later, R' Nachum Parnes died. The Heavenly Court was in a quandary; how was it to deal with R' Nachum's reward for the *mitzvah* of *hachnosas kallah* (providing funds for the marriage of a poor bride)? On the one hand, he had provided the funds for R' Yechiel's daughter's marriage. But, on the other hand, he had caused R' Yechiel terrible anguish just to satisfy his own envy.

The Court reached a compromise. R' Nachum's reward would be held in abeyance. It was as if the angel created by the *mitzvah* of *hachnosas kallah* was blind and could not lead R' Nachum's soul to the proper place for his reward and eternal rest. The blindness of the angel was caused by the eyes with which R' Nachum sinned in coveting a *menorah* that was not his.

It is for this reason that I'm now returning this *menorah* to you. R' Nachum's *mitzvah* is now complete, he will now be assigned his rightful place in *Gan Eden* (Paradise).

[Incidentally, Riva'le's daughter had a speedy and complete recovery.]

The Lottery of a Lifetime

Reb Elchonon Wasserman (1875-1941), the great *rosh yeshivah* of Yeshivah Ohel Torah in Baranovich, Poland, traveled extensively throughout Europe and America to raise funds for his beloved students and also as a representative of the *Vaad Hayeshivos* (United Foundation of Eastern Polish Yeshivos).

Such was R' Elchonon's devotion to his students that when he was in America in 1939 he refused to remain in the safe haven of the United States despite the pleas of many people who feared that he would face certain death if he returned to Europe. Like a dedicated shepherd he chose to return to his four hundred students in Baranovich. He repeated over and over again to those who begged him to stay, "How can I leave my *talmidim?*"

The following episode took place in 1937 on one of R' Elchonon's visits to England, where he spent some time in the Manchester Yeshivah. The yeshivah's administrator, R' Shaul Rosenberg, was a well-to-do businessman who not only raised funds for the yeshivah but attended to the day-to-day details as well. When R' Elchonon was in town, R' Shaul devoted a whole week taking him to the people who would support R' Elchonon's yeshivah in Baranovich.

Shortly before R' Elchonon's arrival in Manchester, R' Shaul had suffered numerous financial setbacks. Business deals had gone sour and his losses were substantial. Hoping to offset his financial losses and re-establish himself, R' Shaul had bought a lottery ticket with a chance to win 50,000 pounds.

On the final day of R' Elchonon's stay in Manchester, R' Shaul went to visit R' Elchonon. R' Shaul explained to R' Elchonon's host, a former *talmid* of Baranovich, that he would like R' Elchonon to give him a *brachah* (blessing) that he win the lottery. The host told R' Elchonon about R' Shaul's financial predicament and how it had taken his time away from doing work for the Manchester Yeshivah. That was why he had bought the lottery and why the cause of Torah would be the biggest gainer if R' Shaul were to win.

When R' Shaul came in, R' Elchonon greeted him warmly, and after a short conversation he said, "R' Shaul, give me your hand."

R' Elchonon took R' Shaul's hand, and, holding it firmly said, "In the *zechus* (merit) of everything that you do for Torah and the *tzibbur* (community), may Hashem bless you with *gezunt* (good health)."

R' Shaul Rosenberg was taken aback. It was a nice *brachah*, but it wasn't what he had expected. "Perhaps," he thought, "the *rosh yeshivah* hadn't fully understood the first time."

He began describing his monetary problems and the reason he had purchased the lottery ticket.

R' Elchonon listened to him and then said again, "Let me have your hand." He held R' Shaul's hand warmly in his two hands and said, "In the great merit of Torah and all that you have done for the yeshivah here in Manchester, may Hashem give you *gezunt.*"

This time R' Shaul didn't say anything. R' Elchonon had undoubtedly heard and understood him, so there was no point in repeating himself. For whatever reason R' Elchonon had said what he did, it was definitely what he meant to say. R' Elchonon left Manchester the next day.

Three days later as he was walking in the street, R' Shaul Rosenberg suffered a severe stroke and fell paralyzed in the street. He was taken to a hospital where he lay in a coma, not recognizing anyone or anything. The family gathered in the hospital where the doctors told them that it was just a matter of time before his end would come. Deeply saddened by the news, the family waited and prayed.

Three weeks later as his doctor and other family members were at his bedside, R' Shaul suddenly opened his eyes and came out of the coma. The doctor, shocked at what was happening right before his eyes, clapped his hands and exclaimed in amazement, "I don't believe it! It's one in ten thousand that pull out of such a coma!"

In a short time R' Shaul made a complete recovery and was back at his office in the Yeshivah of Manchester. Over the years, R' Shaul came to realize that he had indeed won a lottery after all. He had won that one chance in ten thousand of survival. And that was the meaning of R' Elchonon's blessing.

◆§ *When the Tables Turned*

Rav Meir Simchah Hakohen (1843-1926) of Dvinsk, author of the famous *Or Somayach,* was unable to attend the funeral of

R′ Yitzchok Elchonon Spektor, the Kovner *Rav,* but he asked some students who had been there to tell him everything about the event.

When the students began recounting in detail what the *maspidim* (eulogists) had said, R′ Meir Simchah declared, "I am sure that the famous *maggid* R′ Shlomo Zugger* did not speak."

The students were surprised. "Yes," they said, "you are right. He didn't speak after all. But he was going to speak."

The *Or Somayach* smiled, "I knew that Hashem would arrange it that he would not eulogize R′ Yitzchak Elchonon. I'm just curious to know how it came about."

The students related the incident. There were many *maspidim* and the crowd was a sea of people, crushed against each other in the synagogue. It was extremely stuffy and with all the pushing and shoving it was impossible to hear what was being said from the pulpit way up front. There were also hundreds, even thousands of people outside the synagogue, who also could neither see nor hear anything that was going on inside.

It was decided therefore, that in order for everyone to be able to hear the famous R′ Shlomo eulogize R′ Yitzchok Elchonon, everyone would go outside.

Once outside, the men in charge of the funeral arrangements realized that there was no platform high enough for R′ Shlomo to stand on to be visible to all. Some men began to pile one table upon another so that the *maggid* could climb on top of them and be in full view of everyone. With his powerful voice he would then be heard by all.

The *maggid* climbed onto the improvised platform and people began pressing in close to better hear every word. Before he could utter a sound the crush of the crowd caused the makeshift platform to totter. There was some yelling to stop the shoving but to no avail. The tables came crashing down and the *maggid* went tumbling down into the crowd. He was bruised and hurt in the fall both physically and emotionally and was in no condition to deliver a eulogy. He decided against even trying to speak to the gathered crowd.

---

* The name has been changed for reasons that will become obvious.

The students turned to R' Meir Simchah, waiting to hear how he knew that R' Shlomo had indeed not spoken. "Hashem does not forget anything," the *rav* said. "More than twenty years ago this same *maggid* was involved in a *din Torah.* The *rav* who issued the *psak* (ruling) was none other than R' Yitzchok Elchonon. He had ruled against the *maggid* and the *maggid* was incensed. He related the events of the *din Torah* to me, and then in a fury added, 'When he [R' Yitzchok Elchonon] dies, I won't eulogize him.' As you saw, he didn't, because man may forget what he utters, but Hashem does not."

☙ *Suitable Advice*

In the town of Brisk, Poland, a group of zealous individuals approached their *rav,* R' Yehoshua Leib Diskin (1817-1898), with a problem. Because the grandson of the town *shochet* (ritual slaughterer) had been enrolled in a non-religious school, they felt that the *shochet* should be removed from his position. They reasoned that a *shochet* should have impeccable credentials and to have a grandchild in anything but a religious school was certainly a discredit to him.

The *rav* listened to their story and said, "I do not think that is reason enough to remove him from his position as *shochet.* However, should you find him a different job, I agree that it would be perfectly acceptable for you to try to convince him to leave *shechitah* and to assume the other occupation."

Satisfied with his answer, the group spent much time and energy trying to find the *shochet* a suitable, but different type of work. After they had found an appropriate position, they approached the man and tried to convince him to change his occupation to the one they had found for him.

Not being a difficult person, the *shochet* told them that he would consider it, but that he needed time to think it through. He decided that it would be best for him to ask the *rav's* advice, and so he went to R' Yehoshua Leib for guidance.

"Should I leave my position as *shochet* and accept the proposal to do something else?"

"You should remain a *shochet*," replied R' Yehoshua Leib firmly. "It's much better for you. It is a prominent position and you are doing well. By all means don't leave."

The next day the *shochet* gave his reply. "My answer is no," he said flatly. "I've discussed it with the Brisker *Rav* and he told me that it's in my interest to remain in my present position."

The listeners were startled. R' Yehoshua Leib had agreed with their plan. Based on his words they had expended both time and effort to secure the *shochet* another job, and now the *rav* himself had given the *shochet* the advice that destroyed their whole plan.

Baffled, they came back to the *rav* and asked, "How can you have told us one thing and then given the *shochet* advice contrary to what you told us?"

The *rav* smiled and said, "The Torah states: *(Devorim* 27:18): 'אָרוּר מַשְׁגֶּה עִוֵּר בַּדָּרֶךְ — Cursed is he who misdirects the blind on the road.' This is understood to mean that one must give proper advice to an individual. For the *shochet* it is certainly better that he stay where he is. And once he asked me for my advice, I was obligated by Torah law to give the recommendation that was best for him."

R' Sholom points out that both times R' Yehoshua Leib gave advice he acted with compassion. He told the group seeking to oust the *shochet* that it was of the utmost importance for a community to maintain the highest standards and that not only their *shochet,* but his descendants as well, should be unquestionably committed to Torah and *mitzvos.* Had the *shochet* gone along with the plan to take a different job, that would have been ideal for the townsfolk.

However, when the *shochet* came to seek his counsel, R' Yehoshua Leib gave him the advice that would be most beneficial to him, and that was that he should remain on the job regardless of what others may think.

◆§ *A Nightmare to Remember*

The young *shochet* sat up in bed trembling. He had awakened from a nightmare that seemed so real, he found it hard to separate dream from reality. R' Aaron was a pious, dedicated man, whose credentials as a *shochet* were impeccable and whose ways were righteous. Yet in his dream he appeared as a callous and uncaring man. Beads of perspiration ran down his face as he tried to reconstruct and interpret his nightmare.

❦ ❦ ❦

In his dream, he was already in *Olam Haba* (the World to Come), where the celestial angels debated what punishment to give him.

The prosecuting angel presented the facts. He began. "One Friday afternoon R' Aaron left the slaughterhouse and was on his way to the *mikveh*, when a widow approached him and said, "R' Aaron, please *shecht* (slaughter) this chicken for me."

"I can't right now," replied R' Aaron, "it's too close to Shabbos and I must go to the *mikveh*."

"I know it's late," the lady pleaded, "but the man in the market would not sell me a chicken for the little money I had. But just before he closed his shop, he gave me this one. Now my children can have meat for Shabbos if you will slaughter it for me."

"I can't," said R' Aaron tersely. "It's too close to Shabbos for me to go back to the slaughterhouse and then go to the *mikveh* too. Find someone else." As he hurried away he heard her cry out, "But I can't. Everyone has gone home, R' Aaron. Please!"

The prosecuting angel was furious and said angrily. "For this insensitivity to the widow and her family, R' Aaron should be given one of two punishments: Either thirty days in *Gehinnom* or a return to the world below.

No arguments from the defending angels could help his cause, and R' Aaron had to choose his punishment. He chose thirty days in *Gehinnom*.

At this point he awoke.

Sitting up now, he tried to think back over the years during which he had been a *shochet*. Had he ever been insensitive? Had a widow indeed approached him on a Friday afternoon? As hard as he tried to recall the past, he could not remember such an incident. He sought the counsel of numerous *rabbonim* and each one told him that in every dream there is some nonsense (see *Berachos*

55a), and they advised him to put the matter out of his mind. After a while, he did forget it.

More than twenty years later, on a late Friday afternoon, R' Aaron was on his way to the *mikveh*. The now elderly *shochet* was running as quickly as his weary legs would take him. Suddenly a woman approached him. It was a poor widow who had just been able to purchase a chicken for Shabbos at a reduced price. She asked him if he would please *shecht* the chicken for her. "I can't" he replied. "It's very late and I have to be on my way." The woman begged him, explaining that it would be the only meat that she would have for Shabbos, but he refused. Distraught the widow went home, knowing that she would have only *challah* and a little fish for her family for Shabbos.

Without giving the incident another thought, R' Aaron went to the *mikveh*, got dressed for Shabbos and went to *shul*. As he was reciting *Kiddush* in his home that Friday night, he suddenly stopped. His face turned ashen white and his hand began to tremble so violently that the wine spilled. Slowly he sank into his chair in despair. Twenty years ago he had dreamt this scene!

Gathering up meat and chicken from his own Shabbos table he ran from the house and made his way to the home of the widow.* He pleaded with her to forgive him and he presented her with enough meat for her and her family. She accepted it gratefully, thanked him kindly and excused herself for having troubled him.

When he returned home, R' Aaron told his stunned family the entire story. The next night after reciting *Havdalah*, R' Aaron passed away.

Because he had been a *tzaddik*, R' Aaron had been forewarned by a dream twenty years earlier — and he reacted, just in time.

◆§ *Perspective Insight*

Great men are concerned not only with their deeds but with their thoughts. If they fear that a random thought may cause

* Many small towns have an *eruv* that is built around them. The *eruv* serves the halachic purpose of incorporating the individually owned properties into one commonly owned domain, thus permitting carrying through the streets, an activity otherwise prohibited on Shabbos.

them spiritual harm, they look for ways to anticipate the damage and control it.

On Chol Hamoed (the intermediate days of Pesach and Succos) one is not permitted to write (nor do other work) unless it is done to avoid loss or damage, or is required for the holiday. Thus it came as a surprise, when on one Chol Hamoed, R' Isser Zalman Meltzer (1870-1953), the great *rosh yeshivah* of Yeshivah Eitz Chaim in Jerusalem and former *Rav* of Slutzk, asked his nephew for a pen and ink to write something.

"What is the emergency," asked R' Dovid Finkel, the nephew who studied with his uncle, and was always at his side.

"I have something very important to write, so please get it for me quickly," replied R' Isser Zalman.

His curious nephew persisted. He knew that R' Isser Zalman did nothing without prior thought and consideration, hence R' Dovid wanted to know exactly what was going on. "But Uncle, it's Chol Hamoed. I don't see any pressing matter before us that can't wait until after the holidays."

R' Isser Zalman knew he wouldn't be able to appease his nephew without revealing his true intentions and so he told him.

"You know that on Chol Hamoed people customarily come to visit their rabbis and teachers. I know that I will have many visitors, but G-d has blessed me with a penetrating insight into people. After a few moments, I am immediately aware of a person's virtues and faults. It hurts me to know the faults of people who have come to visit me. Additionally, knowing another's faults can lead one to haughtiness. Because of this I have devised an antidote to this problem.

"King Solomon said *(Mishlei* 4:25): 'עֵינֶיךָ לְנֹכַח יַבִּיטוּ וְעַפְעַפֶּיךָ יַיְשְׁרוּ נֶגְדֶּךָ — Let your eyes seek honesty, and your brows search straight-forwardly before you.' לְנֹכַח, used here for honesty, is usually translated 'towards yourself' in which case the verse takes on a new meaning, 'Let your eyes seek yourself.' In other words, look at yourself, see your own faults, instead of the faults of others. I always keep this verse in front of me on a small piece of paper as people are talking to me and it helps me avoid pride. Now I can't find that slip of paper. It is of utmost importance to have it before me throughout Chol Hamoed. I must write it down!"

❦ ❦ ❦

Many years after this incident, and long after R' Isser Zalman had passed away, R' Sholom Schwadron was sitting in the *succah* of R' Yitzchok Meir Ben-Menachem, R' Isser Zalman's son-in-law and retold this story. It was Chol Hamoed and people were amazed at the sensitivity inherent in the story.

R' Isser Zalman's daughter had been listening to the story. Quietly she left the *succah,* and after a few moments returned with a smile on her face and a sugar bowl in her hand. "This is the sugar bowl my father kept on his table." On the sugar bowl, was etched the verse, עֵינֶיךָ לְנֹכַח יַבִּיטוּ, וְעַפְעַפֶּיךָ יַיְשִׁרוּ נֶגְדֶּךָ.

◆§ *Standing Firm*

R' Rafael Hamburger (1724-1804) had been in his new position as *Rav* of Hamburg, Germany for only a few hours, when he was faced with his first crisis.

A woman came to him and complained that R' Nosson *parnes ha'ir* (the town's community leader) had taken advantage of her in some financial dealings. As a result she stood to lose a large sum of money. She apologized for having come so soon after the city had had a *kabalas panim* (welcoming reception) in honor of the new *rav* but she needed the money desperately.

The *rav* listened to the woman's story and agreed that it merited a *din Torah* (arbitration) requiring both parties to appear before a rabbinical tribunal. R' Rafael was exhausted and it was politically uncivil for him to antagonize the powerful R' Nosson, but his responsibilities to his position and the Torah came first.

The *rav* summoned the *shammosh* (attendant) who had been assigned to him. "Go to R' Nosson and tell him that he should come to my home at once. I am summoning him to a *din Torah."*

The *shammosh* looked at the *rav* in disbelief. "*Rebbi* you just got here. Do you know who R' Nosson is? Be patient. Don't rush to challenge him. He can rescind your appointment and that'll be the end of your position."

"Please do as I say," said R' Rafael. "Go to R' Nosson and tell him to come."

The attendant returned shortly and reported with a smirk, "R' Nosson was surprised at your arrogance. He said you shouldn't be so quick to summon certain people to a *din Torah.*"

"Go back and tell him that I demand that he come immediately," said the *rav.* "The woman here has a right to a *din Torah* and I, as the *rav,* have the authority to demand R' Nosson's presence here."

"I can't believe you want to jeopardize your job which is hardly a day old," said the *shammosh.* "R' Nosson will surely get rid of you."

"I am not afraid of him! Go and tell him that he has to come here!" commanded R' Rafael. Once again the *shammosh* went and after a while came back to report to the *rav.* "R' Nosson says you might as well leave Hamburg. He is so angry with you that he'll call a meeting tomorrow and send you packing. He refuses to come see you today."

The *rav* was adamant. "Tell him that if he does not come at once, I'll decree that he is to be in *cherem* (in a state of excommunication from the entire Jewish community). I will be waiting for him right here."

In a short while the *shammosh,* the *parnes ha'ir* and the woman all came into the *rav's* home with broad smiles on their faces and exclaimed, "*Mazel tov! Mazel tov*! You are now officially the *Rav* of Hamburg!"

"What are you all talking about?" stammered the surprised *rav.*

"This was only a test," said the *shammosh.* "You're new here and we weren't sure how you'd stand up to pressure. There's no *din Torah.* The whole thing was only a fabrication."

"But had you buckled under the pressure," said the *parnes ha'ir,* "then we would have known that you weren't able to fill the position as *Rav* of Hamburg. You've proven yourself. *Mazel tov*!"

◆§ A Lion at Dawn

Rav Elya Lopian did everything in his life with deep emotion and much enthusiasm. People listening to him pray, would sometimes tremble, or come to tears at his vibrant, meticulous recitation of the *Shema,* in the *Shacharis* or *Maariv* service. The intensity and depth of his concentration made the words in the *siddur* come alive.

The young *talmidim* in his yeshivah who heard him roar, "וְלֹא תָתוּרוּ אַחֲרֵי לְבַבְכֶם וְאַחֲרֵי עֵינֵיכֶם — Do not follow after your heart or after your eyes," shuddered in awe and never forgot it. His prayers were living lectures.

It was R' Elya's custom to awake early every morning to prepare for his *Shacharis* prayers. But to some, it seemed that he got up too early, for he would awaken quite some time before the time for prayers, even before dawn.

When questioned, he replied. "After 120 years, when I arrive in the eternal world, and stand before the Heavenly Court, they will surely ask me whether I lived by all the laws of the *Shulchan Aruch.* They will take out the *Shulchan Aruch* and start questioning me from the beginning.

"The very first words of the *Shulchan Aruch* are: 'A man should strengthen himself like a lion to arise in the morning to serve his Master and herald the dawn.' And I certainly don't want them to find me wanting on the very first paragraph!"

◆§ A Grenade in the Tzaddik's House

When R' Eliezer Kirzner, a distinguished *talmid chacham* and *rav* in Brooklyn, was once traveling in *Eretz Yisrael,* he made sure to stop at Kfar Chassidim to visit the revered *tzaddik* and *mashgiach* of the yeshivah there, R' Elya Lopian. *Rav* Kirzner and R' Elya had learned together decades earlier in Lithuania. When reunited, they spent much time in warm conversation, renewing their old friendship.

Rav Kirzner was invited to stay overnight and he accepted. He awoke very early the next morning. As he walked into the front room he noticed that R' Elya was not only up but that he was already wearing his *tallis* and *tefillin.* R' Elya was standing by the front window, seemingly looking out towards the yeshivah, saying certain words to himself, and then repeating them over and over again.

Rav Kirzner walked quietly in back of his friend in order to hear exactly what the words might be. He could make out the verse *(Devorim* 7:26), "וְלֹא תָבִיא תוֹעֵבָה אֶל בֵּיתֶךָ — And you shall not bring an abomination (a detestable thing) into your home." And then again, "...וְלֹא תָבִיא — And you shall not bring ..."

Suddenly R' Elya turned around and saw *Rav* Kirzner standing behind him. He began apologizing profusely. "Did I wake you? I'm so sorry, I'm really very sorry."

"Of course you didn't wake me," said *Rav* Kirzner. "I was up already. It's just that I was interested to know what words you were repeating so many times and why."

R' Elya sighed. "You know that we'll soon be going to the *beis midrash* to pray. The boys wait for me to finish both *Shema* and *Shemoneh Esrei.* I am afraid that such honors may lead me to become haughty. A whole congregation waiting for me! That's why I repeat those words, 'וְלֹא תָבִיא תוֹעֵבָה אֶל בֵּיתֶךָ — You shall not bring an abomination into your home,' for haughtiness is indeed detestable, as King Solomon wrote *(Mishlei* 16:5):'תּוֹעֲבַת ה' כָּל גְּבַהּ לֵב — Those who are haughty are an abomination to Hashem.' "

Rav Kirzner smiled in appreciation of R' Elya's meticulousness in the observance of *mitzvos.* Still, he said to R' Elya, "Do you mean to tell me that at your age the *yetzer hara* (evil inclination) is still prevalent? What can he possibly want with old and frail people?"

R' Elya looked straight at *Rav* Kirzner and replied very seriously, "A bad *midah* (character trait) is like a grenade. A grenade may lay in a corner for months, hundreds of people may walk by it and it doesn't go off. But then someone carelessly moves the grenade so that the pin becomes dislodged and the grenade explodes. It makes no difference who caused it, a young child, or an old man. It's the same with a bad trait — a bad temper, haughtiness, or an inclination to deceive. Someone may control it for years, but if just once a person is careless, no matter how old he is, the trait can explode with all its intensity and do tremendous harm."

◆§ *Mind over Matter*

In the introductory prayer that a man recites every morning before putting on his *tefillin,* he declares ... "Hashem has commanded us to put on *tefillin* upon the arm ... opposite the heart ... to subjugate the desires and thoughts of our heart to His service ... and upon the head opposite the brain, so that ... my brain along with my other senses ... may all be subjugated to His service ..."

The following incident crystallizes how the meticulous observance of a *mitzvah,* specifically that of *tefillin,* can have an awesome effect on a man. Here the *mitzvah* had the power to overcome a man's instinctive tendencies.

When the Tshebiner *Rav,* R' Dov Berish Weidenfeld (1879-1965), was in the later years of his life, he was seriously ill and required an operation for which the normal procedure was to anesthetize the patient. However, the *gaon* was so frail that the doctors feared that if he fell asleep under anesthesia, he might never recover. On the other hand, to perform the operation without anesthesia was inconceivable. Such was the medical dilemma the *rav's* doctors faced.

When the Tshebiner *Rav* heard about the problem, he told the doctors that he had a solution to the problem. He could assure them that he would not fall asleep under anesthesia, but he would need his *tefillin. Tefillin?* Neither the baffled doctors nor the family members could understand.

The *rav* explained. "It is forbidden for one to sleep while wearing his *tefillin*" (see *Orach Chaim* 44:1; *Tosafos, Shabbos* 49a). He assured them that if he was wearing his *tefillin,* they could administer the anesthetic and the awe and concentration he always had while wearing *tefillin* would keep him awake.

He donned the *tefillin,* and the operation was performed.

Despite the fact that he was under heavy sedation, the *rav* did not fall asleep for a moment.

The Tshebiner could defy the laws of nature and medicine but not for a moment the laws of the *Shulchan Aruch*.

☙ *A Question of Marriage*

Rav Eizel *Charif* (the sharp one), *Rav* of Slonim (d. 1873), had a daughter of marriageable age. Customarily, a prospective father-in-law would visit the prominent yeshivos and discuss with either the *rosh yeshivah* or *mashgiach* which young man might be most suitable for his daughter.

R' Eizel went to the most prestigious yeshivah in his time, Volozhin, headed by the *gaon* R' Naftali Tzvi Yehudah Berlin, the *Netziv*. When the *Netziv* heard that the great *talmid chacham* was coming, he and many of the senior students went out to greet him.

Word spread quickly that R' Eizel was in Volozhin to find a *chosson* (groom) for his daughter. It was understood that the *talmid* who showed the most outstanding Torah scholarship had the greatest chance of being chosen, and only the most outstanding students dared gather around R' Eizel. They began "talking in learning" and R' Eizel asked a question. The young men were perplexed, but they tried to answer anyway. However, R' Eizel rejected every answer with a proof that the logic was faulty and the answer incorrect.

For two days students came to him, each trying to give the proper answer to the difficult question, for it was understood that the one who would come up with the right answer would be chosen as the *chosson* (groom), but all to no avail. Not one of them could find a solution to the question.

When it was time for R' Eizel to go home, the *bachurim* (young men) in the yeshivah were somewhat embarrassed that he would be leaving Volozhin without a match for his daughter. Dutifully, they followed their *rosh yeshivah*, the *Netziv*, as he accompanied R' Eizel to the wagon that was waiting to take him home.

Suddenly, as they were saying their goodbyes, a young *bachur* came forward and said, "*Shidduch* (match) or no *shidduch*, tell us please, what is the answer to the question?"

R′ Eizel stopped and smiled, pointed to the *bachur* and said, "You're the one I want for my daughter. A *bachur* that's interested in learning Torah for Torah's sake, and not for any ulterior motives, is the *bachur* I want for my daughter!"

Purim Coins

Every Purim, R′ Chaim Volozhiner used to fill his pockets with coins for charity. He would walk in the street and give money to any person who requested it, no questions asked. This was consistent with the teaching, "Anyone who extends his hand for charity on Purim, should be given." (See *Orach Chaim* 694:3.)

One Purim, a poor man approached him and said, "If I tell you a '*gut vort*' (a nice thought) on the *Megillah,* will you then give me a larger amount of money?"

R′ Chaim laughed and agreed. The man said, "The *Midrash* states (*Yalkut Shemoni, Esther,* 1057) that Elijah the prophet appeared before Mordechai and revealed to him this message, 'It is possible that G-d will listen to the prayers of your people and they may be saved, for Haman's decree to kill the Jews was signed not in blood but with the official signet of clay.' This implies that a decree signed in blood is irrevocable, but one signed with the official signet in clay can be overruled. My question is, where is there a hint of this in the *Megillah?*"

R′ Chaim was perplexed and after a few moments of thought said, "I don't know. Tell me where it is."

The man replied, "There is a teaching that every time it says the word הַמֶּלֶךְ, *the king,* in the *Megillah,* it is possible to interpret it as a reference to the King of kings, Hashem. Thus in the *Megillah* 3:9, the verse states, "אִם עַל הַמֶּלֶךְ טוֹב יִכָּתֵב לְאַבְּדָם — If it please the king, let it be recorded that they, the Jews, be destroyed.' The word לְאַבְּדָם, *destroyed,* can be read as two words לֹא בְּדָם, literally, 'not with blood', hence the verse would take on a new meaning. If it please the King (Hashem), let the decree be recorded, but not with blood."

R′ Chaim was ecstatic at the cleverness of the *vort.*

The next time he saw his *rebbi,* the Vilna Gaon, R′ Chaim told him the *vort* he had just heard. The *Gaon* listened and then smiled. "Do you know who it was who told you that *vort?* It was none other than the one who revealed it to Mordechai himself *Eliyahu HaNavi* (the prophet Elijah)."

☙ *Apples and Blessings*

The essence of intelligence is finding the proper perspective on life, people and events. Quite often a random observation from a *rebbe,* parent or friend transcends the here and now, to become an insight for all time, an illuminating message for man's proper behavior in this world.

The following incident is a case in point.

The first Karliner *Rebbe,* who is referred to as R' Aharon *Hagadol* (the great; 1736-1772), was a man of great piety and depth. In his eloquent liturgical songs, he often expressed his longing and love for Hashem, and his soul's constant quest to be close to Him.

One *motza'ei Shabbos* (Saturday night) R' Yaakov, one of R' Aharon's *chassidim* (disciples) came to visit him. During their conversation, the *gabbai* (*rebbe's* attendant) brought him a plate of fruit. The *rebbe* picked up an apple, fervently recited the appropriate blessing, thanking G-d for the fruits of the trees and cut off a slice. He then proceeded to eat the apple.

The *chassid* sat across from his *rebbe* and watched his every move. He had always considered his *rebbe* somewhat akin to an angel, and yet here was his *rebbe* eating a mundane apple just like anyone else. For a fleeting moment a thought flashed through R' Yaakov's mind, "We both eat apples, we both recite blessings. True, the *rebbe* recites the blessing with more fervor than I, but essentially we are both pretty much the same."

The *rebbe,* quick to note the subtle change of demeanor from reverence to careful appraisal, said to his guest, "Tell me, R' Yaakov, what indeed is the difference between you and me? I eat apples, and you eat apples. I recite blessings and you recite blessings. So how are we different?"

"I was just wondering the same thing," replied R' Yaakov, somewhat startled and embarrassed.

"I'll tell you the difference," said R' Aharon thoughtfully, "When I get up in the morning, I look around and see the beautiful trees in the garden, the miracles of creation, and the wonders of the world. I become so enthralled that I want to recite a blessing to express awe. However, I know that it is forbidden to recite G-d's name in vain, so I must take an apple over which I can recite a blessing.

"But, when you arise in the morning, your first thought is, 'I'm hungry. All night I haven't eaten.' You would like to eat an apple, but of course you know that you cannot eat an apple without reciting the appropriate blessing. So you take the apple, recite the blessing, and eat it. Here is where we differ. You make a *brachah* so that you can eat the apple, while I eat an apple so that I can make a *brachah*."

"This," says R' Sholom, "is precisely the question that we should ask ourselves daily. 'Are we living life to serve Hashem, or have we taken the life that Hashem gave us to serve ourselves?' "

For example are we doing business and earning money with an eye towards riches and power, or are we earning money with any eye towards providing proper Torah education for our children, or funds for the needy? Do we eat for our own pleasure, or do we eat to be healthy so that we can study Torah and perform the *mitzvos* better?

Such questions should concern us every moment of our lives.

Apple II

Over the years that I have known R' Sholom, I've heard the previous story, either in person or on tapes, close to forty times. This next story, though, is one that I heard him tell only once. Yet, to me, this second story is inextricably bound to the story of R' Aharon *Hagadol* and the apple, even though that story involved a *chassidishe* leader and the next one a *misnagedishe* Torah giant.

It was told at a gathering, in the home of one of the Telshe *Kollel* fellows in Cleveland.

When the Brisker *Rav* was once in Switzerland, he spent Shabbos in the home of R' Wolf Rosengarten. On Shabbos afternoon, while they were sitting at the table, the *rav* asked for an apple and a banana. R' Wolf, only too eager and happy to serve his illustrious guest, went immediately to get them.

The request seemed somewhat out of character, but R' Wolf did not comment and did as he was asked. When he returned with the fruits, the Brisker *Rav,* the host and the others present, continued talking, and when it came time to *daven Minchah* the fruit still lay on the table uneaten.

The group left for *shul, davened Minchah,* and returned to R' Wolf's home. The Brisker Rav still did not eat the fruit and so R' Wolf asked him if he still wanted the apple and the banana.

"No," said the *rav*, "they won't be necessary." R' Wolf looked surprised. Then the Brisker *Rav* added, "Every day a Jew must recite one hundred blessings. Today I thought I would be two *brachos* short, so I asked for the fruit. But when we were in *shul* at *Minchah* I received an *aliyah* (call to the Torah) and I recited two blessings, the one recited before and the one after the Torah reading, and so they made up the two *brachos* that I was missing to fulfill the requirement of reciting a hundred blessings every day." (See *Menachos* 43b and O.C., 46:3.)

Thus, similar to the point made by R' Aharon Karliner, the Brisker Rav had wanted an apple, but only in order to make a *brachah.*

◆§ *At the Gates of Glory*

When R' Sholom retells the following story, he prefaces it with this remark: "A few years ago I was in *Beth Medrash Govoha,* in Lakewood, New Jersey, for Purim, and I told this story in the presence of the *rosh yeshivah,* R' Shneur Kotler (1918-1982). When I finished, R' Shneur told me that he had heard this same story from his father, R' Aharon, and that there was a small part that I had left out. The addition makes the incident even more memorable and its lesson even more striking."

In the yeshivah of the Chofetz Chaim in Radin, there was a *talmid* who was exceptionally strong and had tremendous stamina. Every night he was one of the last to leave the *beis midrash,* studying well past midnight. He was one of the most prominent *bachurim* in the yeshivah. One particular Purim, this *bachur* drank a bit too much and came into the home of the Chofetz Chaim quite drunk.

The Chofetz Chaim's house was filled with people, but this *bachur* jostled his way through the crowd up to where the Chofetz Chaim was sitting. He stood before the Chofetz Chaim and pleaded with him, "*Rebbi, Rebbi,* promise me that I can sit next to you in *Gan Eden* (Paradise)!" The other guests smiled at the *bachur,* for his words revealed what was in the recesses of his heart. They knew the Talmudic teaching *(Eruvin* 65a) that one who drinks excessively reveals his innermost secrets.

Upon hearing this request, the Chofetz Chaim shrugged his shoulders and said, "Who knows if I will even have any *Gan Eden*? How then can I promise that you will sit next to me?"

The boy was embarrassingly persistent. Every few minutes he resumed his pleading, "*Rebbi,* please grant me just this request, that I will sit next to you in *Gan Eden!*" Each time, the Chofetz Chaim brushed aside the request. After a while people tried to push the *bachur* away, to stop him from pestering the *gadol* (great man), but the Chofetz Chaim told them to leave the boy alone. From that point on, everyone simply disregarded the boy's entreaties and attributed them to his drunken state.

As the afternoon drew on, the Chofetz Chaim prepared to leave the room to eat his Purim *seudah* (festive meal). The *bachur* stood in his way. "No!" he announced, "I am not letting the *rebbi* go, until he assures me that I can sit next to him in *Gan Eden!*"

The others present said to the Chofetz Chaim, "Promise him already that he'll sit by you in *Gan Eden.*"

Suddenly, the Chofetz Chaim became very serious and approached the *bachur.* "I don't know how big a portion of *Gan Eden* I'll get," he said earnestly, "but one thing I do know. I'll probably have some share in *Gan Eden* because from the day that I was old enough to understand, I have not listened to nor spoken *lashon hara* (evil talk, i.e., anything derogatory about another person). Therefore, if you promise me that as of today you will not listen to nor speak *lashon hara* I can assure you that you will be with me in *Gan Eden.*"

The *bachur* seemed to sober up immediately. It became obvious that he understood the ramifications of the Chofetz Chaim's startling words.

The bystanders waited to hear what the *bachur's* reply would be. His eyes had cleared; he paused to think. Then he remained silent, afraid to commit himself to an undertaking that he felt was beyond him. He understood the implications and in his honesty he wouldn't lie to his revered *rebbi.*

It is at this point that R' Aharon Kotler added, "The Chofetz Chaim became very earnest and said, 'Imagine! A man standing at the gates of glory and he doesn't go in. Take him away from me at once!'

"A group of boys quickly hustled the fellow away, and the Chofetz Chaim left the room to go to his Purim *seudah.*"

Sand in the Water

The following episode was described to R' Sholom by R' Yaakov Teitelbaum (1899-1968), my *rav* in Kew Gardens, N.Y., who witnessed it in 1923, at the First *Knessiah Gedolah* (Great Assembly) of Agudath Israel, in Vienna. R' Teitelbaum was there as a delegate from Zeirei Agudath Israel, the organization's youth division.

Many of the greatest Torah authorities of the era had assembled in Vienna, and of them all, the revered Chofetz Chaim was chosen to give the assembly's opening address. In his talk he stressed the importance of every person making a strong effort to teach others about Torah and *yiras Shamayim* (awe and respect of G-d), and to extend a hand to those people who knew little about *Yiddishkeit* (Judaism). He emphasized the obligation of every *rav* to reach out to Jews not familiar with Torah and *mitzvos,* or those who had strayed from the *derech hayashar* (the righteous path).

That evening the Chofetz Chaim asked for permission to speak again. Although the program was full, everyone's respect for the great Chofetz Chaim was such that they promptly deferred to his wishes. The Chofetz Chaim said:

I have heard that throughout the day many people commented on the talk that I gave this morning. They feel that they cannot go out and teach others, for after all the Talmud *(Bava Metzia* 107b) says that one should perfect himself before he turns his attention to others. Although I am sure that these people honestly feel that they are not yet qualified to correct others, for they themselves haven't reached the high standards and goals they've set for themselves — I wish to tell them this story.

A wealthy man came to visit a small town in which he had a large financial interest. When one of the townsfolk recognized him, he invited the gentleman into his home for a cup of tea. The rich man accepted and was served a steaming glass of hot tea. But, he was shocked when he saw what else the glass contained. At the bottom of the glass was a thin layer of sand.

"What is this?" he demanded. "How can anyone drink this?"

"It's not our fault," the host complained. "The water here is impure and contains particles of sand. It is terrible but we have no alternative."

"That's silly," replied the wealthy man. "Get yourself pumps and strainers which will sift out the sand and purify the water. Then it will be clean and drinkable."

A few weeks later the same wealthy man heard that a great fire had consumed a large part of the town. He rushed there to see what had happened. Upon meeting one of the townspeople, he asked, "How did the fire spread so rapidly and damage so much property?"

"I'll tell you," the man answered. "When the fire started we rushed to get water, but we realized that we did not have enough pumps to strain and purify the water as you told us. So we couldn't use it. We followed your instructions."

"That's ridiculous!" screamed the man. "When there's a fire

you use any water at hand to put it out!"

"And that," said the Chofetz Chaim, "is the situation today. When the fire of *apikursus* (heresy) is spreading throughout the land, when the flames of *am ha'aratzus* (ignorance) are consuming our brothers and sisters, when there are so many Jews who know so little and some who know nothing at all, then the obligation to teach falls upon anyone who knows anything. Everyone must reach out to instruct others as best he can about Torah and *mitzvos*. Think not only of yourselves, but think of others as well."

R' Sholom then adds with a self-disparaging smile, "That's why even I can be a *maggid* today. Because in our time *anyone* who can teach, should teach!"

◆§ *To Life, to Life, R' Chaim*

The following story was told to R' Sholom by Rabbi Solomon Shapiro who witnessed it personally. As a young man in the 1940's Rabbi Shapiro was chaplain in what was then called the Home for Incurables, now known as the Kingsbrook Medical Center, in Brooklyn.

One afternoon he received a frantic call from the institution's president, a popular man known as Ike, who told him, "My brother has been in a terrible car accident and is now in a coma in Mount Sinai Hospital (in Manhattan). We have to tell my dad about this, but the news could kill him."

Ike's dad, R' Yosef Chaim, was in his late eighties. He was a gentle man who voluntarily came to give Torah lectures twice a week to the people in the Home. Rabbi Shapiro himself went to R' Yosef Chaim's house, where he found him sitting quietly in his living room. "R' Yosef Chaim," Rabbi Shapiro began, "I'd like you to come with me for a while, I have to take you someplace."

The old man agreed readily and together they drove to pick up Ike, then headed for Mount Sinai Hospital. As they traveled to Manhattan, Rabbi Shapiro explained to R' Yosef Chaim that his son Hirschel had been in an automobile accident and that they were going to visit him. R' Yosef Chaim sat calmly, displaying little emotion or concern. He merely said quietly, "With Hashem's help he will be well," and then began discussing a section of tractate *Pesachim* that he had been teaching the people at the Home.

Rabbi Shapiro thought it strange that R' Yosef Chaim should be so undisturbed about his son Hirschel, but listened to the old man as he described learning parts of this tractate with the Chofetz Chaim, whom he liked to refer to as his *chavrusa* (study partner) back in Radin.

As they were getting closer to the hospital, Rabbi Shapiro thought it might be wise to tell R' Yosef Chaim what to expect when he would see his comatose son. "I hear it was a bad accident," he said, trying to elicit some reaction, but R' Yosef Chaim wouldn't take the bait. He just sat there calmly, waiting to get to the hospital.

Hirschel was in a private room in an oxygen tent and hooked up to a number of tubes, protruding from different parts of his body. Members of the family stood around sadly and looked on helplessly. Nevertheless, R' Yosef Chaim did not seem to be worried. He stood by his son, looked at him for a long moment and said to the somber people around the bed, "Don't worry, he will be fine."

They all pitied the old man; obviously he was not in touch with reality. "Maybe he is becoming senile," Rabbi Shapiro thought. The doctors had given the young man just a few more hours. It did not take much medical knowledge to see how serious the situation was. R' Yosef Chaim looked around at all the shadowed faces and said with a shrug, "What do these young doctors know anyway, you think they know more than the Chofetz Chaim? He knew more than they will ever know. Let's go home."

Noticing that everyone was staring at him in disbelief, he told this story. "When I was a young man," he began, "and the Chofetz Chaim was writing his *Mishnah Berurah* he wanted simple people, not rabbis, to read through the manuscripts to see if the average Jew would be able to understand what he had written. I was one of his favorite readers, and I went through a good part of the *Mishnah Berurah* for him. Years later when I was about to go to America I went to him for a *brachah.*

"He said, 'If you continue to study Torah and remain a *shomer Shabbos* (Sabbath observer), you will have *arichas yamim* (long years) and while you are alive you will not lose any children.' So what do the doctors know?"

Rabbi Shapiro and the others were awestruck. They had never heard this before. They took R' Yosef Chaim home and the next night Ike called the rabbi to let him know that Hirschel had moved his legs and opened his eyes. Within weeks, Hirschel was out of the hospital.

At that time, R' Yosef Chaim was eighty-nine years old. He lived to be ninety-six and not one of his children or grandchildren died as long as he was alive.

◆§ *The Source of Blessing*

It is said that the greatest *talmidei chachamim* in each generation possess *ruach hakodesh,* a divine inspiration, that enlightens them with an uncanny understanding of the past and makes them privy to many of mankind's secrets of the future. The Chofetz Chaim, R' Yisrael Meir Kagan, of Radin, Poland, as humble as he was, possessed this noble attribute of *ruach hakodesh.* The following story was told to R' Sholom by R' Zalman Sorotzkin (1881-1966), the Lutzker Rav, who witnessed it personally.

The story begins in Zhetel, Poland, birthplace of the Chofetz Chaim, where R' Zalman held a rabbinical position early in his career. A citizen of the town, R' Asher, had a nineteen-year-old son who wished to settle in *Eretz Yisrael.* Aware of the economic difficulties there, R' Asher decided to teach his son a trade so that he could find work in *Eretz Yisrael.* He bought his son a car and taught him to drive so that he could be a chauffeur. He would pick up passengers from the railroad station in Zhetel, and take them to their destinations. Soon enough, he became familiar with the various routes and back roads throughout the major cities of the region.

One Friday afternoon, as people were going to *shul,* they noticed that R' Asher's son was still driving people from the station. It was just moments before Shabbos, and it was quite obvious that the boy, who came from a religious family, would not be home in time for Shabbos. Although no one actually saw him driving after nightfall, it would have been almost impossible for him to get home before then.

In *shul,* people told R' Zalman what they had seen. After *davening,* the *rav* had the young man summoned to his home and reprimanded him. The young man claimed that it was an accident, that he thought he could make it home before Shabbos, but there was traffic, he got lost, and so on. He assured the *rav* that it would not happen again.

A few weeks later, he was seen driving on Friday night. This time he was caught red-handed, and the witnesses were infuriated. They hurried to R' Zalman's home to tell him the news. Once again the young man was called in, harshly reprimanded and warned that the community would not tolerate his actions much longer. The father had no control over his now independent son and soon it became common for the boy to be seen driving on Shabbos.

The religious people in Zhetel felt outraged and affronted. They had seen this boy grow up and his open defiance was deeply felt by everyone. Additionally, they felt that such flagrant violations of the Sabbath by one of their own could have a harmful influence on the other young people in the community. They pleaded with R' Zalman to convince the father to send his son away from Zhetel at once. R' Zalman agreed to do so.

However, before R' Zalman had an opportunity to speak with him, R' Asher had a stroke and was rushed to the hospital. He lay there for some weeks, and although R' Zalman came to visit him a number of times, he felt that it was an inopportune time to discuss the doings of his wayward son.

The weeks stretched into months and R' Asher was getting impatient with the medical care that did not seem to be doing anything for him. With each passing day he grew more restless and the idea of leaving the hospital obsessed him. The doctors, however, insisted that he remain.

One night, R' Asher's deceased grandmother came to him in a dream. She told him that he was foolish for staying in the hospital and that he should follow her advice and leave at once. "What you need," she said, "is a *brachah* from the Chofetz Chaim. Go to him and tell him that you are from his hometown of Zhetel. His *brachah* will do more for you than all the medications the doctors have been giving you for the last six months."

The next morning, R' Asher got out of his hospital bed unobserved, took his crutches and hobbled somewhat unsteadily down the back corridors of the hospital and made his way outside. He went home and began to prepare for his trip to the Chofetz Chaim. In a few days he was ready to begin his journey to Radin. His first stop was the train station in Zhetel.

At that very moment, the Chofetz Chaim was traveling home to Radin from a rabbinic conference in Vilna. His train was headed for Otvotzk, a major terminal, where it would stop for about an hour, then continue on to Radin. R' Zalman, who also had attended the conference, was to change trains at Otvotzk, and board another train to Zhetel.

When the train stopped in Otvotzk, R' Zalman and the Chofetz Chaim's grandson, R' Hillel, went out onto the platform for some fresh air, while the Chofetz Chaim remained inside the train.

As R' Zalman was walking in the station he noticed someone familiar in the distance, hobbling on crutches. Upon coming closer to the man he recognized him and called out, "R' Asher!" As they rejoiced at their surprise meeting, R' Asher told R' Zalman about his dream and explained that only once before had his grandmother come to him in a dream and at that time had advised him with what turned out to be exceptional insight. Then R' Asher added, "... and so I am on my way to Radin, to meet the Chofetz Chaim."

"I can't believe it," exclaimed R' Zalman. "The Chofetz Chaim is here right now. It is as if Hashem has sent him directly to you. He is on the way to Radin and is making a train stop here in Otvotzk. Let's go together to greet him."

R' Zalman was hoping to reach the Chofetz Chaim before R'

Asher so that he could tell him about R' Asher's son. Perhaps, thought R' Zalman, if the Chofetz Chaim would admonish R' Asher about the matter, R' Asher would then try to influence the wayward young man.

They entered the train and walked through the corridors until they came to the car where the Chofetz Chaim had just finished *Shacharis* and was putting his *tefillin* away. Respectfully, they waited at a distance until he finished, and then R' Asher hobbled to the Chofetz Chaim and began talking before R' Zalman had a chance to say anything.

"At that point," R' Zalman said when he retold this story, "I knew that I could not interrupt them, but, on the other hand, I knew that Hashem did not arrange this meeting between the two merely by chance. I was positive something would happen, and so I waited."

As R' Asher began talking to the Chofetz Chaim he burst into tears, describing his illness and lengthy stay in the hospital. "I am from Zhetel, your hometown," said R' Asher gasping from his exertion. "My grandmother, who was a deeply religious woman, came to me in a dream and told me that I should come to you for a *brachah*."

The Chofetz Chaim looked up at the man and said, "Yisrael Meir is not a *brachah*-giver. What can I do? How can I help you?"

The man pleaded and begged. Finally the Chofetz Chaim said, "We say every Friday night: 'לִקְרַאת שַׁבָּת לְכוּ וְנֵלְכָה, כִּי הִיא מְקוֹר הַבְּרָכָה — Let us go towards the Shabbos and welcome it, for it is the source of blessing.' If Shabbos, which is the source of blessing is happy with you, then I too can be happy with you."

"What do you mean, *Rebbi?*" asked R' Asher. "Well," said the Chofetz Chaim, "if Shabbos is observed in your home by the members of your family, then Shabbos will bless you. But if your son drives on Shabbos, and your daughter combs her hair in a manner forbidden on the Shabbos, then Shabbos is not happy with you. If so, what kind of *brachah*-giver is Yisrael Meir?"

The man was shocked by the Chofetz Chaim's words and he promised that he would make every effort to see that his children would become true Sabbath observers.

R' Zalman recalled that within a few weeks R' Asher was walking perfectly, without crutches, the very picture of health. "But what I still cannot account for," said R' Zalman, "is how did the Chofetz Chaim knew that even R' Asher's daughter was violating the Sabbath? *Ruach hakodesh* is the only answer."

◆§ *A Cold Day in Siberia*

It was known that R' Yechezkel Abramsky (1886-1966), the noted Slutzker *Rav* and the *Av Beis Din* (head of the rabbinical court) of London spoke to Hashem during his *Shemoneh Esrei,* as a son might talk to his father. He would make his requests and plead for them like a devoted son, addressing Hashem as *Tatte* (Father).

It has been recounted that when R' Yechezkel's wife was ill, he went to the *kever* (grave) of his wife's revered grandfather the *Ridvaz,* R' Yaakov Dovid Willowsky, and prayed to Hashem, "*Tatte* ... You know how much I need my wife Raizel. I beg You, have her grandfather come before You and pray that his granddaughter get well ..."

In his younger years while living under Bolshevik rule, R' Yechezkel was arrested and exiled to Siberia — the nightmarish land of terrifying cold and biting wind. In later years he recalled to R' Sholom two incidents that happened there — one, on the day he arrived; the other, when he was released. One of the first things the heartless Russian officers there did to welcome newcomers was to force them to remove their shoes and socks, and then run barefoot over the frozen tundra. Most people became sick as a result of this ordeal, and many succumbed to pneumonia.

On the very first day that R' Yechezkel was in Siberia, he prayed, "*Tatte,* it says in Your holy Talmud (*Kesubos* 30a): 'הַכֹּל בִּידֵי שָׁמַיִם חוּץ מִצִּינִּים וּפַחִים — *Everything is in the hands of Heaven except for [the effects of] cold and heat'* (meaning that man must find ways to protect himself against the elements). Under normal conditions I would try to guard myself from becoming ill, but in this weather and with my lack of warm clothing, I can do nothing. I am in Your hands. Please, *Tatte,* protect me." And not once, during the years that R' Yechezkel was in Siberia did he ever catch a cold!

❦ ❦ ❦

His release came on *erev* Yom Kippur. A Russian officer came over to him and suddenly announced, "You can leave today." With that he gave R' Yechezkel a train ticket to get home. "Make sure to give the train officials this ticket," the officer said, "and they will let you aboard."

R' Yechezkel quickly assembled his few belongings and made his way to the exit of the camp. As he was walking another police officer approached him. The officer looked around to see if anyone was within earshot and asked, "Are you leaving today?" The officer obviously knew the answer to his own question and R' Yechezkel feared that he was coming to rescind the previous order. "Yes," replied R' Yechezkel nervously. This same officer had not been very kind to him over the last few years, to say the least. He had not been one of the worst ones either, but any officer could make trouble if he so wished. R' Yechezkel repeated as firmly and as respectfully as he could, "I am leaving now."

"Let me see your ticket," the officer ordered. R' Yechezkel searched nervously for it while the officer said to him, "Are you a *duchovner* (rabbi)?"

There was no point in lying, thought R' Yechezkel, they probably had all the information anyway. He answered that, yes, he was a *rav.* Once again the officer looked around to make sure that no one else was around. He looked down at the purple ticket that R' Yechezkel was now holding in his hand, took it from him and said, "Here, take this other ticket, the yellow one. The one they gave you would have put you on a car without heat where you could freeze to death and no one would know the difference. This will get you on a heated passenger car." Then looking around again to make sure they were still alone he whispered, "I too am a *Yid.* I am truly sorry that I was mean to you. Please, please forgive me. I had to follow my orders." The two men shook hands in a rare moment of mutual compassion and friendship and then R' Yechezkel turned and left the camp.

At the train, just as the police officer had said, people were being directed to the freezing cars, while he with his yellow ticket went into a regular passenger car.

"What horrible people, those Russians," R' Yechezkel thought, "if they don't actually kill a person during his stay in Siberia they try to have him die on the way home. And then with self-righteousness they can claim they had nothing to do with his unforeseen death."

When R' Yechezkel finally got on the train, he realized there was no way he could reach his home before Yom Kippur. Things had been so rushed and hectic for him during the day that he had no time at all to contact his family and let them know that he had been released.

He decided to get off in a town that he knew had a *shul* and stay there until after Yom Kippur. The day wore on and shortly before nightfall R' Yechezkel got off the train in the small town, made his way to the local *shul* and without having eaten anything began the fast.

After Yom Kippur he boarded a train going to Lithuania where he changed to a train bound for Warsaw. During the long ride he noticed a tall man walking through the train corridors. He couldn't believe his eyes! It was R' Elchonon Wasserman, his longtime friend, the *rosh yeshivah* of Baranovitch. They fell on each other in a warm embrace, thrilled to be together after not having seen each other for years. As they began their excited conversation R' Elchonon said to R' Yechezkel, "You were freed *erev* Yom Kippur, isn't that right?"

"Yes, that's right," answered the startled R' Yechezkel, "but how did you know that? I didn't have a chance to notify anyone about my release!"

R' Elchonon then said, "I was with the Chofetz Chaim *erev* Yom Kippur in Radin, when he suddenly stopped and said, '*Boruch Hashem* the Bolsheviks couldn't carry out their plans.' I looked at him with surprise. I had no idea to what he was referring, until he added, 'They just released the Slutzker *Rav*!' "

R' Yechezkel was later told that the Chofetz Chaim had prayed frequently for his release, saying four chapters of *Tehillim* (Psalms) on his behalf every day.

◆§ *Chutzpah*

R' Sholom had not remembered this story for years, until one Friday night, when he was visiting the Beth Medrash Govoha in Lakewood. A young man came up to him and posed a provocative talmudic question. At first, R' Sholom was perplexed, for the young man had asked well. But then suddenly, with a flash, the following story came back to him, and with it the answer to the young man's question.

The young man was troubled by a passage in Mesechta *Kallah Rabbasi* (Ch. 2): "עַז פָּנִים לְגֵיהִנֹּם, בּוֹשׁ פָּנִים לְגַן עֵדֶן — The brazen are destined for *Gehinnom;* the modest are destined for *Gan Eden*" (see also *Avos* 5:20). The *gemara* then asks: "But suppose the one who is brazen, repents, does he still go to *Gehinnom*?" To which the answer is given: "There is no repentance for such people."

The puzzled young man asked, "Isn't there a Talmudic teaching *(Yerushalmi Peah* 1:1), 'אֵין כָּל דָּבָר עוֹמֵד בִּפְנֵי בַּעֲלֵי תְשׁוּבָה — Nothing stands in the way of those who wish to repent?' "

R' Sholom thought for a moment and then remembered a story that was told to him by R' Elya Lopian, many years earlier. He went on to tell it to the young man as well as to the others who had crowded around him.

For many years the Chofetz Chaim was assisted by his son-in-law R' Hirsch in administering the yeshivah in Radin. One day R' Hirsch came to the Chofetz Chaim and suggested that they ask a certain boy to leave the yeshivah. His learning had slackened off, his *davening* wasn't what it should be and his general attitude seemed to be indifferent. R' Hirsch felt that the boy might become a bad influence on others and it would be better to have him out of the yeshivah.

The Chofetz Chaim, however, disagreed. "The boy," he said, "has potential. He will even someday be a *rav* for his fellow Jews." (R' Elya Lopian told R' Sholom that he knew the boy and that eventually he did become a *rav* in the United States.)

A few weeks later a woman came to the Chofetz Chaim to complain about a yeshivah student. Her home was a *stancia* (inn) where some yeshivah *bochurim* received room and board.

The woman complained that the boy was fresh and disrespectful to her. The Chofetz Chaim listened to the woman and then, after verifying the woman's complaint, directed R' Hirsch to expel the student. R' Hirsch could not believe it. Why was this situation different from the one about which he had spoken to the Chofetz Chaim just a few weeks earlier? Puzzled, he asked his father-in-law why he had ordered this boy to leave and insisted on keeping the one R' Hirsch had wanted to expel.

The Chofetz Chaim answered, "There is a *mishnah (Avos* 5:20) that states, 'The brazen are destined for *Gehinnom;* the modest are destined for *Gan Eden.'* Why does the *mishnah* say only that the brazen go to *Gehinnom;* don't other people who commit other sins go to *Gehinnom* as well? And besides, if he repents will the brazen man still go to *Gehinnom?*

"But the answer is that the *mishnah* is teaching us what we can expect of a sinner. An ordinary sinner will most likely repent. But those who are brazen will, in all probability, never repent. Brazenness is a personality trait, it is not a specific sin; and this characteristic leads to sinning in general.

"That is why the *mishnah* states firmly and with conviction, 'the brazen are destined for *Gehinnom!'* And *talmidim* with *chutzpah,* who will not repent, do not belong in this yeshivah."

R' Sholom finished his story and smiled at the young man, for the story had answered his question. True nothing stands in the way of a *baal teshuvah* (penitent), but one who is brazen can be expected to stubbornly remain in his ways forever.

R' Sholom looked around at the nodding faces and then smiling broadly exclaimed with resonance, "The Chofetz Chaim understood the *mishnah* and he acted accordingly. But only because he had a source to back him up. *Gevaldig!*"

◆§ *Showdown*

There is a proverb based on a Talmudic teaching (*Shabbos* 59b), "צַדִּיק גּוֹזֵר וְהַקָּדוֹשׁ בָּרוּךְ הוּא מְקַיֵּם — That which a tzaddik decrees, Hashem fulfills." This was dramatically demonstrated one day in the home of R' Akiva Eiger, the great *gaon* of Posen, in western Poland.

A number of *rabbonim* had brought to R' Akiva Eiger (1761-1837) a man who was refusing to give his wife a *get* (religious divorce). He had become a secularist, was no longer living at home, and was holding back the divorce in order to make it impossible for his observant wife to remarry.

R' Akiva Eiger spoke with the man and soon saw that nothing he said would be to any avail. The man was spiteful and vindictive and paid no heed to the *rav.*

Finally R' Akiva Eiger took out tractate *Kiddushin,* opened it to the first page and said to the man, "The *mishnah* here clearly states that a marriage can be ended in two ways: by a divorce or by the husband's death. I am asking you now," said R' Akiva Eiger sternly, "by which method do you choose to free this woman?"

The man snarled at R' Akiva Eiger's veiled threat, "I have no use for you or for the *mishnah!*"

R' Akiva Eiger closed the volume and the man stalked out of the house defiantly, leaving the other *rabbonim* in the room appalled at his audacity.

Moments later there was a scream outside. People ran from the house and saw that the man lay slumped on the bottom of the stairs in front of R' Akiva Eiger's house. As he was walking down the steps he had suffered a massive heart attack. Within minutes he was dead.

◆§ *Concern for a Student*

When R' Akiva Eiger gave a *shiur* (lecture) to the young men of his yeshivah, a certain wealthy businessman made sure that he was always present to listen very carefully. This gentleman, R' Alter, was very close to R' Akiva Eiger and made sure to have his business matters attended to by others for a few hours each day so that he could attend and review the *shiur*.

One day, R' Alter was delayed by more than a half hour because of a pressing business matter. As soon as he could get away, he came running to the yeshivah in order to hear the last part of the *shiur*.

To his surprise, however, when he came to the *shiur* room it was empty. Puzzled, he went to the *beis midrash* (study hall) to ask what had happened. Upon arriving, he found everyone in a turmoil. "What's going on?" he asked, "Where is everyone today?"

After some confusing and contradictory stories, he was able to determine that indeed there had been a *shiur*. However, about ten minutes into the *shiur* a young *bochur* had asked a question to which R' Akiva Eiger gave a prompt answer. The *bochur* did not understand the reply and he asked the *gaon* for further explanation. R' Akiva Eiger went over his answer patiently once more. Again and again, the boy tried to grasp the explanation but couldn't. To his credit, he did not give up. He desperately wanted to understand and persisted in asking, arguing and verbally fencing with R' Akiva Eiger.

It was a hot day, R' Akiva Eiger had not been feeling well even before the *shiur*, and in great frustration at not being able to make the *talmid* understand, he fainted.

The fainting, however, heralded a more serious physical reaction and soon R' Akiva Eiger was finding it difficult to breathe.

The *bochurim* ran to get a doctor, who came at once. He ordered that the *gaon* be taken home. But instead of reviving at home, word had it that the *gaon's* condition was deteriorating rapidly.

R' Alter thanked the student for the information and then asked, "What was the question the boy had asked, and what did the *rebbi* answer?"

The bochur couldn't believe his ears. "Now with the *rebbi* so sick, what difference does it make what the question was?"

Now it was R' Alter who persisted and finally found someone who would repeat both the question and the answer. R' Alter listened, shook his head in disbelief and said, "I can't understand it. The *rebbi* was right, he answered the boy to the point."

R' Alter then rushed to R' Akiva Eiger's home and found that the situation had worsened. Family members had already been summoned to come to the bedside, and even the *chevra kadisha* (burial society) had been summoned. Candles were lit (a tradition followed by some in the room of the dying person) and people stood around reciting *Tehillim*. R' Alter glanced at his *rebbi* lying in bed and noticed that he was murmuring some words. He pushed his way through the family members who stood around the bed and bent his ear to hear what R' Akiva Eiger was saying. "*Ribbono Shel Olam*, please let me live in the *zechus* (merit) of the Torah that I repeated to the *bochur*, for it was truth. And besides, if anything should happen to me, the young *bochur* will not be able to live with himself, for he will always blame himself and say that I died because of him."

When R' Alter heard these incredibly touching words he stood up straight and announced, "You can put out the candles. The *rebbi* will have a *refuah sheleimah*. The *Ribbono Shel Olam* will surely listen to such a selfless prayer!"

And He did. Shortly thereafter, R' Akiva Eiger recuperated and eventually returned to saying his *shiur*.

◆§ *A Spreading Fire*

Rav Sholom was once asked to address a group of young Torah scholars in the Boro Park section of Brooklyn, on the topic of Torah study. He prefaced his remarks with these words:

"You may wonder why it is necessary to speak of the great merit of Torah study in a neighborhood where there are so many *shiurim* and where so many individuals set aside time every day for learning. Perhaps some of you may even consider it an insult that you should be addressed on this topic. Let me tell you of an incident that happened with one of my *rebbeim* (teachers), R'

Elya Dushnitzer, the *mashgiach* in the yeshivah of Petach Tikvah, where I studied as a young *bochur*."

✿ ✿ ✿

One Shabbos, when R' Elya was in Vilna, a *maggid* came to speak. The main thrust of his speech concerned the observance of Shabbos, the importance of constantly reviewing the laws of Shabbos, and giving the proper respect for Shabbos.

As R' Elya left the synagogue after the *drashah*, two people approached him and said, "Why did the *maggid* speak about Shabbos observance? Doesn't he know that every member of his audience observes and respects Shabbos?"

R' Elya thought for a moment and then said, "When there is a big fire and the firemen see that it cannot be put out because the building is entirely engulfed in flames, they don't spray water on the blazing inferno; it's too late for that. Rather, they spray water on the adjacent buildings so that the fire won't spread. It's a question of protecting what has not yet been damaged by the flames. That's why the *maggid* spoke here about Shabbos observance to an audience full of Shabbos-observers. He wanted to be sure that people wouldn't be influenced by the large number of their neighbors who are not Shabbos observant."

✿ ✿ ✿

And then R' Sholom added, "And that's also why it makes sense to talk about Torah study here in Boro Park."

◈§ *Daily Judgment*

The Baal Shem Tov (1698-1760) once related a conversation that took place between an old water-carrier and his friend. The old man had been walking with difficulty up a steep hill to the village to make his deliveries, his breathing heavy and labored, when his friend called out, "So, how are things with you today?"

"Look at me," complained the old man. "I am on in my years,

frail, no savings and still struggling to make ends meet! Where is the rest and relaxation I was praying for in my old age?"

A few days later, the same man was climbing up a hill to yet another village, but this time he was singing a song to himself as he carried his water bucket. The same friend greeted him. "I see you're smiling today. How are things with you?"

"See how lucky I am," came the jovial reply. "Thank G-d, although I am an old man I still don't have to rely on anyone. My faculties are fine, I'm able to support myself, and I don't have to take charity from my family or friends."

A contradiction? A change of heart? "Well," said the Baal Shem Tov, "there are two Talmudic statements that also seem contradictory, yet when they are reconciled they explain the very different attitudes of our friend, the water carrier."

"The Talmud states (*Rosh Hoshanah* 16a): 'בְּרֹאשׁ הַשָּׁנָה כָּל בָּאֵי עוֹלָם עוֹבְרִין לְפָנָיו כִּבְנֵי מָרוֹן – On Rosh Hashanah all mankind passes before Him (G-d) like a flock of sheep [as G-d judges each person individually].' Yet the Talmud there also declares that according to R' Yossi, G-d sit in judgment on every single individual, every day. When *does* G-d sit in judgment, only on Rosh Hashanah or every day?"

"The answer," said the Baal Shem Tov, "is that both are true. On Rosh Hashanah G-d decides how much a person will earn for the entire year, will he be blessed with riches or will he have to suffer with poverty – that is the decision made on Rosh Hashanah. But every day G-d decrees in what frame of mind the person will be when he receives his ordained portion. Will it make him happy? Or will it bring sadness to him? This is part of the reward and punishment that the person's actions have earned for him. And that is why the water carrier had different attitudes on different days."

In our own lives, too, quite often the same person who has a large home will become depressed and jealous because he sees others with larger homes and even more furnishings that he has. But on another day this same person will be joyful and consider himself fortunate, realizing that there are many people in the world who have so much less than he has.

His position and possessions have not changed, his mood and attitude have changed and that is because of the judgment G-d decrees for him that day.

◆§ *The Future is Now*

It was June of 1942, during the height of the second World War. The Nazi general Erwin Rommel — whose brilliant strategy earned him the nickname Desert Fox — sought to thrust his armed forces into the heart of Egypt, his main objective being the Suez Canal. If he could overpower the Allied forces and cross through Egypt, he could then overrun Palestine fairly easily.

A sense of foreboding prevailed in Palestine. The German forces were stronger than the British. People in Palestine prayed, trembled, and cried with every successive radio broadcast. It was only a few days before the fast of the seventeenth of Tammuz, and already people were acting as if it were Tishah B'Av.

One afternoon the Ponevezher Rav, R' Yosef Kahaneman (1886-1969), met R' Betzalel Zolty (1920-1983), later to become the chief *rav* in Jerusalem, and told him that he had just borrowed five hundred pounds and bought land in Bnei Brak on which he would eventually build the Ponevezher Yeshivah.

R' Betzalel was astounded. "Today, of all days, you spend money to buy land in *Eretz Yisrael? Klal Yisrael* is in such danger, everything points to a bleak future, how can you even think of building anything now?"

The Ponevezher smiled and told R' Betzalel, "Now, more than ever is the time to look towards the future." And then the Ponevezher cited a story found in chapter 32 of *Jeremiah*.

❦ ❦ ❦

In the eighteenth year in the reign of Nebuchadnezzar, the Babylonian army surrounded Jerusalem. Although the Jews of that era were going to be destroyed, Hashem told Jeremiah that when his uncle Chanamel came to sell him some land he should buy it.

Not only did Jeremiah buy the property, but, again following the orders of Hashem, he made sure that the transaction was duly and validly recorded and preserved so that people would be aware of it in the future. Then Jeremiah proclaimed, "this is what Hashem said, 'In that future time, Jews will yet purchase homes, fields and vineyards in this land.' "

The Ponevezher then said, "You know, R' Betzalel, the Talmud in *Megillah* (14a) says that the Jews had thousands of prophets, yet only those prophecies needed as lessons for future generations were recorded in *Tanach* (Scriptures). Whatever was not necessary for future generations was not recorded. Thus, the narratives in *Tanach* are there for us to learn from. That lesson of Jeremiah — not to forsake the future, even when the outlook is bleak — is valid for us today. That is why I bought the land, for we have a future in *Eretz Yisrael!*"

How right he was!

Idle Moments Adding Up

Rav Zelig Reuven Bengis (1864-1953), *rav* of the Eidah Hachareidis community in Jerusalem and author of *Liflagos Reuven,* was an exceptional *masmid.* He spent every possible moment studying Torah, and every year he would call together a *minyan* to celebrate a *siyum,* commemorating his completion of the *Shas* (the entire Talmud).

One afternoon he called together a group for a *siyum* just a few weeks after having celebrated his usual *siyum* of *Shas.* The group knew of his extraordinary capacities as a Torah scholar, but there was no way even he could have finished *Shas* again so quickly since the last *siyum.*

When the group asked him about it, he replied, "Oh, this is a *siyum hashas* from a different study rotation, and this *siyum* took me much longer to accomplish than all the others. You see," he said, "as a *rav,* I'm often called to participate in happy occasions, such as weddings, *bar mitzvahs* and circumcisions. Quite often there's a delay; an important guest is late, a relative has not arrived yet, and so on. Instead of wasting precious time, I decided seventeen years ago that I would begin a special cycle of *Shas* during these waiting periods. The other day I was at a *simchah* and finished this separate cycle. Therefore I am celebrating with this *siyum.*"

☙ *What's the Rush?*

Sometimes a timely question is as brilliant as any answer. R' Sholom enjoys the following incident both for its wisdom and underlying message of *emunas chachamim* (faith in the Torah sages).

A prominent philanthropic woman known as Chavale was once given a blessing by the *Sha'agas Aryeh* (1695-1785) because she took the time every week to bring him two *challos* for Shabbos. He blessed her that someday she would attain wealth and merit the building of two synagogues, one in Minsk, where she lived, and one in *Eretz Yisrael.*

Time passed and the woman indeed became wealthy and she did indeed build a synagogue in Minsk, which came to be known as *Chavale's Shul.* As she became older, she decided that it was time for her to make a pilgrimage to Jerusalem so that she could fulfill the second part of the blessing and see a synagogue built there with her wealth.

Before she left Europe, however, she decided to say good-by to all the prominent rabbis she had become acquainted with over the years. When she came to R' Chaim of Volozhin, he asked her where she was going. She explained that she had the assurance and the blessing of the *Sha'agas Aryeh* that she would live to see two synagogues built, one in Minsk and the other in Jerusalem, and now that she was getting on in years, she wanted to see the second part of the dream and blessing fulfilled.

R' Chaim turned to her and said, "If you have the assurance of such a great *tzaddik* that you will live until it is built — then what is your rush?"

Part E:
Common Folks, Common Goals

◆§ *A Mother's Kiss*

This is an incredible story of a self-imposed restraint undertaken by a woman already living in a land of restraint. It was told to R' Sholom by the Kaliver *Rebbe*.

In Soviet Russia, it is forbidden for a Jew to have a *bris* (ritual circumcision) performed on his newborn son. The punishment for having an infant son circumcised is immediate layoff from work, with the possibility of subsequent criminal charges, trials and perhaps even a jail sentence. For this reason, the great majority of Jewish boys born in Soviet Russia remain uncircumcised.

Nevertheless, some Jews take the risk of gathering a few highly trusted friends and having the *bris* performed clandestinely. Although a *bris* should be performed on the eighth day of a child's life, many times parents wait three weeks, three months or even six months before they can accomplish what is for them a risky *mitzvah*.

For the first few weeks after the birth of a son, parents can almost feel the presence of the authorities and no hint of a *bris* can even be mentioned. The family watches not only for officials, but for "friends" who might actually be informers.

In one particular town there was a "trusted *minyan*" of people whom the Shlayder * family wished to invite to their son's *bris*. They were discreet, dependable and responsible people. They would never betray a family and no police authority could get any

* The name is fictitious, but the story is true.

information from them. Often, it was one of these men who advised the family when it was "safe" to have the *bris.*

The Shlayder boy was almost a year old and he had not yet been circumcised. Suddenly the atmosphere became a bit less tense and Mr. Shlayder was informed that it was safe to have the *bris.* The *mohel* was called, the guests gathered in a basement, and the child was brought there to have his *bris.*

The *bris* was performed, the proper blessings were recited and everyone wished each other *mazel tov.* The child was then brought back to the room where his mother was waiting for him. Suddenly there was a piercing scream, a wail and a cry. There was a thud, as though someone had fallen to the floor. Pandemonium broke out as people ran to the room where the mother lay in a dead faint. After they revived her, she told an incredible story.

The young mother had feared that her son might never have a *bris,* that she would be lulled into negligence because of her fear of the authorities, that she might capitulate to fear, and not have the *bris* at all. She was determined not to let that happen to herself and she undertook something that would compel her to long for the *bris,* to make it paramount in her mind at all times. She vowed not to kiss her son until he had had his *bris.*

For close to a year she suffered the pent-up emotions that only a mother can feel. Finally, after the *bris,* she had taken her son into her aching arms and kissed him fervently.

Overcome with emotion, she had fainted.

◆§ *Upside-down Roots*

The assembled guests in Bnei Brak were proud to have been invited to the *seudas mitzvah* (festive meal to celebrate a *mitzvah).* The young *baal teshuvah* was making a *siyum* on his first *masechta* (tractate of Talmud), and for him it was the joyful culmination of a long, hard road back to the authentic *Yiddishkeit* of his forefathers. His parents were not religious and he had never attended a yeshivah. But now in *Eretz Yisrael,* he had discovered Torah and Judaism, had been inspired, and had made long steady progress that brought him to this major milestone. He had progressed from *siddur*, to *Chumash*, to *Mishnah*, *to Gemara* and now this *siyum*. His joy was boundless and all his friends shared his happiness.

All except his father. His father sat glumly, seemingly oblivious to the evening's festivities. To him, the study of Talmud meant nothing. At first he had refused to attend this party, but his son had begged him, and reluctantly he had consented to make an appearance.

Every speaker spoke of the pride they had in young Ephraim. His *rebbi* likened him to a man who builds his home painstakingly, cementing brick to brick, until the house is complete. He said; "Each new line of the *Gemara* that Ephraim learned was added to all the others, finally making the *mesechta* complete."

Ephraim himself could not contain his joy. With tears, he recalled his humble start, his new-found meaning in life. As he spoke, he stole a quick glance at his father. His father seemed uneasy.

Now it was time for *Bircas Hamazon* (Grace after the meal), but suddenly the father was moving in his chair. He stood up. He raised his hand to ask for silence. Knowing his uncaring, even negative attitude, the guests were surprised by his sudden desire to speak. He was wearing shorts and a cap, and now — as a speaker — he seemed even more out of place than before, when he'd been just a detached onlooker. He looked over the crowd and asked for permission to say a few words.The people turned to him and waited in curious and respectful silence. He cleared his voice and this is what he said.

"I have been watching this event for the past two hours and I did not think it would affect me. Some of you may know that I was reluctant to come here, but now that I have seen the *siyum* and met some of you, I am happy that I came. If you will allow me, I would like to tell you a story."

❦ ❦ ❦

I come from Russia. I was an assimilated Jew there, but it did not do me any good with the Russian authorities. To them an assimilated Jew is still a Jew. They accused me of disloyalty to Communism and sent me to a labor camp in Siberia. For a year I shared a working area with another fellow who was as afraid to talk to me as I was to him. We froze together, worked together, starved together, and still we never spoke.

At the end of the year, I was granted my release. I felt I should say good-by to my silent companion. When I did, he said that he wanted to tell me a story. I never understood the story — perhaps he was afraid to explain it — but tonight I think I understand.

He said, "Once upon a time there was an apple orchard. The trees in the grove grew beautifully, each apple shinier and more delicious than the next. Every year a new crop grew, and every year it was finer than the previous one. One summer day, a gardener turned to his friend and said, 'You know, the roots of these trees are filthy and dirty. They are black and muddy and yet they manage to produce such beautiful apples. If we were to take one of the trees, uproot it, turn it over and put the top of the beautiful tree in the ground, how much more magnificent would the apples be!' The other gardener was impressed with the logic, and so, together, they uprooted a few trees and placed the trees in the ground upside down. The roots were now skyward, and the lovely leaves and branches were embedded in the earth.

"Nothing grew. But the gardeners were stubborn and they repeated the process again and again, planting uprooted trees with their heads in the earth, not willing to give up until they would succeed. But they failed dismally, and soon there were no apples, except one. That lone apple was saved somehow, and its seed was planted. The next year a new sapling grew, and from that sapling there was new hope for the future."

With that he ended his story and we had to part, I to freedom and he to further slavery.

❦ ❦ ❦

I never knew what he meant, although I thought about it many times. Tonight I know. My generation thought it had the right ideas; we would overturn the ideals that our forefathers had lived with for centuries, we would plant new, modern, logical ways of living, hoping to produce even better generations. It has not worked. But one apple was saved, and from him shall grow a future.

The crowd was stunned into silence. The father waited as he tried to compose himself and say his next words. He looked at his son and said in a voice choked with emotion, "My son, you are the future. I am proud of you." And with that he wept and embraced his son.

☙ *A Cab Ride to Jerusalem*

At the corner of *Rechov* Rabbi Akiva and *Rechov* Herzl in Bnei Brak, one can pick up a *sheirut* (direct taxi ride) to Jerusalem at almost any hour of the day. Seven people share a *sheirut*. When the car is filled, the cabbie buckles his seat belt and, like a rocket catapulting off its launching pad, the *sheirut* slashes its way through Bnei Brak and out onto the highway to Jerusalem.

Our story takes place on one of these *sheirut* rides a few years after the passing of the *Chazon Ish*, R' Avraham Yeshaya Karelitz (1878-1953). Two religious people in the back of the cab were talking to each other, and one of them sighed, "Bnei Brak is not the same since the *Chazon Ish* passed away."

"Yes," agreed his friend, "our generation needs great ones like him."

Listening attentively from his seat in the front was the cab driver, Natan, a non-observant Sefardi. He was dressed much differently from his Orthodox passengers in the back. He wore no *kippah* and sported an open khaki shirt, over a pair of Bermuda shorts, unlike his bearded riders who were dressed in black suits and hats. Natan turned to the fellow sitting on his right. "Did you hear what the men in the back say? That the *Chazon Ish* is gone. They are wrong, they don't know what they're talking about!"

Surprised that the obviously irreligious cab driver would even know who the *Chazon Ish* was, the man being addressed retorted,

"Well, maybe you haven't heard, but the *Chazon Ish* passed away a few years ago."

"Well, then you are wrong too," said Natan emphatically. "The *Chazon Ish* is still around and I can prove it." By now, all ears were listening to the cantankerous cab driver, and once he had their attention he offered to prove he was right. They all agreed to listen, and the cabbie began his story:

❦ ❦ ❦

My daughter was having a difficult labor. She had been rushed to the hospital in Tel Aviv and the doctors had been with her for hours. But the child would not come. She was in agony and the doctors who seemed helpless told me that there was nothing they could do. As they discussed her situation, an old nurse, who saw my predicament, came over to me and said, "Why don't you go to the *Chazon Ish*?"

"The who?" I asked. "What is the *Chazon Ish*?"

"He is a great rabbi," the nurse said, "and he helps people."

At my wit's end, I asked her, "But where does he live?"

She told me, "Just get to Bnei Brak and once you get there any child in the street will be able to direct you."

I got into my cab and raced to Bnei Brak. In no time I was at the *Chazon Ish*'s house. It was late at night, but he answered my knock himself. In a quiet and friendly manner he asked how he could help me. I told him of my daughter's pain and how the doctors could not help her. He looked at me, smiled and said, "Go back to the hospital. The child was just born."

He shook my hand and wished me *mazel tov*. My heart leaped with joy, but I could not believe him. I dashed back to the hospital and when I got there, sure enough, the child had already been born — exactly as he had said!

❦ ❦ ❦

In the *sheirut* all were spellbound — but Natan was not finished. He went on with the second part of his story:

❦ ❦ ❦

Two years later, my daughter was again expecting a child. Once again she had a difficult labor and once again the doctors could do nothing to speed up the birth of the child. I remembered what had happened the last time and so, this time, I didn't wait for the old nurse. I got into my cab, rushed to Bnei Brak and went to the *Chazon Ish*. I came to the corner where I thought he lived and just to be sure I asked a passerby, "Is this the home of the *Chazon Ish*?"

The man looked at me as if I had come from outer space. "What's the matter with you? Don't you know that the *Chazon Ish* passed away a year ago."

My heart fell. I felt as if it were the end of the world for me. It was as if I had lost my best friend. I began pleading to this total stranger. "I came here to speak to him; it's an emergency. To whom do I go now?"

"People go to his *kever* (gravesite) and pray there," he told me.

"Where is he buried?" I queried.

The man pointed me in the direction of the cemetery. I ran there at breakneck speed and jumped over a fence to get to some people who might be able to tell me where he was buried. They pointed to a grave that was covered with stones and pebbles.

When I saw his name on the stone, I fell on the grave, prostrating myself over it and began crying uncontrollably. I lay on the stones begging the *Chazon Ish* to pray for my daughter. "*Rebbi*," I said, "You saved my daughter once before, please pray for her again."

I was there a short time, and I could swear that I suddenly saw his face with that same smile and could hear his voice saying to me, "*Mazel tov*, the child has been born," and that I should go back to the hospital. Startled, I got up, ran to my cab and rushed back to the hospital. When I got there, they told me that my second grandchild had indeed been born.

❦ ❦ ❦

Then the cabbie turned to his companion in the front seat and said, "And these people in the back say the *Chazon Ish* is gone!"

◆§ *The Light of Her Life*

Over the past two decades, thousands of non-observant Jews throughout *Eretz Yisrael* and the Diaspora have come to espouse and observe the traditional way of Judaism. Each, in his own way, has become part of what is today known as the *baal teshuvah* (penitent) movement.

Most such people can point to a particular act or incident that ignited the dormant spark of Judaism that had lain unnourished deep inside them. At a recent seminar for *baalei teshuvah* in *Eretz Yisrael*, a young mother related the following story.

She was by nature a *pachdanit* (coward) who had more fears and apprehensions than the average person. She had only one daughter and was extremely hesitant to enroll her in a school to which she would have to travel by bus. Terrorist activities in her area, fatal highway accidents, and the concern that her child might miss the school bus and be alone in the streets, all caused her to insist that her child attend a school within walking distance.

For the first few grades, all went well. But then the family moved to the outskirts of Bnei Brak, where the only school within walking distance was a *dati* (religious) school. The mother understood that a problem might develop since both she and her husband were completely non-observant. Nevertheless, she felt that she would be able to cope with whatever situations might arise.

Things went smoothly, with the occasional rough edges being brushed over by love and understanding pats on the head, until the nine-year-old girl came home from school one Friday afternoon. Enthusiastically, she told her mother how her *morah* (teacher) had taught the girls the blessing for the Friday-night candles. She began reciting the blessing with pride.

"That's very nice," said the mother, "but you know that we don't light candles Friday nights."

"But," complained the child, "my *morah* said that everyone lights candles Friday night. Why don't we?"

The mother was somewhat hesitant to explain to her daughter

that she was irreligious, and instead decided to accentuate the positive.

"We don't light candles Friday night," said the mother emphatically, "but we do light them on *Yom Ha'atzmaut* (Israeli Independence Day) in memory of the fallen soldiers who fought for our land." The little girl left the room dejected, but determined. The teacher and her classmates had seemed so excited about candle lighting that she decided she would take matters into her own hands.

Later that afternoon as the shops and stores were about to close, she walked down to the local grocer and asked him for two candles for the Sabbath. "Are these for your mother?" the surprised grocer inquired. He knew the family had never bought *Shabbos* candles before.

"Yes," answered the little girl softly. But the grocer found it hard to believe. He thought to himself that the girl had most likely misunderstood her mother. He gave her the candles that he thought her mother had probably wanted. He gave her two *yahrzeit* candles.

As the child walked home, she practiced the blessings over the candles once again. She was proud to be fulfilling a Jewish woman's *mitzvah.*

That evening, after the girl's father had come home, her mother called the family in for dinner. The little girl, who was busy in her own room, didn't respond to her mother's call. After repeated calls, both the mother and father walked to the girl's room where they found her sitting at her desk, staring at the two lit *yahrzeit* candles.

"What are these?" exclaimed the mother. The *yahrzeit* candles sent a shiver through her. In her mind she saw her own mother, many years back, as she stood beside the two *yahrzeit* candles she had lit for her own dead parents. She recalled the tears of sorrow and pride that had accompanied that rite.

The child stood up, uneasy that she had been caught. "What are those?" asked the father, who was unaware of the afternoon's conversation. The child looked at the candles and then back at her parents. Then she uttered the words that reverberated throughout the auditorium as the mother told the story, *"Echad l'Abba ve'echad l'Imma"* — one is for you, Father, and the other is for you, Mother." She meant that she wanted to share the *mitzvah* with her parents, but her mother took it differently: One for her father who was for all intents and purposes dead as a Jew, and one for her mother who had killed all the beauty of traditional Judaism with her "modernistic" approach to life.

"Those candles made me see the light," said the mother as she told of the resolution made at that moment to return her family to authentic Judaism. And from that week on, the father has provided *Shabbos* candles for everyone living in their building.

◆§ *Honor Roll*

The following story was told to R' Sholom by R' Aharon Porush, an outstanding scholar of Yeshivas Eitz Chaim. R' Porush gave a *shiur* in the old folks' home of *Battei Natan* in Jerusalem, and a regular member of the *shiur* was a certain R' Shmelke.

R' Shmelke actually understood very little, for he had been raised in Czarist Russia where he had been taken forcibly when just a child into the Russian Army. Children like him were know as Cantonists — or in Yiddish, *Gechapte* (the caught ones). They had to serve in the army throughout their teen years and into adulthood, some for as long as twenty-five years! There was no yeshivah and no Torah training for them at all.

Now, as an adult, the most he could do was sit in the synagogue and listen as others discussed and debated the myriad of wonderful topics in the Talmud. To R' Shmelke, the give and take between *rebbi* and student, and one *chavrusa* (study partner) and another, was music to his ears.

He attended as many *shiurim* as he could, barely understanding any of them. He would sit unobtrusively and try to absorb whatever would sink into his unsophisticated mind. At times his wife would become impatient with him, for as she said, "You admit that you don't understand much anyway, so what's the point of going? I could use your help here at home with the chores."

It was to no avail. Every day he went, and he went enthusiastically. Finally his wife complained to the *rav,* who one day took Shmelke aside: "Tell me," the *rav* said, "I understand that you enjoy coming to the *shiurim* but at times it is inconvenient for your wife. She is ill and she needs you at home. Wouldn't it be better if you sometimes stayed home and did *chessed* for your wife?"

"I'll tell you," said R' Shmelke as tears welled up in his eyes. "When I was a young man, I was conscripted into the Russian army. Every morning there was a daily routine which all officers had to follow. In order to show loyalty to the Czar and his ruling family, we had to recite the names of the monarch, the chief officers, their family members and cabinet officials. Every morning we stood at attention and recited the whole long list by heart.

"When I get to *Olam Haba* (World to Come), I want to show my loyalty to G-d. I'll stand up and recite the names of G-d's monarchs, officers and cabinet members. They are the rabbis of the *Gemara* — R' Papa, Abaye, Rava, Rebbe, R' Yochanan, R' Eliezer, Rabban Shimon ben Gamliel, and so on. By going to these *shiurim* I learn their names and I gain a knowledge of the royal family and their prominent members!"

With Pure Intent

The Volozhiner Yeshivah had a fund-raiser, whom we shall call R' Hershel. For many years R' Hershel traveled throughout the neighboring cities, towns, and villages to collect funds for the yeshivah. R' Hershel was a simple man, always modestly dressed, traveling mostly by foot. Every year he made his rounds, until he became a familiar figure, almost an institution to the people from whom he solicited funds. As the yeshivah grew, and hundreds of boys came to study in Volozhin, the financial burdens of the yeshivah became much greater. Now R' Hershel was obligated to travel much farther afield and to approach many more people than he had before.

He now had to seek out wealthy people who lived in magnificent homes. So, R' Hershel bought himself a fine suit, a stately hat and provided himself with a coach and horse. In this array, he felt he would make a better impression on all the people, both new and old, and he could cover much more territory in less time.

One day, he went out to visit one of his "regular customers," a farmer right outside Volozhin. Every year the farmer gave generously to the yeshivah, and R' Hershel expected that this year he would get the same or even more. To his surprise, the farmer, even when told of the additional burden of the yeshivah, gave a minimal amount, much less than he had ever given before. R' Hershel accepted the donation graciously and did not complain. He continued on his rounds and eventually came back to the yeshivah in Volozhin where he sat down with R' Chaim to summarize what he had accomplished.

In their discussions, R' Hershel told R' Chaim that one of his regulars had given him much less than in previous years.

"Do you know why he gave less?" R' Chaim asked R' Hershel.

"No," came the reply. "I was surprised myself. He didn't say that it had been a bad year for his crops, nor did he complain about his business. When I got the small donation, I just couldn't bring myself to ask why he had given less, but I was puzzled."

"I would like to see him," said R' Chaim.

R' Hershel sent word to the farmer that R' Chaim would like to speak to him the next time he was in Volozhin.

A few days later, seated across the table from the farmer, R' Chaim asked him, "Why this year, of all years, did you choose to give less money?

"Let me explain," said the farmer. "Every year, when R' Hershel came to see me, I gave generously, as you must surely know. I thought that all my money went for the yeshivah. But this year R' Hershel came to me dressed in an expensive suit, with a fine horse and carriage. I know the yeshivah had to pay for all the finery and I certainly don't want my money to be spent on a horse and carriage."

R' Chaim smiled at the farmer and said, "I understand your feelings but let me explain a *posuk* (verse) in *Chumash (Shemos*

31:1,4) to you. The Torah says that when Hashem wanted the *Mishkan* (Tabernacle) to be built for the Jews who were traveling through the desert, He said to Moses, 'See, I have called by name Betzalel, son of Uri ... and I have filled him with wisdom, insight and knowledge ...' Rashi notes that the word 'knowledge' refers to *ruach hakodesh* (divinely inspired intuition).

"Why," asked R' Chaim, "was Betzalel granted all these various levels of intelligence, even *ruach hakodesh?"* R' Chaim answered his own question, "The answer lies in the very next *posuk:* '... לַחְשֹׁב מַחֲשָׁבוֹת to ponder thoughts regarding gold, silver and copper.'" R' Chaim then offered a novel interpretation: "Through his *ruach hakodesh,* Betzalel had to determine the intent of each person who donated money (i.e., gold, silver, copper) and decide if the donation was made with appropriate sincerity. If one's intent in giving charity was pure, then Betzalel would designate that the money go for something in the *Mishkan* that contained the highest level of holiness such as the Ark. If, however, it was given with less sincerity, then Betzalel would designate that the money be assigned to an item in the *Mishkan* that was on a lesser level of holiness.

"The same applies to money that you or anyone else gives for the yeshivah. There are many reasons that people give charity. Some give because they sincerely feel a responsibility to assist those in need. Others give only because they feel compelled to match what their friends have given, but not because of the goodness of their hearts. [R' Sholom adds, "And still others give because they want a tax deduction!"] Hashem judges each donation and assigns it accordingly, either for a higher level of holiness or for a lower one. Every penny given to charity is considered a *mitzvah,* but in a yeshivah some money must go for *sefarim* while other money goes for heating and plumbing. If your intentions are pure," said R' Chaim to the farmer, "the money you give will still be reckoned as having gone for Torah study. People who give insincerely may have their donations used to buy hay for the horses. When your intent is pure, the money will go where you want it to go, and thus it is up to you and not us, where the money goes."

◆§ *The Cliffhanger's Dream*

This remarkable story was told by a woman at the conclusion of a weekend seminar in *Eretz Yisrael* for *baalei teshuvah* (penitents). All the participants had been non-religious and, through incidents that occurred in their lives, had been inspired to return to authentic Torah Judaism. The weekend had been spent in a friendly atmosphere with rabbis and scholars who fielded questions, gave advice and delivered enlightening and inspirational lectures. At the closing banquet each person was given an opportunity to "tell his story." This was one woman's emotional story.

She and her husband had been sent by the Israeli government on a mission to America. They were to be in the United States for a year and then would return home. They and their young children lived in a rented apartment in New York.

They soon realized that unlike Israel, where Sunday is a day like any other, in America, Sunday is a day for family trips. One Sunday afternoon, they got into their station wagon and headed for the mountains. The weather suddenly changed and torrential rain began to fall. The husband, who was driving, was unfamiliar with the winding roads and was going too fast under these conditions. On a left turn, the car went straight out over a cliff and crashed far below the road. The parents, who had not been wearing their seat belts, were thrown out of the car and knocked unconscious. After a few moments the mother began to regain consciousness and heard her three small children crying, *"Imma! Imma!"*

She looked around and saw her husband lying motionless, but she knew that her first priority was to get the children out of the car which balanced precariously on a huge rock and from which it could fall, at any moment, down a steep cliff. She struggled to get up, and, in great pain, managed to get to the car in which her frightened children were trapped.

She was afraid to open the door for fear it might cause the car to topple over. But she had no other way of getting them out, so, ever so slowly and carefully, she opened the front door. Reaching in she was able to get two of her children out, but the third was strapped into an infant seat, beyond her reach.

She tried to open the back door, but it was hopelessly smashed and totally jammed. She went back to the front seat and tried to stretch over the seat. The frightened child leaned forward but she was beyond her mother's grasp. Again the mother stretched as far as she possibly could and suddenly the baby was in her hands. She couldn't believe it, for she knew that she could not possibly have stretched that far, but there was the little girl, clutched tightly in her arms.

Once outside she placed her baby near the other two children who sat huddled together near a tree, and went to her husband, who still lay motionless. She feared the worst although she hoped for the best. In her heart she knew he was dead. She collapsed in shock. She never knew how long she lay there. All she remembers is hearing her children cry out, *"Abba! Abba!"*

Startled, she roused herself, cleared her eyes and saw a man limping toward them. In an identical accident, his car had skidded off the roadway and come to rest near theirs. He had injured his foot and, while looking for some assistance, had spotted this family. In their confusion, the children had thought that he was their father. He assessed the situation and, despite his injured foot, went back to the road to flag down help and eventually both he and the Israeli family of five were taken to a nearby hospital.

Numerous plastic surgery procedures had to be performed on the woman's face and it was three months before she was released from the hospital. Her husband, though, had perished in the accident and she would have to make a new life on her own.

During her hospital stay she kept thinking back to how her third child had been saved. It had to have been a miracle, she reasoned. Maybe it was an angel who handed her that child over the front seat. She remembered clearly that it was not humanly possible for her to reach her daughter. With a strong resolve, she decided to change her life. She returned to *Eretz Yisrael* and became a religious woman. In the Holy Land, she enrolled her two older children in religious schools.

Because they had previously attended secular schools, they were behind their new classmates, especially ten-year-old Ami, who was placed in a class that was studying *Gemara*. Though he was a bright boy, he found it difficult to adjust to the reasoning and language of the Talmud, and could not catch up to his class. He became frustrated because he wanted to succeed, but couldn't.

Several months into the school year, Ami came home in tears. His class would soon take a comprehensive test on the fifth chapter of tractate *Bava Kamma* — and there was no way he could pass. "How can I pass the test when I'm so far behind?" he cried.

"Don't worry," his mother said lovingly, "No matter what mark you get, I know the *rebbi* will understand. After all, he knows quite well that you started learning much later than all the other boys, and besides they have someone to study with at home, but you don't."

Only slightly pacified, Ami went to sleep feeling miserable about his whole situation. The next morning he was overjoyed. Surprised at the turnabout, his mother asked him if he had had a restful night. "Oh, I had a wonderful dream," he said brightly, "and I know I will do well on the test."

Surprised, she asked, "How is that?"

"Well," said the boy a little hesitatingly, "I had a dream. I dreamt of *Abba*."

"You did?"

"Yes. We were walking along a street and I said to him, '*Abba* do you know that we are now religious?'

"And he said to me, 'Yes, I know, the day that all of you became religious, I was permitted to enter *Gan Eden*.'

"I said that I was enrolled in a yeshivah and he said he knew that too. Then I told him that I was now learning *Gemara* and was going to have a big test. *Abba* said, 'The *Gemara* you're learning in school is the same *Gemara* they are teaching me in *Gan Eden*.'

" 'Then can you teach it to me?'

" 'Yes, of course,' *Abba* said, and he proceeded to teach me everything I needed to know about the fifth *perek* in *Bava Kamma*."

As she told the story at the seminar, the woman paused a moment and her voice choked. With tear-filled eyes, she said, "My Ami got 100% on his test."

◆§ *Priorities! Priorities!*

There is an expression that wise men learn from the mistakes of others, but fools do not learn even from their own. The following bit of advice from a simple man could just as easily have come from a great sage.

When R' Sholom was a young boy, a man working at home wiped the sweat from his forehead and said to him wistfully, "Sholom'ke, when I was young I often worked late into the night, I worked overtime, I gave up my health for the sake of making more money. But now that I am older, I would give all my money for the sake of my health. But it's too late."

◆§ *The Lost Moment*

Sometimes we are inspired by a lecture, an event, or an experience. The time to react is at once. The more time that elapses from that moment of fervent enthusiasm, the more lukewarm our response will be. People tend to continue in their habitual ways. In order to change ourselves or to improve in any real way we must be ready to put into practice without delay what we have learned in theory. (See *Iggeres Haramban).*

In a similar vein, we are taught in *Avos* (2:4): "אַל תֹּאמַר לִכְשֶׁאֶפָּנֶה אֶשְׁנֶה, שֶׁמָּא לֹא תִפָּנֶה — Don't say, 'When I am free, I will study,' for perhaps you will not become free." In other words, seize the moment! Don't let time slip by, for when an opportunity is lost, a life may be directed to a different destiny.

R' Sholom recounts this incident which took place close to fifty years ago. Its message is as timely now as it was when it happened.

The Auerbachs, a prominent religious family in Israel, sought an apartment for their growing family. They finally found a three-room apartment that met their needs, but only two of the rooms were vacant. A young couple lived in the third room. They were *chalutzim* (pioneers) who had come from Europe to settle and build the land of Israel. These *chalutzim* would be moving to their new quarters within a week, and they asked the Auerbachs if they could stay in the third room until their new home was ready. Rebbitzen Tzivia Auerbach agreed, but she made one stipulation.

She knew that the young *chalutzim* weren't observant, so she told them, "You may stay here for the week, but I ask one favor. When the Sabbath comes, please do not transgress the holy day." Respectful of the *rebbetzin's* wishes, the couple consented.

On *Shabbos* afternoon, however, the *rebbetzin* happened to glance through her door and noticed that the young *chalutz* (pioneer) was writing in his room! She was shocked and disappointed. He had promised not to transgress the *Shabbos,* and now he was doing just that. Quickly she called her son Shlomo Zalman (today *rosh yeshivah* of Yeshivah Kol Torah in Jerusalem) and asked him to please go in and ask the young man to stop his *chillul Shabbos* (desecration of the Sabbath).

R' Shlomo Zalman, by nature a compassionate and soft-hearted person, walked slowly and hesitantly to the room, knocked on the door and was welcomed in. After an exchange of greetings, he began talking about the sanctity of the day. He then courteously mentioned that his family would be grateful if the young *chalutz* would stop his writing until after *Shabbos,* because writing was a violation of the laws governing *Shabbos*. The young man excused himself profusely, explaining that he had not known that writing was forbidden on *Shabbos.* He explained that he had only the vaguest notion about the meaning of *Shabbos.* He was under the impression that only making a fire or using machinery was a violation. He certainly hadn't meant to break the agreement with R' Shlomo Zalman's mother, and he apologized.

The two continued talking and then the *chalutz* said, "Perhaps you think I don't believe in G-d as you do. You may well be surprised, but be assured that I believe in Him just as strongly as you do!"

"If you do," asked R' Shlomo Zalman, "then how is it that you know so little about the *Shabbos?*"

"It's a long story," the *chalutz* sighed, "but if you want to hear it, I will tell it to you. Let's take a walk." The *chalutz* and the yeshivah student walked through street and field, and a soul was bared.

❦ ❦ ❦

I was a young man, attending secondary school in Russia, when I was drafted into the army. Shortly afterwards, World War I broke out. Every day I shot and killed and hid in my foxhole trying to avoid being killed myself. For hours and hours the shooting would continue, then there would be a cease-fire. At that point both sides would emerge to remove the fallen soldiers from the field. After a short reprieve the shooting would begin again. We were exhausted and spent. But I noticed something interesting. In the foxholes next to me were young religious Jews. During the cease-fire they would take out a *Tehillim* and pray with great intensity. When they finished I could see that they were comforted. Their faces were relaxed and they approached the next round with confidence in G-d.

I didn't have that comfort and I needed it very much. My parents were not religious at all, although my grandmother used to light candles every Friday night. Every time I thought about it, I became angry that my father had not taught me anything about *Yiddishkeit.* This thought gnawed at me every time I saw those young Jews reciting their *Tehillim* so fervently. Finally, one day when I was in the foxhole after a particularly hard round of fighting, I cried out, "G-d, You know that it's not my fault that I don't know how to approach You. My father didn't teach me anything, and it's not my fault that I don't know how to be a good Jew. I am facing the enemy, trying to stay alive. I don't know them and they don't know me. I don't want to kill anyone. If a bullet hits my hand so that I can no longer shoot, it will be a sign from You, G-d, that You are indeed here, even on this battlefield."

I finished my prayer. It was quiet. A few minutes later the sound of a single shot shattered the silence. The bullet hit my finger!

[The *chalutz* showed R' Shlomo Zalman his finger which had remained useless from that day on. Then he continued.]

My gun fell from my hand and I lost consciousness from the

excruciating pain. I was in a military hospital for days and I promised myself that as soon as the war was over I would go home, and find someone to teach me as much as possible about *Yiddishkeit.* I was never sent back to the front.

Finally, the war ended. I came home and had to make a decision. Should I learn about my religion? But what would I do for a living? If I went back to school for three months I would get my diploma in agriculture and be assured of a livelihood. I decided to get my diploma and then go to a *shul* or yeshivah to learn about Judaism.

I went back to school, and in three months I finished. Then I began to study Torah. My head was clear and logic dictated that I study with intensity, but now after three months of my original resolve, my heart was not in it any more. I thought I could continue learning, but it just didn't go. Had I started three months earlier, maybe I would be a different person today. The first *Yom Kippur* after the war, I went to *shul,* but as I held the *Machzor* I became frustrated with my inability to read Hebrew. The next *Yom Kippur* I didn't go any more.

Had I started learning about *Yiddishkeit* right after coming out of the army, while the fire of inspiration was within me, perhaps today I would have known that writing is forbidden on Shabbos!

❦ ❦ ❦

The two new friends walked back in silence. R' Shlomo Zalman went home and told his mother the story. Then he cried. *Klal Yisrael* (the Jewish People) had lost a golden *neshamah* (soul) only because a young man had not seized the moment ...

R' Sholom knows this story well, for his wife, *Rebbitzen* Leah, was the daughter of *Rebbetzin* Tzivia Auerbach and the sister of R' Shlomo Zalman.

◆§ *Costly Candy*

During World War I, *Eretz Yisrael* was still under Turkish rule. Most of the country was poor and undeveloped, and those who lived there were in serious financial straits, especially since their support from Europe was completely cut off. Hunger was so rampant that hundreds actually died of starvation in Jerusalem; many people had no steady income and many more were unemployed altogether. It was the era of the *yishuv,* the settling of *Eretz Yisrael* by thousands of idealistic immigrants and the poverty was heart-wrenching.

Yet, as in every society, there were always some individuals who with great business acumen were able to raise themselves above the prevailing economic level and accumulate considerable wealth. One such family was the Friedmans.*

One afternoon, seven-year-old Naftali Friedman asked his father for some candy. Mr. Friedman told him to take a coin from the desk and buy some from the local grocer.

A few hours later, when Mr. Friedman went to his desk, he saw that a golden napoleon coin was missing. About the size of an American half-dollar, a golden napoleon was worth enough to sustain a family for six months. He quickly summoned Naftali, and demanded to know which coin he had taken. After questioning the child it became obvious that he had mistakenly taken the wrong coin. Instead of taking a metal coin similar in size to the napoleon, but worth just a few pennies, he had taken the napoleon.

"But didn't the grocer say anything to you?" shouted Mr. Friedman, losing his self-control.

"No, Father," answered the frightened Naftali. "I gave him the coin and he gave me the candies. He didn't ask me anything."

Now beside himself with rage, Mr. Friedman rushed down to the grocer and demanded that he return the napoleon.

"Your honor," insisted the grocer, "your son gave me a *chirale* (a coin of miniscule value), nothing more." An argument erupted and it was decided to present the situation to the rabbinical court of R' Shmuel Salant, chief *Rav* of Jerusalem.

As Mr. Friedman and the grocer presented their sides of the story, it became obvious to the *rabbonim,* that each man would continue insisting on his version of the facts. After listening

* The name is fictitious; the story is true.

attentively to both people, one of the *rabbonim* called Mr. Friedman to the side and said, "Torah law stipulates that in such a situation, the grocer has the prerogative of swearing that he does not owe you any money. If he does indeed swear, he is free from any financial obligation to you. But, Mr. Friedman, you know that when one swears, he must swear by the name of G-d, and to swear falsely and profane the name of G-d is a terrible sin (see *Exodus* 20:7). Times are bad, people are in economic trouble. I beg you, don't make him swear for he could swear falsely. Please forgo the money!"

Reluctantly, Mr. Friedman agreed to drop the matter. However, things went badly for the grocer. Deep in their hearts, people felt that the grocer had taken advantage of an innocent, unsuspecting child. They held him in contempt, and he lost many customers. Three years later, after the war was over, Mr. Friedman received the following unsigned letter.

Dear Mr. Friedman:

Three years have passed since that terrible day when your son went to get candy from the grocery. It was an unhappy day in many ways, for you, your son, the grocer, and me.

I was a desperate and despondent man. I had no job, my children were starving and I saw no future for myself. As I walked the steets engrossed in my misery, I noticed your Naftali playing with his friends. He was casually tossing about the coin you had given him for candy and I could not help but notice that it was a shiny gold napoleon. I thought to myself, "Here I am slowly starving to death and this mere child has the audacity to play with a coin that could support my family for months!"

I joined the playing children and began chatting with them. One thing led to another and as the children were playing with their coins I exchanged my *chirale* for Naftali's napoleon. Being a child, he had no idea what had happened and when he went to the grocer, he did indeed give him the coin that he had with him, the *chirale*.

I beg your forgiveness for having caused you so much grief. I hereby return the value of the coin that I took from your son.

Please forgive me. I was not rational that day because of my pain and the cruel circumstances of my life.

Yours truly,

❦ ❦ ❦

Indeed when Mr. Friedman discovered the truth he tried his best to let people know of the grocer's integrity, but unfortunately the grocer had paid a dear price for three long years, all because people rushed to accuse him and did not judge him *lekaf zechus* (favorably).

❦ ❦ ❦

Whenever R' Sholom cites this story, he discusses how hesitant one must be in judging others and jumping to conclusions. Who would have believed that the grocer was not guilty of cheating the young boy? Yet in fact he was actually honest and truthful.

R' Sholom then asks his audience, "Which of the characters in this story is deserving of punishment in the Hereafter? Certainly not the grocer or Naftali — they were but innocent victims. Nor would Mr. Friedman be punished, for he followed the advice of the rabbinical court. And the thief! Why he already suffered three agonizing years, and he made full retribution for what he stole! Surely the Heavenly Tribunal will not punish a true penitent!

"The answer is that the only ones who will be punished, will be the people who spoke and believed the slander, and caused the grocer untold misery when they stopped buying from him."

Part F: Perspectives and Insights

◆§ *A Kosher Pot*

R' Sholom often begins his remarks by declaring that "I do not express my own thoughts, but rather those of my great *rabbeim* (teachers), which makes them well worth hearing. But this I will say," he adds, "at least I know that I am a kosher pot."

A kosher pot? He explains with a parable.

A *maskil* (so-called "enlightened one") once came to the Brisker *Rav*, seeking permission to address the congregants in the synagogue of Brisk. The *maskil*, known for his anti-religious beliefs, was flatly denied permission.

"But," complained the *maskil* to the *rav*, "I cite only 'kosher' sources in my talk. I will quote only such sources as the *Alshich*, the *Abarbanel*, etc."

"Yes," the Brisker *Rav* retorted sharply, "but kosher meat cooked in a *traife* pot becomes *traife* and may not be eaten."

◆§ *Lost in a Forest*

Often R' Sholom prefaces his talks with an apology that he is about to speak words of *mussar* (chastisement). This is true especially if he's speaking at a gathering of *bnei Torah* (Torah scholars). "After all," he says, "who am I to admonish people of your caliber, you who spend so much time in Torah study?"

He excuses himself in advance by citing this parable, which R' Itzel Peterberger (1837-1907) said when he was invited to speak during *Asseres Yemei Teshuvah* (the Ten Days of Repentance from Rosh Hashanah until Yom Kippur) at the *Bais Hamussar* (House of *Mussar* Study) in Kovno.

A little boy was wandering in the forest. He had taken a walk off the beaten path and soon realized that he was lost. He became frightened as each turn he took seemed to take him deeper into the labyrinth of the forest.

After two days of wandering, he saw the figure of a man in the distance. He mustered up his strength, ran to the man and embraced him with joy. "I'm so happy to see you!" he cried. "Finally I've found someone who can get me out of this forest."

"I wish I could be as happy as you are, my child," said the tired old man. "You have been lost for only two days, but I've been lost for over two weeks."

The boy was filled with despair. "But perhaps," the old man continued, "we can work on it together. I at least know where *not* to go. By helping each other we will find a way out of this predicament."

"So too," says R' Sholom to his listeners, "let us discuss where I, a tired old man, and perhaps you, have wandered off the proper path of life, and then perhaps we can find our way back together."

Meirka

Every *maggid* is a reservoir overflowing with stories. Some are long, some are short, some are happy, some are sad. But over the years a *maggid* has a precious few stories that are his individual classics. They become inseparable from the man, identified with him forever. No one tells them as he does. He relishes them and retells them hundreds of times.

"Meirka" is one of R' Sholom's remarkable stories, not only because of its message, but because it is more poignant than many of his other stories since he was involved with it personally.

One afternoon as R' Sholom was sitting in his home in the Shaarei Chessed section of Jerusalem, working peacefully on his grandfather's *sefarim,* he suddenly heard a piercing scream coming from the alleyway outside his window. In a moment his wife ran into the house, yelling that little Meir, the grandson of the *gabbai* of their *shul,* had fallen and was bleeding profusely from a gash over his eye.

The *rebbetzin* rushed to get a wet towel and together with R' Sholom ran back out towards the fallen child. R' Sholom, still in his shirtsleeves, picked up the child, as his wife held the wet towel over the child's cut trying to control the bleeding. It seems that Meir and his friend had been playing horse and wagon, and Meir had fallen and struck his head against a rock.

Carrying the child, R' Sholom, his face furrowed in deep concern, began making his way up the alleyway to the main street rushing as fast as his legs could carry him in order to get the child to a doctor. As they rushed up the hill, Meir's grandmother was walking down towards them. She was a wonderful lady, always doing *mitzvos* and always with a kind word. She saw the Schwadrons holding a child and assumed that it was one of their own. From a distance she called out in Yiddish, "R' Sholom, R' Sholom, *ess is kain baiz nit, ess iz kain baiz nit* (there's nothing to be worried about), *der Oibeshter vet helfen* (Hashem will surely help)."

"I wondered," says R' Sholom, "whether her reaction would change when she realizes who the child really is! Will she still be calm then?" As the lady came a bit closer, she began to suspect that maybe the child was not one of the Schwadron children, and so her reassurances that "nothing was seriously wrong" and that "Hashem would surely help" became a bit muted. Now the woman herself began rushing to see just who the child was, and as the Schwadrons passed directly in front of her, she looked down and realized that the bleeding child was none other than her own grandson. In a flash she lost herself completely and began shrieking uncontrollably, "*Gevalt!* Meirka! Meirka! *Gevalt!*" as she struggled to take hold of the child.

The neighbors, observing their windows, echoed her cry, "*Ess iz kain baiz nit, ess iz kain baiz nit, der Oibeshter vet helfen!*"

R' Sholom has transformed that scream of "Meirka" into a catchword lesson. He says, "If it's not 'my Meirka' it's easy to say, 'Don't worry, nothing is wrong, Hashem will surely help.' But when it is 'my Meirka' it's a different story. The picture changes and the scream that pierces the air has no objectivity; it becomes a personal hurt."

Shortly after that incident there was a large demonstration in Jerusalem against municipal employees who were desecrating the Shabbos. R' Sholom was among the primary speakers who loudly decried and admonished those who violated the Shabbos and those who sat idly by doing nothing about it. A few acquaintances came over to him and said, "R' Sholom, what is your problem? Let the matter alone, this is not your concern." The next week, the same municipality instituted an increase in taxes to pay for police and fire protection. A hue and cry went up from the citizens as they complained that they were already being taxed enough. Now it is they who raved and ranted against the government, but this time it concerned not Shabbos but the tax increase.

R' Sholom overheard them talking in *shul* — and realized it was the same two people who had admonished him the week before. "Why is it your problem?" he asked them. "Leave it to the city, what is your concern here?"

"Are you serious?" they retorted. "You are talking about hard-earned money. No one is going to take it away from us!"

"That's exactly what I wanted to point out," replied R' Sholom with a laugh. "You complained because money is your Meirka, while I complained because Shabbos observance is my Meirka!"

◆§ *Angels in Waiting*

Ranking near the top of our oft-repeated sins is that of reciting words of our daily prayers without concentrating on their meaning. One of R' Sholom's most memorable parables, adapted from the Chofetz Chaim, illustrates this point beautifully.

R' Zorach was a wealthy businessman who remembered the poor. People knew that he could be relied upon to help any of his fellow Jews. One morning R' Zorach received a telephone call.

"Good morning, R' Zorach," came the voice on the line.

"How are you, R' Baruch?" said R' Zorach, recognizing the voice on the other end.

"Oh, I'm fine, *baruch Hashem* (thank G-d), just fine, thank you," said R' Baruch. "And how is your family, R' Zorach?"

"Just fine, *baruch Hashem,* and yours?"

"Very well, *baruch Hashem.* Thank you for asking. And how is your business, R' Zorach?" continued R' Baruch, hesitating to get to the point of the call.

"Fine, fine," said R' Zorach a bit impatiently. "I know you called me for something, R' Baruch. I am busy today, but I would like to help you. Tell me, what can I do for you?"

"To tell you the truth," R' Baruch began diffidently, "I'm marrying off a daughter and I find myself short of funds. I was wondering if you could lend me three hundred rubles for a few months. By then I would surely be able to pay you back."

"Of course, of course!" replied R' Zorach. "*Mazel tov!* May G-d bless you and the family. Tell me, when do you want to pick up the money?"

"How is twelve noon?"

"That would be perfect," agreed R' Zorach. "I'll wait here for you." And they both hung up.

Twelve o'clock found R' Zorach sitting patiently in his office waiting for R' Baruch. At 12:15 R' Zorach began getting edgy. He waited until 12:30, but still no R' Baruch. R' Zorach had other pressing business matters, so he decided to leave his office. Upon returning to the office that afternoon, R' Zorach was told that no one had come while he was away. Indeed no one came for the money the rest of the day.

The next morning, the phone rang.

"Oh hello, R' Zorach, it's me, Baruch. How are you R' Zorach?"

"Me, I'm fine, *baruch Hashem*. What about you? Where were you yester ..."

R′ Baruch interrupted, "Tell me, R′ Zorach, how is your family?"

"Fine," came the quick reply, "but, R′ Baruch, yester ..."

"How is your business, R′ Zorach?"

"Just a minute, R′ Baruch," R′ Zorach interrupted curtly. "I waited for you yesterday. What happened?"

"Oh," replied R′ Baruch, somewhat embarrassed. "Something unexpected came up and I just couldn't get to your office. But don't worry, I'll be there today. Would you be so kind and wait for me at twelve?"

"Why, of course, R′ Baruch, and once again, I wish you a lot of *mazel.* I look forward to seeing you."

Twelve o'clock came and went, but there was no sign of R′ Baruch. R′ Zorach just couldn't believe it. Two days in a row — it was incomprehensible. What was wrong with R′ Baruch? ... 12:15 ... 12:30 ... still no sign of R′ Baruch. "What *chutzpah* this man has," R′ Zorach thought to himself. He left his office for the afternoon and went home. Once again, his secretary told him that there had been no sign of R′ Baruch all day.

The next morning the phone rang at 9:00 a.m.

"Good morning, R′ Zorach. How are you, R′ Zorach? How's business, R′ Zorach?" Once again, the same scenario, R′ Baruch apologizing for not coming, agreeing to meet at twelve o'clock and for the third day in a row, no R′ Baruch. The next morning when the phone rang at nine o'clock, R′ Zorach picked up the phone and shouted, "Baruch! Are you trying to make a fool out of me? Three days in a row you called and three days in a row I prepared money, sat here and waited for you and you didn't show up. Are you playing games with me or trying to aggravate me? I have other things to do with my time!" and in a fury he hung up.

Aren't many of us like R′ Baruch? Every morning in our *Ahavah Rabbah* prayer (the blessing just before *Shema)* we pray, "[Hashem] You loved us ... You have pitied us ... Our Father, our King ..."

"Yes," Hashem says, "Tell me, how can I help you? What are your desires?

"Our Father ... have mercy on us ..."

"I will," Hashem says, "just tell me what you want ..." (A new home? More customers? Good children?)

We pray: "וְתֵן בְּלִבֵּנוּ בִּינָה לְהָבִין וּלְהַשְׂכִּיל — Instill in our hearts to understand and to elucidate [Your Torah] ... לִשְׁמוֹעַ לִלְמוֹד וּלְלַמֵּד — to listen, to learn, to teach ... וְהָאֵר עֵינֵינוּ בְּתוֹרָתֶךָ — Enlighten our eyes in Your Torah ... וְדַבֵּק לִבֵּנוּ בְּמִצְוֹתֶיךָ — attach our hearts to Your commandments ..."

Such worthwhile requests elicit an immediate response from Hashem, Who immediately orders His angels "to fill their barrels with intelligence" and commands them, that if we just open our minds a bit, if we open a *Chumash*, or turn the pages of a *Gemara*, the flow of intellectual comprehension will be nonstop.

The angels rush to be on time, because they know that *Shacharis* will be over soon and we will rush for our *sefarim*. Indeed we finish *Shacharis*. We close the *Siddur*, remove our *tefillin* ... and rush for the synagogue exit, many times not even remaining for the *Kaddish* after *Shacharis*. The angels are waiting with their barrels, ready to pour knowledge into us — but we rush right by them. They wait, but we are already in the car ... subway ... or on the bus heading for our businesses.

"Fine," say the angels. "Perhaps he had pressing business matters today. No doubt he will study Torah during his lunch hour."

They wait until 12:30. Once again the angels are ready to present us with all the knowledge for which we prayed so hard this morning. But what's this? A sandwich, idle chatter, a look at the newspaper, some letter-writing, maybe even *Minchah*, but no learning.

Now the angels are becoming impatient. "When will he open a *sefer?*" they ask each other. "Here we are ready to be at his service, and he completely disregards us."

"Maybe tonight," another angel comments, "the night is made for learning."

Comes the evening, and we return home. We are tired, the wife needs this, the children need that, there are phone calls, supper is ready, the newspaper has to be finished ... and before we know it, the evening has slipped away. *Shema*, sleep and maybe tomorrow there'll be time for learning ...

The next day, the same *tefillah.* Every day the same routine. Each day we run through the words of our prayers, but do not even try to follow up our own requests.

Have we opened a *sefer* to seek the enlightenment in Torah for which we prayed so devoutly this morning? Do we take any steps towards repentance after having said three times today, "הֲשִׁיבֵנוּ אָבִינוּ ... קָרְבֵנוּ מַלְכֵּנוּ— Bring us back, our Father ... Bring us near, our King ...?" Have we tried to improve ourselves in consonance with the words we utter "... סְלַח לָנוּ אָבִינוּ ... מְחַל לָנוּ מַלְכֵּנוּ — Forgive us, our Father ... Pardon us, our King?"

Don't we sound foolish?

Aren't we foolish?

◆§ *Hearing is Not Enough*

The Torah *(Sh'mos* 18:1; see *Rashi)* relates that when Yisro, the priest of Midian, heard about the miracles that Hashem had performed for the Jewish people, such as their triumph against Amalek and the splitting of the Sea of Reeds, he decided to become a Jew himself.

The Midrash asks, "Was then Yisro the only one who heard the news? In reality everyone throughout the world heard about all those miracles. Why does the Torah stress that Yisro heard? The answer is that only Yisro *acted!* Others heard, but it had no effect on them whatsoever. Yisro heard and became a Jew. This is why the Torah emphasizes that Yisro heard."

R' Sholom notes that in our lives, too, we often hear things but fail to react. It is almost as if we aren't paying attention. The message may be vital, but it does not penetrate. R' Leib Chasman, the *mashgiach* of the Chevron Yeshivah, graphically illustrated such a situation.

A simple peasant from a small farm town, tucked away in the mountains, was given an opportunity to visit the big city. Not being familiar with modern society or its conveniences, he anticipated his trip with great excitement, for surely he would see things that would amaze him.

The day of his trip arrived. He dressed in his finest clothes and arrived in the big town at mid-day. He strolled the streets gazing in awe at the huge buildings, the hordes of people and the hustle and haste that surrounded him. Eventually he found himself on the outskirts of the city where he saw something that made him stop short in curiosity.

He looked down and noticed two long, shiny, silver rails that stretched endlessly into the distance. On further examination he noticed that there were wooden ties evenly spaced across the ground between the two rails. The large bolts that held these slats in place fascinated him and he sat down next to one of the bolts to see if he could loosen it to take it home as a memento of his trip.

He sat there busying himself with the bolts until he heard a rumbling in the distance. He looked up and it seemed to him that a huge face was coming closer and closer to him, with smoke billowing from its head. As the locomotive sped toward him, the engineer in the cabin realized that a man was sitting on the tracks and would be killed if he did not move immediately.

The engineer blew his whistle as loudly as he could. The peasant was overjoyed. Surely, he thought, this is a wedding, otherwise why would anyone be playing music? He stood up, and right in the path of the train he began to dance.

Two passersby observed what was happening. "The man is deaf!" yelled the first man to his friend, "He's not even trying to get out of the way!"

"He's not deaf," shouted back his friend, "you can see that he is responding." As they dragged him off the tracks, the second man wisely said, "He simply has no idea what the whistle means. He thinks it is a time for jubilation, when really it is a time of danger. He hears — but he does not understand."

All the world heard about the greatness of the Jews and the miracles Hashem had wrought for them, but only Yisro reacted. In essence this means that only he heard and understood it.

◆§ The Greatest Artist of Them All

The good with which Hashem surrounds us every day is too often taken for granted. From the blossoms on the tree, to the rising and the setting of the sun, we accept the beauty of nature with casual indifference. Even in our personal lives, we fail to pause and consider the miracles of our daily existence. Only when these "daily miracles" are taken away do we realize the magnitude of the gift that we had all along, but failed to appreciate.

How often have we heard a person on crutches say, "Now I appreciate the value of a healthy body"; or an older person say, "If only I had taken advantange of youth when I had it."

The *Chassan Sofer* (1835-1883) once used a parable to portray man's inattentiveness to the "natural" things in life.

A world-renowned sculptor was commissioned to design a statue that would be placed in the city square. After much thought he decided on a work that would pay tribute to the animal that had given civilization its mobility and versatility — the horse.

For months he worked meticulously, paying attention to every detail, sculpting every sinew and muscle of his bronze stallion, so that it would be a lifelike replica of Hashem's miracle.

After two years of painstaking effort, the statue was complete. The artist presented it to the city officials who agreed unanimously that it was truly magnificent. They promptly placed the bronze stallion in the city square, where people — much to the shock of the sculptor — completely ignored it.

He could not believe it. Each day he would walk by his masterpiece to see if anyone would stop to admire his work, and every day he would return home dejected. No one had given his horse a second glance.

In despair, he confided to his friend, "I cannot believe that people are so insensitive," he began. "I worked on the project for two years, and today it stands in the square ignored. Everyone passes it by without even giving it a second glance."

"My dear friend, the problem is that your horse is too perfect," his friend answered. "People think it is a real horse — and who is going to stop to look at a horse?"

"So what should I do?" exclaimed the exasperated sculptor.

"I will tell you," replied his friend. "Make a crack in it, and then people will realize that it is not a real horse, but a grand piece of art."

And so, with a heavy heart, the sculptor did indeed chisel a split across one side of the horse. The result was immediate; people stopped everyday to marvel at the work of art that had been there — taken for granted — all along.

Hashem did the same thing at the Sea of Reeds. For centuries the world had witnessed the phenomena of nature. Grass grew, cows grazed, brooks flowed and seas surged — and mankind forgot that it was only by the grace of Hashem that nature took its course every day. And so He made a tumultuous split in the Sea of Reeds, which reverberated around the world.

The Midrash *(Shemos Rabbah* 21:6) notes that all waters everywhere in the world suddenly split in unison with the Sea of Reeds. It startled people, and for the first time they considered the possibility that perhaps the rolling stream and the ocean wave were not natural at all, that a river was not eternal.

It was only then that the world realized that nature was indeed not natural and automatic, but a master design with Hashem its artist.

Wrong Number, Right Party

Every action, every event of a person's life, even the seemingly insignificant ones are guided by Hashem. The Talmud *(Arachin* 16b) notes that even if one puts his hand into his pocket to take out three coins and only takes out two, that too has happened because of Divine Providence. In this vein the Chofetz Chaim translates the words of one of our daily morning blessings, "הַמֵּכִין מִצְעֲדֵי גָבֶר, He (Hashem) prepares the footsteps of man" (see *Psalms* 37:23).

"Preparing man's footsteps" must be understood in a broader

sense: Hashem guides not only footsteps, but even the insignificant motions of one's fingers, as is evident in this incredible incident involving R' Asher Fleishman,* a prominent Israeli rabbi.

R' Asher traveled throughout the world for the benefit of his yeshivah. During one of his trips to New York, he suddenly became ill. He had been under a New York doctor's care for many years because of a heart condition and always carried his physician's phone number with him so that he could call him if necessary.

The very sharp chest pains that he felt made him realize that he had to get medical attention at once. He broke into a cold sweat as weakness began to overtake him. He fumbled for his telephone book to get the right number. Although feeling faint, he mustered enough strength to reach for the phone. Slowly he dialed the number, trying to control his panic. He prayed that the line would not be busy.

The phone rang. After it rang a second time a woman picked up. "Hello?"

"Is Dr. Miller there? This is Rabbi Fleishman," he said in a low, husky voice.

"Yes," the woman said in surprise. "The doctor happens to be here. I'll get him to the phone."

Told who it was, the doctor ran to the phone to see if the rabbi was all right. "How are you? Is everything all right with you?" the doctor asked quickly.

R' Asher described his pains and the doctor assured him that he would be over to see him in a few moments. "But how did you know that I was here?" the doctor asked. "I didn't tell anyone where I was going."

"You're not in your office?" asked the surprised R' Asher.

"No," replied the doctor. "I'm on an emergency call a few blocks from my home. Not even my wife knows where I am. I said nothing to her because I thought I'd be right back."

"I just dialed your regular number," the incredulous R' Asher

* The names are fictitious; the story is true.

insisted.

Then the doctor looked down at the phone from which he was speaking. The numbers were precisely the same as his office phone except for one, in which the number was one digit off. By inadvertently dialing one of the numbers incorrectly, R' Asher had actually dialed the "right" number!

Later, after having been taken to the hospital, the rabbi was told that his life had been saved only because he had reached the doctor in time.

> Wrong number. Right party. An overt lesson in *hashgachah pratis* (Divine Providence).

◆§ *At the Last Moment*

> Man's *yetzer hara* (Evil Inclination) is ever present. No man should ever feel sure that he cannot be lured into sin. R' Sholom retells this incident to describe the *yetzer hara's* tenacity.

A prominent student of the *Arizal* (1534-1572) lay on his deathbed. His friends and family gathered around him to say their final words. One scholar bent close to the dying man and said, "Is the *yetzer hara* still with you, even at this moment?"

The elderly man, weak and frail, shook his head, nodding, "Yes."

"But what can he possibly be telling you at this point?" asked the surprised scholar.

"The *yetzer hara*," he said in a soft voice, "is telling me to recite the *Shema* in a loud voice, to make sure that people will speak of me with praise and say, 'He died with holiness and purity on his lips!' "

◆§ *Mumble-Jumble*

> R' Levi Yitzchak of Berditchev always saw the good side of his fellow Jews, even the most non-observant ones. If a man talked during his prayers, he would say, "Look how G-d-fearing this Jew is, even while talking he finds time to pray ..."

One day, during morning prayers in the synagogue he became exasperated as he watched a young man mumbling his prayers, flying through them at the speed of sound so that not one word made sense. R′ Levi Yitzchak was upset that the young man could stand before the King of kings and delude himself that he was indeed praying.

When the young man finished, R′ Levi Yitzchak walked over to him and said, "Minaminaminaminamina ..."

The fellow looked at him in wonderment. "Excuse me, *Rebbe,* what did you say?"

R′ Levi Yitzchak again murmured "Minaminaminaminamina-minaminamina ...

"*Rebbe,*" said the young man, "I'm sorry, I can't understand you."

"Then why do you think Hashem understands when you say minaminaminaminamina when you are praying?"

An older man, standing nearby overheard their conversation. "*Rebbe,*" he said, "what you just said is true when one person speaks to another. But when a child in a cradle or a playpen makes sounds, the mother who is close to the child and loves him dearly can understand him clearly. She knows from his mumble-jumble whether the child is hurt or hungry or whatever. We are Hashem's beloved children. Even if we make unintelligible sounds with our mouths, as long as our hearts are turned toward Him, He knows what we need."

R′ Levi Yitzchak was overjoyed. He hugged the old man and said. "The seventy years that you have spent in this world are justified, just by your finding favor and merit for this young man. May Hashem bless you for teaching me to see the good side."

When R′ Sholom tells this incident, he adds whimsically, "Yes, yes, but when a twenty-year-old acts like an infant, he is a fool."

R′ Sholom goes on to explain that the person in the story who stood and prayed so poorly was a simple man. He had little Torah knowledge and no understanding of what he was saying. For him one can rationalize and say that Hashem understands his babbling, as a mother understands her child's garbled words. But, if a *ben-Torah,* or one who has the capacity to understand prays this way, slurring his words and babbling like a child — even R' Levi Yitzchak," says R' Sholom with confidence, "would consider this man foolish."

⊰§ *The Thought Counts*

R' Sholom is fond of repeating a question asked and answered by his late father-in-law, R' Chaim Yehudah Leib Auerbach (the head of Yeshivah Shaar Hashamayim, the *Kollel* for *Kabbalah* in Jerusalem).

On *erev* Yom Kippur people tend to eat excessively, preparing themselves for the long fast ahead. Although it is a *mitzvah* to eat the day before Yom Kippur (see *Berachos* 8b), not everyone eats heavy meals only to fulfill the *mitzvah,* rather they do so for fear they might go hungry.

By twilight, when *Kol Nidre* begins, some people are satiated to the point of gluttony. Yet during *Maariv* when we recite the *Shema,* we are told to say the verse, "בָּרוּךְ שֵׁם כְּבוֹד מַלְכוּתוֹ לְעוֹלָם וָעֶד — Blessed is the name of His glorious Kingdom forever," out loud because we are like angels. After Yom Kippur, however, following an entire day of serious prayer, fasting and repentance, we must recite the same phrase ... בָּרוּךְ שֵׁם in the *Maariv* service quietly, for we have once again returned to the status of human beings.

But if there is any time that we should be regarded as angels, it should be *after* a day of conducting ourselves in holiness, not before.

The answer is in the expression quoted by the Baal Shem Tov from the *Zohar,* "מַחְשָׁבָה דְאָדָם זו הִיא אָדָם — The thought of man, that is man." What is man? His physical self, his flesh and bones? No — it is his capacity to think, and what he thinks makes him what he is.

If a man eats only to enjoy his food and sleeps only to prepare his body for fun and frolic, then he is like an animal, except that he walks on two feet instead of four. But, if he exercises and sleeps with the intention of having the strength better to serve his Maker, then he is truly a man, and a holy one at that.

Thus, on the night of Yom Kippur, when people's thoughts are of holiness and seriousness, even if their stomachs are filled, they are considered to be on the level of angels. At such a time it is proper that they should recite the phrase ... בָּרוּךְ שֵׁם — out loud. However, after Yom Kippur, when they have breathed a sigh of relief that the fast is soon over, and their thoughts are on the meal awaiting them at home then indeed they should say ... בָּרוּךְ שֵׁם quietly, for they have come back down to the level of human beings once again.

R' Sholom describes how his *rebbe,* R' Leib Chasman, the *mashgiach* of the Chevron Yeshivah, sat eating the *seudah hamafsekes* (final meal before the fast) on *erev* Yom Kippur. R' Sholom entered to wish him a *"Gut Yom Tov."* R' Leib was sitting at his table, oblivious to anything around him, eating his soup. Tears were rolling down R' Leib's cheeks from the fear and awe of the upcoming Yom Kippur. When he looked up, his eyes were red, as though he had been weeping for some time.

That awesome sight causes R' Sholom to shudder every time he thinks about it.

The Calculated Risk

Hashem's first *mitzvah* to Adam was simple and straightforward, "מִכֹּל עֵץ הַגָּן אָכֹל תֹּאכֵל, וּמֵעֵץ הַדַּעַת טוֹב וָרָע לֹא תֹאכַל מִמֶּנּוּ — Of every tree of the garden you may freely eat, but of the tree of knowledge of good and bad, you must not eat" (*Bereishis* 2:16-17). Yet, only a few hours later (See *Sanhedrin* 38b), the snake was able to use contorted reasoning and sly calculations to lure man to violate this directive. That devious characteristic of twisted rationalization has become part of man ever since.

King Solomon wrote: "עָשָׂה הָאֱלֹקִים אֶת הָאָדָם יָשָׁר, וְהֵמָּה בִקְשׁוּ חִשְּׁבֹנוֹת רַבִּים — G-d made man straight and upright, but they sought many intrigues." (*Koheles* 7:29).

R' Sholom often cites the Omler *Rav,* R' Avraham Eliyashuv (d. 1943), of Jerusalem, who claimed that people of our generation have made up "new" *aveiros* and "new" *mitzvos* using faulty logic.

A man is called upon to donate money to *tzedakah* for an important cause. He refuses, claiming, "That cause is not worthy at all; it's an *aveirah* to give money to it!"

Another person is overheard defaming an individual and speaking *lashon hara.* Someone tries to stop him, but he says, "No, the fellow I'm talking about is really bad, it's a *mitzvah* to talk against him!" New *mitzvos!* New *aveiros!*

Good examples of man deluding himself with his flawed reasoning.

R' Yosef Yoizel of Novharadok (1848-1920) used to tell his students a beautiful parable on this point.

A young prince was once assigned to travel on behalf of his country to various lands throughout the world. A month before his departure, the prince was summoned by his father, the king.

"My son," he began, "I know that you are a fine young man, and have always been loyal to me and to our kingdom. I want you to realize that everything you do or say on this trip will be a reflection on us back home. I have complete confidence that you will uphold our honor, but I must stress one thing." The prince sat quietly and listened closely. "Never," stressed his father, "never agree to make a bet. You will meet all types of people with all sorts of whims and desires. Never fall into the trap of making a wager with them, no matter how sure you are that you will win."

The prince was surprised at what seemed a relatively simple request. "Of course, Father," he replied, "I will surely obey your wish."

Two days later, the king again called the prince into his chambers. "My son," he said, "you're going on a mission that will keep you away for a number of years. You will meet all kinds of people. Remember, for your sake as well as for the sake of your people back home, never get involved with a bet."

"Of course not, Father," replied the young man, again surprised at the strange request. As the trip drew nearer, the king called in his son many times, and each time with a similar introduction, he made the same request. "Don't get involved with bets!"

Finally the prince was on his way, visiting countries and cities throughout the world. Once in a while, at a social gathering, people would tempt him with a wager, but remembering his father's stern warnings, he was always careful to say no.

Months went by. The prince met with kings, heads of state and government officials, all of whom came to respect and admire him. Often they sought his advice and counsel, as his reputation spread throughout the world. Memories of his days back home began to recede as each new day brought new and exciting experiences. No longer did anyone try to convince the prince to make a wager, for everyone already knew of his strong resolution not to do so.

One day he was at a meeting with a prominent governor. A municipality had a problem to which the governor had proposed a solution. The lieutenant governor suggested a different approach. The prince offered a third solution, a novel approach to the problem.

The lieutenant governor looked at the prince with scorn. "How are you qualified to offer your suggestion here?" he snapped. "This is a local problem and you should not even be sitting in on this meeting!"

The prince was taken aback. "And why shouldn't I be here?" he demanded. "As a member of a royal family, my experience and expertise in municipal problems is such that I am as capable as anyone else here."

"That's just my point," the lieutenant governor flung back. "I have been investigating your background and I have learned that you are nothing more than a servant; you are not royalty at all! You are a fraud!"

The prince was shocked. "This is totally absurd!" he exclaimed. "I am a prince and you know very well that my father is a king."

"Not only don't I believe it," said the lieutenant governor, "but

I can prove that you are a mere servant. In your country every slave is branded behind his left shoulder. I know that you have that mark which proves that you are indeed a slave."

"That is a lie!" the prince shouted, as the governor listened in dismayed silence to the war of words between his lieutenant and the young prince.

"I'll bet 5000 rubles that you have that mark on your shoulder," challenged the lieutenant governor.

The prince's heart sank. He suddenly remembered that he'd been warned by his father never to be trapped into making a bet. But this was surely different, he reasoned. A bet is always a thing of chance, a situation in which there is some doubt, but this was a definite thing; he was a prince, just as sure as the sun came up every morning. He further rationalized that in this case his honor and, even more so, his father's honor were at stake. Surely, in this situation, even his father would agree to make an exception.

After thinking for a few moments the prince announced defiantly, "I am a prince, the son of a king, and I accept the bet to prove my royal lineage."

The governor and his lieutenant looked on in anticipation as the prince removed his jacket, his vest, his shirt and then his undershirt. There was no mark. He had won the bet! The lieutenant governor blushed with embarrassment and the governor said angrily, "You owe the prince an apology, besides having to pay him the 5000 rubles."

The lieutenant governor apologized profusely and handed over the money that he had lost on the wager. The conversation eventually returned to the problem at hand.

A few months later, the prince returned home. Expecting to find a welcoming committee and a very happy father to greet him, he was surprised to find his father crestfallen and unhappy. After the initial greetings, the prince asked his father why he seemed so sad.

"I understand that you made a bet after all, my son." The prince then explained the circumstances and the considerations that had caused him to make an exception just that once.

"But my dear son," said the father, "it was all a ploy. That same lieutenant governor had made a bet with me for 10,000 rubles that he could get you involved in a bet. Although you may have won 5,000 rubles, I lost 10,000."

❦ ❦ ❦

The King is Hashem, the lieutenant governor is the *yetzer hara* and the prince is each one of us. The bet involved symbolizes any particular sin. How often do we rationalize that in one particular instance Hashem would agree to bend His rules *(mitzvos)* just a small amount? One day, like the prince, we too will have to return home. Our actions will determine the welcome awaiting us.

◆§ *The Return Trip*

This true narrative was told to R' Sholom by the principal participant in the story. Recently, this same gentleman was in my home, and my family and I sat spellbound as he detailed the incident and the incredible events that followed. When he finished answering all our questions, he made a request — that if this story would ever be published he would be grateful if his name were not used. Hence the facts in the story are true, but the names are fictitious.

Perhaps all that needs to be said in introduction are the words of King David *(Psalms* 92:6-7), "מַה גָּדְלוּ מַעֲשֶׂיךָ ה׳ ... וּכְסִיל לֹא יָבִין אֶת זֹאת — How great are Your deeds, Hashem ... a simple man cannot understand them."

R' Sholom Schechter, a prominent elderly *rav,* was on a TWA flight to *Eretz Yisrael,* with a stopover in Athens where he would board a connecting flight.

It was two days before Rosh Hashanah, and the last few days in New York had been exhausting. Expending his energy in raising funds, selling *sefarim,* packing, and preparing for his trip had all taken their toll on this seventy-year-old man. Extremely tired, he fell into a deep sleep as the plane crossed the Atlantic.

He asked to be awakened when the plane landed in Athens, but someone forgot to do so. On board were many people of many nationalities, heading towards many different destinations, so it didn't seem unusual that the rabbi with the long beard remained asleep even as the plane landed in Athens and people disembarked. He remained asleep throughout the stopover and awoke only as the plane roared down the runway, taking off to its next destination.

The captain greeted everyone and then detailed the flight plan. The next stop was Lebanon!

Rabbi Schechter blinked his eyes a few times in disbelief. Lebanon? Were they being hijacked? What had happened to Athens? He soon realized that he had slept through his changing point and unlike a bus, he couldn't just get out and walk back to his correct stop. His baggage was probably on its way to *Eretz Yisrael,* but he most certainly was not.

This obviously Jewish-looking man would certainly be in danger in Lebanon, a land of fanatical, Jew-hating Arabs. He mentioned his predicament to the flight attendant who discussed the situation with the captain and then came to Rabbi Schechter with their advice. They suggested that since all the passengers were either American or European tourists who would in all probability not report the Jewish passengers to the Lebanese authorities, the crew might be able to protect him from being seen by any Arabs who might assist the disembarking passengers, or by those who might come on board to check and clean the plane. They told him to pretend that he was asleep and they heaped blankets all around him, covering him almost completely.

As the trip continued, Rabbi Schechter busied himself studying the *sefarim* he had taken along. When the plane eventually came to a halt in Lebanon, his heart was in his throat. For this landing he was wide awake. He sat trembling with fear, covered in darkness by the two blankets that the stewards provided for him.

No one gave the "sleeping" traveler more than a passing glance and then once again the plane took off, the next stop being India. Rabbi Schechter knew that there were Jewish communities in Bombay and Calcutta, but enroute the captain informed the passengers that due to civil disturbances in India, only those people holding Indian passports would be permitted to disembark.

Rosh Hashanah was only a day off. Checking plane flights and schedules, Rabbi Schechter realized that he had no chance of getting back to *Eretz Yisrael* in time for *Yom Tov.* He couldn't help but wonder where in the world this incredible journey might take him. He was confused and emotionally drained. Why was this happening to him? Was this wandering a punishment for something? Or was he destined to accomplish something special at some unknown destination? He would have to get off at the first stop after India, regardless of where it might be. He soon found out — Bangkok, Thailand.

By the time the plane taxied to a stop at Don Muang airport and Rabbi Schechter was cleared through customs, it was only a few hours before Rosh Hashanah. After some desperate inquiries he was told that there was indeed a synagogue in the center of town. He made his way there, hoping that someone would be kind enough to invite him home. The people turned out to be more than kind.

He had no trouble conversing with the congregants, for most of the men who attended the synagogue were in Thailand on business, and they spoke English. He was invited by the president of the synagogue, a Mr. Atlas, to be a guest in his home, and it was there that Rabbi Schechter stayed for the next few days.

At Mr. Atlas' table, Rabbi Schechter ate only some cake, fruit and vegetables, that his daughter had packed for his trip, and *matzah,* which his host provided. He was introduced to Mr. Atlas' children, two of whom were brilliant young scholars studying at Oxford University in England. Among many things they discussed was the fact that in the synagogue tomorrow, aside from the regular Rosh Hashanah services, there was going to be a *bar mitzvah.* "This trip gets more interesting every step of the way," Rabbi Schechter thought to himself.

When he came to the synagogue the next morning, he had another surprise waiting for him. Not only was there no *mechitzah* separating the men from the women, but the congregants were all sitting together. As an Orthodox Jew, Rabbi Schechter prayed alone in an anteroom to the side of the main sanctuary. After *Shacharis* (morning prayer), he asked the rabbi if he could address the people, to explain why he had not joined them for the prayers. He was granted permission.

"My dear brothers and sisters," he began, "I am grateful to G-d that He granted me the privilege to be with you wonderful people this Rosh Hashanah. Surely many of you know that it was my original intention to be in *Eretz Yisrael* with my family, but G-d in His wisdom decreed that I be here with you in Bangkok. Perhaps some day I will know the reason. I appreciate your hospitality and friendliness. Because of your overwhelming kindness to me, I feel that I must explain why I did not pray with you this morning, but rather prayed alone in the anteroom.

"Every synagogue is meant to be a model of the Holy Temple that once stood in Jerusalem. The sanctity of the synagogue is similar to the sanctity of that holy place. And because of the temple's holiness, men and women were separated during all services, to insure that there be no frivolity or diversion of attention from the prayers and the holiness of the place. A synagogue in which men and women sit together loses some of its holiness. Therefore, as you can see, I must pray in the anteroom."

Rabbi Schechter spoke about the importance of a child becoming *bar mitzvah* and studying Torah to understand and appreciate his Jewish heritage.

Rabbi Schechter's words were eloquent, moving, and respectful. He did not talk down to the congregants nor criticize them, rather, he pleaded with them to start Torah-study groups so that they could become more familiar with the traditions, customs, and laws of their forefathers. He raised their spirits and when he finished his talk, an unbelievable thing happened. A Dr. Frankel, one of the members of the synagogue, walked up to the podium and began speaking spontaneously. "I'm sure that many of you feel as I do that it is an honor to have such a distinguished guest in our presence. In his honor, may I suggest that we separate the men from the women before we continue with the Torah reading and *shofar* blowing, so that he can pray with us."

The local rabbi was offended that something so drastic was done in "his" synagogue without consulting him. He got up to protest, but it was too late. Two hundred people were already on the move, the men stationing themselves on the right side of the synagogue, the women to the left. And they remained so for the entire holiday service.

The next morning Rabbi Schechter spoke again, and once again the Atlas boys, sons of his host, were present. The older of the boys, Morris, possessed an inquisitive, analytical mind and was much taken with Rabbi Schechter. The conversations which had flowed between the young thinker and the older scholar had established a strong bond between the two.

Morris had never been to a yeshivah and he had no idea what Orthodoxy was all about, but here was an Orthodox man who touched his heart. By the time Rosh Hashanah was over, Morris had made a decision. He was going to interrupt his studies at Oxford and transfer to Ohr Somayach (a yeshivah with a program for boys with little Torah background) in Jerusalem. After much discussion, Mr. Atlas agreed that his son could try it for one semester. The young scholar went off to Israel and the one semester lasted three fruitful years. During those years he became a true *ben Torah* and eventually influenced his younger brother to come to Ohr Somayach as well.

Today, years later, the Atlas brothers are Orthodox Jews living in London, strongly committed to Torah and *mitzvos* and deeply indebted to the rabbi who slept through his stopover in Athens. Back in Bangkok, the classes which Rabbi Schechter organized have also borne fruit; some women now observe *taharas hamishpachah* (family purity) for the first time in their lives.

❦ ❦ ❦

When retelling this story Rabbi Schechter observes reflectively, "It is true," he says, "that I was punished. I could not be with my family in *Eretz Yisrael* for the holidays. Yet, because of my unscheduled trip, a chain of events was put into motion that accomplished much for *Yiddishkeit*. Hashem let me be involved in returning two Jews to authentic Judaism.

"As King David wrote (*Psalms* 94:1-2), 'קֵל נְקָמוֹת ה' — Hashem is a G-d of vengeance.' The two Divine Names used in this verse both are generally indicative of compassion and mercy, yet here they surround the word vengeance which indicates strictness and punishment! From here we see that G-d's ways are great, for even in punishment, we are surrounded by His mercies."

◆§ Seeing in the Dark

In *Bereishis* (32:28-30) we learn that an interesting dialogue took place between our patriarch Jacob and Esau's celestial angel after the two of them had tangled with each other.

> The angel asked him, "What is your name?"
>
> The reply came, "Jacob."
>
> The angel then said, "Your name shall no longer be Jacob, rather it shall be Israel."
>
> In turn, Jacob asked the angel, "Please tell me, what is *your* name?"
>
> The angel seemingly refused to answer and instead asked, 'Why must you ask my name?"

Most commentaries understand the angel's reply to Jacob as an attempt to brush him off and avoid his question, as if to say, there is no need for you to know my name. However, R' Leib Chasman understood that "Why-must-you-ask-my-name" was really the angel's name and interpreted the reply in a unique manner. He understood the angel's words not as a question but as an answer.

By its very nature, a name should define its subject, be it a person, an object, or even an angel (see ArtScroll *Bris Milah* p. 35,39). Esau's celestial angel was actually the *yetzer hara* (the Evil Inclination) which by definition represents all that is unethical and immoral. If any person were to truly understand what evil lurks behind the devious plans that the *yetzer hara* has for him, he would surely avoid following its wishes. Nevertheless, the *yetzer hara* is able to sway people and lure them into sin only because he camouflages his true self. He appears as something good, something exciting, and conceals the real evil inherent in his suggestions. When a man lies or cheats he doesn't see himself as doing an injustice; he feels that he's avenging a wrong or getting something that is rightfully his.

That is what the angel meant when he said to Jacob, "My name is 'Why-must-you-ask-my-name.' " The angel was saying, "As long as people do not seek to delve into what I really represent I can be successful in dragging them to sin. I say to them what I say to you, 'Why must you ask my name?' Don't ask questions, don't give matters too much thought, just do as I say; it's for your benefit."

R' Leib then explained this thought further with the following parable.

> A farmer came to the big city for the first time. He had heard about the cinema and decided to see for himself what talking and moving pictures were all about. He entered the theater, walked through a well-lit lobby and was directed into a large, dark auditorium.
>
> He watched with amazement as the picture flashed, danced and changed on the huge screen in front of him. People on the screen were actually moving and talking right before his incredulous eyes. He became so excited that he wanted to see the pictures even more clearly. Running down the aisle, the unsophisticated farmer shined his flashlight directly onto the screen, thinking that he would get a better view.
>
> All at once everyone began shouting. "Stop that, you fool! Shut that light! We can't see a thing! You're ruining the picture!"
>
> "What's wrong?" he cried. "All I want to do is see a little better. I'm giving you all extra light."
>
> "No, you fool!" someone shouted. "In this place we can see only in the darkness. The light ruins everything!"

The world of the *yetzer hara* is like a motion picture — there is nothing real on the screen, no real people, no real movement, it is only a deception. The light makes people realize that, but they would rather be in darkness, which is exactly where the *yetzer hara* wants them to be. Only in spiritual darkness can people be lured to sin. Knowledge of truth is the ultimate "light" and in the revealing glare of light, the *yetzer hara* can have no effect.

⁂

In retelling this parable, R' Sholom whimsically describes his initial contact with television, during his first trip to London. Accompanied by a friend, R' Dov, he was on the way to a philanthropist, to collect funds for an organization in *Eretz Yisrael.* As they approached the home, no lights were visible, but R' Dov insisted on ringing the door bell. "There is no one home," protested R' Sholom. "All the lights are off."

"No, no!" said R' Dov, "I know for sure they are home."

"Then maybe they are all asleep. How can we wake them up? Let's leave," said R' Sholom.

"Of course not," said R' Dov. "They are awake. You will see."

"But it's as dark as *Gehinnom* inside," protested R' Sholom. R' Dov rang the bell and soon the philanthropist himself came to the door and welcomed them inside. As they walked past the living room, R' Sholom, still surprised at how few lights were on in the large house, noticed that the family was sitting on the floor in a darkened room, and staring straight ahead.

"They must be sitting *shivah,*" he thought. "What a pity. A family tragedy, no doubt." Concerned, he inquired as to what had happened and was told not to worry about anything, everything was quite fine. They were sitting in the darkened room simply to watch something called television.

"And I say," comments R' Sholom, "there *is* indeed something to be concerned about. A person brings darkness into his home, has his family sitting on the floor like mourners, G-d forbid, and convinces himself that he has brought light, joy and gladness into his home. What deception! What foolishness! They have fallen into the clutches of Why-must-you-ask-my-name because they are afraid to 'see the light'."

◆§ *Asleep for the Trumpets*

A benevolent king traveled throughout his country once a year, going from city to city, to meet his subjects, listen to their pleas, and fulfill their requests.

The date of the royal visit would be announced well in advance. When the day finally arrived, people dressed in their holiday best and went out to the town square in the morning to maneuver themselves into a place up front where they could stand and wait to see and meet the king. No one knew exactly what time he would arrive, since he had so many places to visit. But the townspeople knew that it was customary for foot soldiers and trumpeters to march ahead of the king to herald his arrival.

The people of one town waited for hours, but still the king had not come. One person was too tired to wait any longer. He left the crowd and said, "The king probably won't come today; he'll be here tomorrow."

"Stay, don't leave," his friends urged. "You'll miss a golden opportunity."

"I'm tired," he said. "I'm going back home to rest. Besides, if I hear the trumpeters, I'll get up quickly and run back."

The man went home, fell into a deep sleep and didn't hear anything the rest of the day. The royal soldiers and trumpeters came, followed by the king in all his splendor. The people made their requests, while the sleeping man was left with nothing but empty dreams and dashed hopes. The only thing he could do was to attempt to follow the king to another city.

The Chofetz Chaim explained that this behavior describes many of us during the period prior to, and even during, the *Asseres Yemei Teshuvah* (the Ten Days of Repentance from Rosh Hoshanah to Yom Kippur). We are told that once a year Hashem, the King of all kings, gives us a special opportunity for prayer, introspection and repentance so that He can grant our request of being entered into the Book of Life for the following year.

But many Jews remain in their spiritual slumber and do nothing to prepare for the Days of Judgment. Throughout Elul, the month preceding the *Asseres Yemei Teshuvah,* they continue in their sinful ways. They don't resolve to strive for a more profound observance of Torah and *mitzvos.* They are content with their spiritual status quo.

After a month of such apathy, Rosh Hashanah arrives. The *shofar* heralds the coming of the King. One would expect those who were spiritually lethargic during Elul to come alive and make amends during the next ten days, the *Asseres Yemei Teshuvah.* After all, the sound of the *shofar,* notes the *Rambam (Hilchos Teshuvah* 3:4), is symbolically a message to those who may have fallen asleep, to bestir themselves, awaken and become vigilant in their performance of *mitzvos*.

But these stubborn people remain in their stupor and refuse to change their ways. The opportunity of the Ten Days slowly ebbs away, culminating with the one last chance, Yom Kippur. Sadly they don't take advantage even of that day.

How embarrassing it must be to have to come later on in the year to repent and seek the "King in other cities." Surely it would have been far more prudent to heed the prophet Isaiah, who said (55:6): "דִּרְשׁוּ ה׳ בְּהִמָּצְאוֹ, קְרָאֻהוּ בִּהְיוֹתוֹ קָרוֹב – Seek Hashem when He can be found, call Him while He is close," which the Talmud *(Rosh Hashanah* 18a) says refers to the Ten Days of Repentance between Rosh Hashanah and Yom Kippur.

❦ ❦ ❦

"However," said R' Sholom in one of his annual month of Elul *drashos*, "even those who seek to come closer to Hashem must remember that merely regretting their transgressions of the past is not enough. By discarding his sins, one fulfills only the first half of King David's directive *(Psalms* 34:15), "סוּר מֵרָע – Turn from evil." However, one must actively accomplish the second half – "וַעֲשֵׂה טוֹב – and do good". He must chart a new course of action and follow it, performing *mitzvos*, concentrating more on his prayers and alloting more time for Torah study."

To stress the need for changing direction, R' Sholom cites the parable of R' Yosef Yoizel of Novharadok.

❦ ❦ ❦

A man who wished to travel down south mistakenly got on a boat that was traveling north. As the boat made its way out to sea, the traveler realized he was heading in the wrong direction.

"Quick, jump off, you can still swim back to shore," someone yelled to him from the port. "No, it's all right," he called back. "I'll stay on the boat. It may be going north, but I will walk in a southerly direction."

"What good is man's changing his direction," asks R' Sholom, "if he is still on the same boat? The man on the boat also regrets his mistake, but his actions are not substantial enough to rectify anything."

◆§ *The Soul — The Spiritual Eye of Man*

The eye is man's window to the world. The beauty, the miracles, the awesome accomplishments of G-d and man are there for us to behold. The eyes are one of man's most precious possessions. Indeed, the Talmud notes that blindness is akin to death (See *Nedarim* 64b).

One could not even read these words unless his eyes were focused properly on this line. And yet, noted R' Leib Chasman, the tiniest speck of dust can cause a man to shut his eye tightly and close out everything; the beauty, the glory, all the potential knowledge that just moments ago were open before him.

Similarly, said R' Leib, man's soul yearns for spiritual heights and is eager for the spiritual growth that lies before him. Torah and *mitzvos* beckon, but the smallest sin, like the speck of dust, causes the soul to cringe, darken and close up within itself. As long as that 'speck' is not washed away, it impedes further vision. As long as the sin is not removed by *teshuvah* (repentance) it may prevent spiritual growth.

◆§ *Son or Servant*

The Talmud *(Bava Basra* 10a) notes that at times *Klal Yisrael* (the Jewish Nation) is referred to lovingly as *banim,* "children" of Hashem. Yet at other times they are described contemptuously as *avadim,* "servants" of Hashem. The Talmud explains that when Jews fulfill the will of Hashem they are called "His children", but when they do not fulfill His will, they are called "His servants".

R' Elya Lopian once asked, "How can one who does not fulfill the will of Hashem be considered a servant, a term that indicates one who serves his master? Furthermore," he noted, "the term 'Hashem's will' seems somewhat ambiguous. Would it not have been more accurate to say that the criterion of whether we are considered children or servants is whether or not we fulfill Hashem's commandments? What exactly is meant by Hashem's will?"

Allegorically, R' Elya depicted scenes in two different stores to bring out the message concealed in this Talmudic dictum.

❧ ❧ ❧

In a busy hardware store on *erev* Pesach, people were rushing through the aisles frantically doing their last-minute shopping, pushing, excusing themselves, and pushing again. One wanted dishes, a second needed lightbulbs, a third was returning damaged goods. The people behind the counter had their hands full trying to cope with the mild hysteria of customers' demands. Someone noticed a teenage boy who at first seemed to be helping to stack some merchandise, then he was off helping a customer carry his packages to his car, and then returning, went behind the counter to see where else he could be of assistance. He seemed to be everywhere. The observer wondered who this boy was and which of the many jobs he was attending to was actually his responsibility.

The same person went next door to a grocery store to observe the scene there. Once again people were running around for last-minute items. Bedlam ruled as one person bought fish, another *matzah,* a third grape juice, and a fourth was trying to pay his bill. Here too the aisles were crowded with shoppers. The owners and workers didn't know where to turn to first. In the back of the store there was a young man, about the same age as the boy in the hardware store, who was sitting quietly doing the bookkeeping. He sat calmly amidst the storm of noise downstairs, oblivious to everything else as he proceeded with his work. Once again, the observer couldn't help but wonder. Why didn't this young fellow come forward to help with the customers? How could he sit there so calmly?

Upon inquiry he found out that the boy in the hardware shop was the owner's son, and, as a customer there said in describing the lad, "He is always around to help. He has a keen sense of where to be and is always available to fill the gap where it's required. You don't have to tell him every little thing."

The second boy, he was told, was a paid worker. "He comes in at 9:00 a.m. and leaves at 5:00 p.m.," a customer said. "He does what he is told to do and no more."

❦ ❦ ❦

"And that," said R' Elya, "is the difference between a loyal son and a dutiful servant. Both do their jobs and take care of their obligations. But the son runs with enthusiasm, trying to be of service at all times, while the dutiful servant carries out his task, but does it in a perfunctory manner."

R' Sholom points out further that the Talmud was not discussing a Jew who does not perform the *mitzvos.* Such an individual would be considered a rebellious son to Hashem, not even a servant. Rather, the servant is someone who performs the *mitzvos* in a dull, lifeless way. He prays three times a day, but merely recites the words, not thinking much about their meaning. He buys his *esrog* and builds his *succah,* but doesn't spend much effort or money to make them beautiful. He learns his *mishnah* or *gemara* but makes no special effort to remember them and put them into practice.

A son is different. He fulfills Hashem's will with joy and goes beyond the letter of the law. He does everything he can to improve the prospects of the "family business," because he is a part of it and it is a part of him.

◆§ *On Target*

Perhaps the most famous of all *maggidim* in Jewish history was R' Yaakov Krantz (1741-1804), the *Maggid* of Dubno, a small town in Poland.

In his lifetime the Dubno *Maggid* must have told hundreds of parables *(meshalim).* Although none of them were printed while he was alive, his son, Rabbi Yitzchak, and a devoted disciple, R' Avraham Dov Berish Flamm, collected many of them in such *sefarim* as *Ohel Yaakov, Kochav MiYaakov, Emes LeYaakov* and others.

Perhaps more than anyone the Dubno *Maggid* personified the idea of teaching with a parable. He was once asked how he was able to invent a parable for every point — a parable that invariably fit its moral perfectly.

His reply? "I'll answer you with a parable."

❀ ❀ ❀

A man was wandering in a forest, and as he strolled he noticed that many trees had been used for target practice. As he came closer he noticed that every arrow was nestled right in the bull's-eye. He marveled at the marksmanship of the archer and wondered who it might be.

Then, in the distance, he saw a young archer taking aim at a tree. He ran over to the boy and exclaimed, "Are you the sharpshooter with all those arrows in the bull's-eyes?"

The young boy grinned and said, "Yes, but the way I do it, it's easy. First I shoot the arrow into the tree and then I paint the bull's-eye and target around it."

❀ ❀ ❀

"It's the same with me," said the Dubno *Maggid*. "There are those who, in order to teach a lesson, try to find a suitable parable to bring out their point. I do the opposite. To me every incident in life is a parable, and the only question is, what lesson can be learned from it? Thus there is no end to the parables available."

◆§ *Borrowed Yom Kippur*

In most synagogues around the world, the scene on Yom Kippur is the same: men wear white *kittels,* immersed in prayer and serious thought. A passerby, observing the assembly for a few moments, might think that all those present are righteous, repentant people, all committed to a new year of meticulous Torah study and *mitzvah* observance.

But as the Dubno *Maggid* pointed out, looks can be deceiving — a point he illustrated with a beautiful parable.

❀ ❀ ❀

When the richest man in the city marries off his daughter, no one wants to miss the festive occasion with its lively singing, good food and ambiance. All the guests dress in their finest clothing, adorn themselves with their best jewelry, make sure they look just right and then attend the wedding.

But what about the poor people? They too would like to join in the wedding festivities. Unfortunately though, they have no fine clothes to wear, no jewelry to adorn them. They are reduced to borrowing pretty dresses, dignified suits, bracelets, necklaces, and trinkets from whomever they can, so that they too can attend the event in splendid finery.

Anyone observing the guests would think that everyone at this gala affair is wealthy and lives comfortably. But if he would stay until after the wedding and watch where the poor people go, he would see that they rush to return their borrowed clothes and ornaments. It is only after the wedding, not during the main event, that the spectator can really tell who is fortunate and who is not.

"Thus," says the Dubno *Maggid*, "only on the day after Yom Kippur, when people return to the regular patterns of life and conduct their business in their usual fashion, can one observe and realize who the true penitents were. If one is dishonest, deceptive and deceitful, it becomes obvious that yesterday's remorse was only temporary.

"For such people it was only a 'borrowed' Yom Kippur."

If the Coat Fits ...

In the *Shema* we are exhorted: "וְאָהַבְתָּ אֵת ה׳ אֱלֹקֶיךָ בְּכָל לְבָבְךָ וּבְכָל נַפְשְׁךָ וּבְכָל מְאֹדֶךָ — And you shall love Hashem your G-d with all your heart, with all your soul, and with all your resources." In other words, to have total commitment to Hashem and His commandments. Yet sometimes, when we try to fulfill this edict, we find that this noble goal is elusive.

The Dubno *Maggid* pointed out that the reason for the

difficulty lies in the very next phrase of *Shema*, "וְהָיוּ הַדְּבָרִים הָאֵלֶּה ... עַל לְבָבֶךָ — *Let these words ... be on your heart.*" The term on your heart means directly on your heart without any barriers or interventions of any kind. Unfortunately, a person's evil traits, such as jealousy, greed, and the pursuit of glory, are barriers to attaining a closeness and intimacy with Hashem (see *Avos* 4:21). If man could only rid himself of those characteristics, the words of *Shema* would indeed be "on his heart". As usual the Dubno *Maggid* explained his thought with a beautiful parable.

A farmer from the backwoods once came into a big city in the springtime and observed prominent-looking people wearing beautifully tailored coats. He himself was accustomed to wearing only baggy overalls and thickly padded coats. He had never owned a nicely tailored garment. He inquired where he could purchase one of the coats that had impressed him and was told to visit a certain tailor who would make it to order.

"I'd like a nice coat," he announced upon entering the shop. "Just like the ones all those important-looking people outside are wearing."

"Fine," said the tailor, "let me take your measurements." After doing so, the tailor told the farmer to come back in two weeks for the finished product.

Two weeks later, the farmer returned, paid for the coat and with great excitement tried to put it on. But, it didn't fit!

"What's the matter?" he stormed. "I can't even get this on me! This isn't my size. It would hardly fit a child. Give me back my money."

"I measured it perfectly," said the tailor from the other side of the shop. "Let me see what the problem is." The tailor came forward, took one look at the farmer and said, "Of course it won't fit you the way you are trying to wear it. You are still wearing your big overalls and stuffed jacket. Remove your old farmer's clothes and then you will see that the city clothes will fit you perfectly."

The Dubno *Maggid* then added, "Let every man remove his 'rough garments', his bad characteristics, and then the fine cloak of devotion to Hashem will fit him perfectly."

☙ Heavy Load?

The Kotzker *Rebbe,* R' Menachem Mendel Morgenstern (1787-1859), considered the following parable to be one of the finest the Dubno *Maggid* ever told.

A dealer in precious stones once went out of town on business. He had with him a valise filled with his wares — diamonds, rubies, emeralds — to show to potential buyers.

When he came to his hotel, he was assigned a room on the fourth floor. The hotel clerk summoned a porter and asked that he carry the businessman's valise up to his room. When the businessman came to his fourth floor room, he found the porter there waiting for him, huffing and puffing from exhaustion. "That was one heavy suitcase!" the porter complained. "I'm collapsing! What do you have in there, rocks?"

"If you are tired," said the diamond dealer, "you must have taken the wrong valise. Mine is filled with diamonds and precious stones which are lightweight; they wouldn't tire anyone out. You probably took someone else's valise, and that is why you're so tired."

❦ ❦ ❦

"This," said the Dubno *Maggid,* "is how to understand what G-d said to the Jewish nation *(Isaiah* 43:22): 'וְלֹא אֹתִי קָרָאתָ יַעֲקֹב כִּי יָגַעְתָּ בִּי יִשְׂרָאֵל — You, Jacob, (should know) it is not I (Hashem) whom you have called, because you, Israel, became tired."

The *Maggid* explained, "G-d said to the Jews, 'The *burden* of observing My Torah and doing My *mitzvos* is a light one to carry. If you find it heavy — then you are probably carrying the wrong load.' Torah study and the performance of *mitzvos* are a pleasure to carry, for they make a Jew's life complete and happy — not weary and burdensome."

After years of worldly experience, King Solomon wrote (*Koheles* 1:2), "הֲבֵל הֲבָלִים הַכֹּל הָבֶל — Futility of futilities, all is futile." And (ibid. 12:13): "סוֹף דָּבָר הַכֹּל נִשְׁמָע, אֶת הָאֱלֹקִים יְרָא וְאֶת מִצְוֹתָיו שְׁמוֹר, כִּי זֶה כָּל הָאָדָם — The sum of the matter, when all has been considered, is to fear G-d and keep His commandments, for that is man's whole duty" But man doesn't always see things clearly. He exchanges the ways of his forefathers for the ways of the nations. He abandons the traditions and customs of the previous generations for the modes of his own time.

The prophet Jeremiah, who forewarned the Jews of the destruction of the first Holy Temple, cried out (*Jeremiah* 2:11): "הַהֵימִיר גּוֹי אֱלֹהִים וְהֵמָּה לֹא אֱלֹהִים, וְעַמִּי הֵמִיר כְּבוֹדוֹ בְּלוֹא יוֹעִיל — Did the nations of the world exchange their gods even though their gods were useless? Yet my nation has exchanged His (i.e., Hashem's) glory for something that has no worth." Hashem said to Jeremiah (ibid. 2:13): "כִּי שְׁתַּיִם רָעוֹת עָשָׂה עַמִּי אֹתִי עָזְבוּ מְקוֹר מַיִם חַיִּים לַחְצֹב לָהֶם בֹּארוֹת בֹּארֹת נִשְׁבָּרִים אֲשֶׁר לֹא יָכִלוּ הַמָּיִם — My nation has performed two wrongs; they left Me, the source of fresh well water, and then sought to dig for themselves broken pits (idolatory) that cannot contain any water."

The Dubno *Maggid* told a whimsical story to illustrate this sorry state of affairs.

❦ ❦ ❦

A wealthy man had a simpleton for a son-in-law. Seeing that nothing he did was right and everything he touched went wrong, the father-in-law was afraid to allow his son-in-law into his business for fear of the results. But, after supporting him for two years, he felt he could tolerate the situation no longer. He called his son-in-law into his office.

"Listen," he said, "I will give you money and I want you to act intelligently and prudently. Go to the market and buy an item in large quantity for a cheap wholesale price, but be sure that each one can be sold individually at a higher price so that you can make a nice profit."

The son-in-law, not well endowed with business sense, went to the market, and after some investigating decided he had a marvelous idea. He took all the money his father-in-law had given him and bought three hundred *shofars*. "Rosh Hashanah is coming soon," he reasoned, "and everyone has to hear the sound of the *shofar*, so surely they will be in great demand."

When he came home with a cartload of *shofars* his father-in-law almost fainted. "How in the world will you get rid of these?" he fumed.

"Everyone has to have a *shofar*," the son-in-law replied in all innocence.

"No," answered the exasperated father-in-law. "Everyone needs to *listen* to the *shofar*, but only a few actually buy them."

And so, as the father-in-law predicted, after Rosh Hashanah the son-in-law was left with 275 *shofars* and no money in his pocket.

Resigned to his fate, the father-in-law decided to support his son-in-law once again. After another year, he decided to try his luck once more and called his son-in-law to his office.

"This time," he said, "think of something that everyone needs and don't worry about making a big profit on each item. The main thing is to be able to supply a product to people for which there is a demand."

The son-in-law took the money and on his way to the market repeated to himself, ... "Remember, something that everyone needs, everyone." This time he was more careful. He didn't buy one-time items like *shofars* or even *megillos;* instead he bought a whole wagonload of toothpicks.

When he returned home, his father-in-law nearly collapsed. He could hardly believe that a person could be so foolish. Once again he resigned himself to keeping his son-in-law home and supporting him. But now he had to get rid of all the merchandise that his son-in-law had bought.

One evening he called a broker and asked him to come over to his home. "Look," said the unhappy father-in-law. "I'm embarrassed by what my son-in-law brought home. Please take the 275 *shofars*, go to the market and try to get rid of them. Whatever money you make or merchandise you can exchange it for is fine with me. I realize that I will probably suffer a loss, but I want to recoup any money I can from this investment."

The broker took the *shofars* and promised to try his best. The next evening the father-in-law called another broker and once again explained. "I'm embarrassed by what my son-in-law brought home. I have a wagonload of toothpicks. Please take them to the market and see if you can get rid of them. I'll take any money or merchandise you can get for the whole load of toothpicks."

The next morning both brokers, each unaware of the other's assignment, went to the market to see what they could accomplish. As luck would have it, the two ran into each other. Not realizing that they were acting for the same person, the first broker with the *shofars* said to the second one, "I have to get rid of a cartload of an extraordinary number of *shofars* and I don't have a buyer. What do you have to sell?"

"I've got the same problem," said the broker of the toothpicks. "No one even wants to look at my merchandise."

They agreed to exchange the wagonload of toothpicks for the entire cartload of *shofars.* That night the two brokers made their way to the father-in-law. One can imagine his shock and dismay when they both stood at the door and explained what had happened. Flabbergasted, he exclaimed, "What fools you are! I thought you were intelligent brokers, but instead one comes back with *shofars* and the other with toothpicks. You have no business sense whatsoever."

Suddenly, from the other room came the son-in-law and exclaimed, "You see, you said I was foolish, but here you have two supposedly smart business brokers and they brought back the same things I did."

"No," screamed the father-in-law, losing his last bit of patience. "The difference between you and them is they exchanged useless *shofars* for useless toothpicks, but you exchanged good money for useless goods."

❦ ❦ ❦

"And that," said the Dubno *Maggid*," explains the shame of the Jewish people. Their values were wrong. They forsook the

King of kings for utterly worthless idols. Although the nations of the world could not be blamed for exchanging one useless idol for another, they stood steadfast in their loyalty to their futile gods and didn't exchange them."

Before we substitute our traditional ways for those of others, we should calculate their values, plus the compensation of a *mitzvah* against its loss and consider the punishment of a sin against the merit of refraining from it (see *Avos* 2:1).

☙ *Diamonds in the Street*

In our lives each of us must establish our priorities, then constantly keep them in mind and see to it that our decisions and actions reflect those priorities.

Every Jew attains his personal set of priorities by studying the Torah, the laws of the *Shulchan Aruch* and the traditions and customs of his forefathers. The purpose of a Jew in this temporary world, *Olam Hazeh,* is to maintain and uphold Torah standards throughout the course of his life, never deviating from them despite compelling outside influences.

In this famous, unforgettable parable of the Chofetz Chaim we learn about maintaining our perspective. I first heard this parable as a youngster in an *Oneg Shabbos* group in Kew Gardens and it made an impression then. When I heard it again recently from R' Sholom I realized that its message is timeless.

R' Nachman lived in a small town in Poland, where he found it very difficult to make a living. He tried his hand at many things but nothing seemed to work for him. Financially strained, he decided he would travel to an island near Africa, where, it was said, diamonds were so plentiful they lay scattered in the streets. Even though the sea voyage was risky and would last more than a year, it would be well worth taking. When he would return home with the diamonds he could sell them and attain great wealth and be able to live the kind of life he had always dreamed of.

He told his family of his decision and began making preparations for the trip. After weeks of excitement and planning, the day of departure arrived. He said his farewells to friends and family, assuring them that he would return in a few years. His ship sailed off beyond the horizon for his long journey across the seas.

Ships did not travel often to this remote island and so he would have to be there for a year at least. With great anticipation he watched as the ship drew closer to land and in the distance he imagined he could see diamonds glistening in the streets.

He disembarked and as he walked the streets he observed that the rumor was true, there were diamond chips everywhere he went and people were actually casually stepping all over them. Not able to contain his exuberance he dropped his packages, bent down and began gathering diamonds; big ones, little ones, perfect ones, imperfect ones, he took anything he could get his hands on and stuffed it in his pockets.

As he was picking up the stones, he noticed that the people standing near him were laughing. He couldn't understand it. "What's your rush?" one person asked R' Nachman. "You're going to be here a whole year!"

"Yes," added another man, "look at everyone else, they came here for the same reason you did, but here we take our time."

"Well," thought R' Nachman, "maybe they're right. I'm going to be here for a while and there seems to be an endless amount of diamonds here, so there's enough for everyone." The following day, as he familiarized himself with the island, he again began to pick up diamonds.

But he noticed that no one else was doing it, and he began to feel foolish. Didn't diamonds mean anything here? How could everyone just ignore them? As he asked questions, he came to realize that, truly, diamonds had no value on this island. The commodity that the islanders regarded most highly was fats (oil or shortenings) used in baking and frying. They were of basic importance and extremely hard to obtain. Anyone who could make fats, produce it, store it or sell it could become wealthy. The people on the island were so far from civilization that they had no cooking oil — something that was so easily obtained everywhere else.

R' Nachman was a man of determination and he set out at once to seek the ingredients for fats, even developing methods of storing and selling them. The work was hard and he spent a few weeks exploring the island until he found the proper ingredients.

As the weeks rolled by, he became so completely immersed in his attempts to develop fats that he completely forgot why he had come to the island in the first place. Every day he would pass the diamonds in the streets and ignore them, just as everyone else did. If he happened to see an exceptionally shiny one he'd examine it and slip it into his pocket. It brought him back to his senses for a moment, but then he would say to himself, "There is always tomorrow. Meanwhile I have to build up my supply of fats."

The weeks turned to months and eventually news came to the island that in two weeks the boat was coming to pick up all the "foreigners" who did not belong there. R' Nachman was too caught up in his pursuit of fats to pay much attention to what he heard, but a few days later when the boat arrived, it suddenly occurred to him that he had better pack his fats and get ready to carry them back home. He was proud of himself, for he had a successful year. The people on the island had given him much honor and now his wife and family back home would surely be proud of him.

But as he was carting all the fats to the boat, it suddenly occurred to him that the accumulation of fats had not been the reason for this trip. He had come for diamonds, not fats! Now it was too late, but he rationalized that the wealth of the fats would surely help him anyway. He picked up a few diamonds on the way to the boat, and then, after an enthusiastic send-off, began the long journey back home.

After a few weeks on the boat, the fats began to smell. The odor became so bad that the people on board complained to the captain. The captain ordered his crew to locate the source of the stench and they found the rotting fats which R' Nachman admitted was his. He pleaded with them not to throw it overboard for he had worked so hard to accumulate it. The workers tried to contain the odor by covering the fats, but in a little while the stench was so bad, there was no choice but to throw it all overboard. The fats for which he had worked so hard had become nothing but a lingering bad smell.

As he watched the last box go overboard, he realized that he had been a failure. He had wasted his precious time on the pursuit of worthless goods.

The days dragged by in dreaded anticipation. In his mind he saw his wife and children awaiting him and looking towards the "good years ahead" and their "happy" future. The ship finally docked, but embarrassed and forlorn, R' Nachman was one of the last to leave the ship.

His wife and children greeted him excitedly but he could not share their happiness. All he wanted was to be left alone. Friends and relatives gathered at his home to hear all about his experiences but he went to his room, downcast and deeply humiliated.

In his room, R' Nachman lay on his bed and cried himself to sleep. His wife, thinking that he was simply exhausted, left him alone. After a few hours she went up to talk to him. When she saw that he was still asleep she decided not to disturb him and instead picked up his coat and looked into his pockets. She found two big diamonds. With great joy and excitement she ran to the local jewel dealer to ask him for an evaluation. The dealer could not believe his eyes. "Lady," he said after examining the stones, "you are a lucky woman. Whoever got you these diamonds brought you great wealth. You will be wealthy for years to come with the proceeds of these diamonds!"

The woman ran back to her husband who had awakened, and she thanked him profusely for his great efforts. But he was still downcast. "Why are you so unhappy?" she asked him anxiously. "We are so lucky and you are so smart to have accomplished so much."

"I was not smart at all," said R' Nachman sadly. "If I had been intelligent I would have kept my mind on what I had come to the island to do. I got caught up in what those people considered in their world to be important rather than what was really important for us. It's true, I do have a few diamonds, but I could have amassed a fortune that would have provided not only for us and our children but even for our grandchildren and friends, forever."

"The reason that we came to this world," said the Chofetz Chaim, "is to collect diamonds — which are *mitzvos*. While we are here, however, we let ourselves become influenced by others who disregard these *mitzvos* which are readily available, and we get caught up instead in their way of thinking and try to gain wealth in what they think is important.

"Throughout a man's life *mitzvos* are just 'lying in the streets' waiting for someone to perform them. There are *mitzvos* that involve *chessed* (kindness) such as visiting the sick, helping the poor, or consoling the bereft. There are moments of free time that add up to hours, days, and even months which can be used advantageously for Torah study, be it *Chumash*, *Mishnayos*, *mussar*, *halachah* or Talmud. If man would only utilize his time properly on his 'trip' here in the temporary world, he could make himself forever fortunate in the *Olam HaEmess* (the True World).

"But man passes through life, letting time and opportunities slip by. When it's time to return to the real world, he tries to snatch a few 'diamonds' but by then it is too late. He should have kept his goal and priorities in mind all the time. Picking up a few diamonds here and there is wonderful, but imagine what level could have been reached had he made 'diamonds' his life's endeavor."

◈§ *A Wasted Loan*

R' Eliezer became aware that his good friend R' Yaakov needed money, and he offered him a loan. After some discussion, they agreed that the loan would be repaid in two years. When R' Yaakov received the money he promptly placed it in his security box where it would be perfectly safe.

Every week R' Yaakov would check to see if the money was still there, and sure enough it was always right where he had left it. Finally, after two years, he went to the security box for the last time, removed the money and hand-delivered it to R' Eliezer, "Here it is," he said with pride, "exactly as you gave it to me. I guarded it very carefully."

"I can't believe you were so foolish!" said R' Eliezer, when he realized what had happened. "I didn't give you the money just to guard it for me. I gave it to you so that you could invest it, build a small fortune, or at least in some way improve your financial status. By merely holding it all this time you wasted the opportunity to do something with it."

"The same," said the Chofetz Chaim, "is true for the *neshamah* (soul) that is 'lent' to all of us. At the beginning of our lives we are given a soul so that we can enhance it and nourish it by observing Torah and *mitzvos*. To return it unchanged to Hashem after our days are over is a waste of a golden opportunity."

With this thought in mind, the Chofetz Chaim had a novel interpretation of the words of King David (*Psalms* 24:4): "נְקִי כַפַּיִם וּבַר לֵבָב אֲשֶׁר לֹא נָשָׂא לַשָּׁוְא נַפְשִׁי — One with clean hands and pure heart, who has not sworn in vain by My soul." The word נָשָׂא means "sworn" but may also mean "carry". Hence the meaning of לֹא נָשָׂא לַשָּׁוְא נַפְשִׁי can be, "One who has not carried in vain the soul that I, Hashem, lent him," but has accomplished something with it.

Thus, adds the Chofetz Chaim, if a person does not perform *mitzvos*, then even if he hasn't done any *aveiros* (sins) throughout his life, it is still considered as if he carried his soul in vain, for man is expected to elevate his soul, and that is accomplished only through *mitzvos* and good deeds.

The End of the Line

The Talmud (*Sanhedrin* 98b) notes that R' Yochanan, among others, feared the coming of *Mashiach* (the Messiah), because the Jewish nation would have to endure much suffering in the period before the Messianic age.

In explaining why there would be such hardship in the Messianic era, R' Sholom once related a parable from the Chofetz Chaim.

Shimon, who owned a local hardware store, often bought his merchandise from a wholesaler named Boruch. Every month, Shimon would order goods for his store, depending on the needs of the local villagers. Often, when he had to place large orders, he could not pay his bills at once. Boruch, the wholesaler, extended Shimon a line of credit, and Shimon would make partial payments, trying to keep as up to date as possible, but there was always a balance left.

Over the years this balance grew, until it came to a very large sum of money. One day, when Shimon placed his order, Boruch called him in to his office and announced, "I'm sorry, but I can't give you any more merchandise. You must pay your old bills."

Shimon was surprised. "But, Boruch," he protested, "we have had such a wonderful relationship over the years. You have always trusted me and I have paid as much as I could, as often as I could. Why the sudden change?"

"It's different now," said Boruch. "From now on I won't be supplying you with any materials at all. I am going out of business. It's the end. That is why I have to call in all the debts now."

The Chofetz Chaim said it is the same with the pains and problems that Jews will face at the end of days. When that time comes, Hashem will "collect" the penalty for all the sins that people have committed throughout all the centuries. The debt will be so great that we can only pray that the troubles and hardships we have already seen may be considered as full payment.

A Sign of the Times

A man once returned to his former neighborhood looking for an old restaurant. He walked down the familiar streets and recognized many of the shops. He saw people going in and out of the hardware store, the grocery and the furniture store, but when he came to the restaurant, the door was closed and locked. He looked in through the window but nothing stirred. The sign on top of the store reading RESTAURANT was still there, so he conjectured that since it was summertime, the owners were probably on vacation.

He planned to come back another time.

A few months later he did come back, but noticed that while other stores were doing a brisk business, the restaurant was not only closed but the sign over the store had been taken down as well.

"It's obvious," said the man to himself, "they've gone out of business. If the sign isn't here, it's all over."

"The same indicator," said the Chofetz Chaim, "is valid with regard to a Jew's adherence to Torah and *mitzvos*. While it's possible that at times a person may accidentally fall prey to an evil temptation, he can still be considered a committed Jew provided that he performs *mitzvos*. But if one removes the signs of Judaism, the basic fundamental tenets that symbolize our affinity to Hashem, and are referred to in the Torah as 'signs,' then he has disavowed his association from those who observe Torah and *mitzvos*.

"The 'signs' are the practice of *bris milah* (ritual circumcision) *(Bereishis* 17:11), the observance of Shabbos (*Shemos* 31:13,17), and the wearing of *tefillin* (ibid. 13:19).* Without these 'signs,' " says the Chofetz Chaim, "it is a certain indication that the Jew is out of business."

A Tourist's Priorities

Quite often R' Sholom decries the perpetual pursuit of material goods in this world. Instead of concerning himself with

* See ArtScroll *Bris Milah*, p. 84 — Circumcision and *Tefillin*.

spiritual matters such as the performance of *mitzvos,* or the study of Torah, man regards the accumulation of money, elegant cars and fine furniture as his primary goals. Torah and *mitzvos* seem to be of only secondary importance. Yet, if a Jew stops to think he soon realizes that the world in which we live is only a preparation for the World to Come. "Prepare yourself in the lobby so that you may enter the banquet halls" *(Avos* 4:21). It behooves us to be involved in matters that have eternal value rather than those that are at best temporary and transient.

R' Sholom cites R' Yosef Leib Bloch's (1860-1930) parable of an Israeli tourist traveling by boat to America, to portray this point. The tourist is meticulous in his preparations. He buys a map, studies the cities at which the boat will dock and makes elaborate plans for the trip. When he realizes that he will be in France for a few days, the tourist studies basic French, so that he can learn to converse with the average Frenchman. For two months he studies all the useful expressions and idioms.

When he finally feels secure with French, he suddenly remembers that his final destination is actually America. He has completely forgotten about learning English! In a panic, he feverishly studies English, trying to pick up as much as he can. But it is late, the boat is about to sail, there are so many things to do ... He boards the boat, fluent in French, but with almost no knowledge of English.

When the boat reaches France, he puts on his beret, is happily able to ask for change, get directions to the hotel and he quickly becomes the envy of his fellow passengers. "How clever," they all think, "how well prepared."

But once the boat leaves the French port and begins the last leg of the journey to America, the tourist realizes the futility of his efforts. He is hardly prepared for his final destination. He had confused his priorities. He had prepared for the short stay, not for the long one.

R' Sholom concludes, "The tourist, red faced with embarrassment disembarks at his final destination with little to show for his efforts."

◆§ *Whose Money?*

The talents we possess or the wealth that we accumulate did not become ours because of any inherent greatness that lies within us. Rather, they are gifts that Hashem, in His infinite wisdom and grace, has bestowed upon us to use, and that, for only as long as He deems useful — for everything is His.

R' Sholom uses a bank scene to illustrate this message.

A child in the bank for the first time, watched the teller dispensing thousands of dollars to one customer and collecting thousands of dollars from another. He was astonished at the amount of money that was handled before his eyes. As he left the bank, the child turned to his father and said, "That man behind the counter must be a millionaire; did you see all the money he had?"

"It's not so," the father said, "you and I may very well be wealthier than he. The money he takes in and dispenses is not his. If he misuses this privilege and gives away one extra dollar or keeps one for himself, he can lose his job and with it the privilege of handling any money at all. He must always bear in mind just where the money originates and to whom it ultimately belongs."

❦ ❦ ❦

We too must use the money and the talents which Hashem has granted us in accordance with the rules and guidelines of the Torah. If we abuse the privilege, then like the bank teller who violates the banking code, we stand to lose whatever has been granted us.

◆§ *Out to Market*

R' Sholom once described a man walking in the markets of Jerusalem.

The man stopped to admire a fruit stand. The apples were shiny and fresh, the bananas glistened in the sun and the tomatoes were plump and luscious.

Suddenly he felt a punch to his chest. "What's this?" he wondered. "Who is shoving and punching me in the open market?" He looked around and saw no one near him, and then he realized that he had hit himself.

Hit himself?

Yes, he was in the middle of *davening* and had just reached the sixth blessing of *Shemoneh Esrei,* the blessing in which we request forgiveness for our sins. During this blessing one strikes his chest as a gesture of contrition. As he had been praying, his mind had wandered to the market on Ben-Yehudah Street, yet he had continued mumbling the words of the *Shemoneh Esrei.* His automatic gesture, the blow on his chest, brought him back to where he was supposed to be.

Could this be a description of how some of us *daven?*

"When someone stands before Hashem in prayer," says R' Sholom, "especially during *Shemoneh Esrei,* he should think of the meaning and intent of his words, and not let his mind wander to contemplate anything but his prayers."

◆§ *A Share for Whom?*

One of the Talmud's most famous expressions is from a mishnah in *Sanhedrin* (10:1): "כָּל יִשְׂרָאֵל יֵשׁ לָהֶם חֵלֶק לָעוֹלָם הַבָּא — Every Jew has a portion in the World to Come." Seemingly, it is reassurance given to us by *Chazal* (our Sages) that every Jew, even if he is sinful, corrupt, or immoral has a share waiting for him in the World to Come, except for those guilty of the sins that are specifically enumerated later in that same *mishnah.*

R' Sholom once pointed out that if the world's understanding of the mishnah is correct, that every Jew indeed has a portion set aside for him in *Olam Haba,* then the wording should be "בָּעוֹלָם הַבָּא — **in** *Olam Haba.*" But the phrase reads differently; it says "לָעוֹלָם הַבָּא — **towards** *Olam Haba.*" Why the prefix of לָ, *towards,* instead of the prefix בָּ, *in?*

R' Sholom cites a beautiful parable from R' Chaim of Volozhin to answer this question.

❦ ❦ ❦

A father had twin sons, and supported them until their twentieth birthday. After that date, he told them, "It is now time for you boys to be on your own. I will give each of you a large parcel of land and it will be your obligation to plow, seed, plant and then eventually reap the harvest of your individual fields. The land is fertile and it can surely produce enough to support you and your families. But you must get started at once. I will support you for only one more year because crops do not grow overnight. But a year from now you will be on your own."

One son heeded his father and did everything necessary to insure that his land would indeed grow bountiful crops of fruits and vegetables. He hired workers and supervised them to make sure that the land was worked properly.

The second son sat by idly, doing nothing with his land, reasoning that there was no rush to work since his father was supporting him — for now, anyway.

When the year elapsed, the first son had a field with crops to be proud of, while the second son had nothing but weeds and thorns in his field, and no means of support.

❦ ❦ ❦

The same is true with us. When we are young, Hashem gives us a "parcel of land". The parcel consists of our physical body and spiritual soul, together with the Torah which serves as our guide on how to perform and fulfill *mitzvos.* Every one of us has only a specific amount of time to "plow, plant, seed and tend the parcel" in this world and then eventually reap the harvest of our efforts in the World to Come.

As the *mishnah* states *(Avos* 4:21): "הָעוֹלָם הַזֶּה דּוֹמֶה לִפְרוֹזְדוֹר בִּפְנֵי הָעוֹלָם הַבָּא, הַתְקֵן עַצְמְךָ בִּפְרוֹזְדוֹר כְּדֵי שֶׁתִּכָּנֵס לַטְּרַקְלִין — This world is like a lobby before the World to Come. Prepare yourself in the lobby so that you may enter the banquet hall." Or, as the Talmud *(Eruvin* 22a) states in reference to *mitzvos,* "הַיּוֹם לַעֲשׂוֹתָם לְמָחָר לְקַבֵּל שְׂכָרָם — Today is to perform them and tomorrow is for receiving their reward."

The message in the *mishnah in Sanhedrin* is as follows: Every Jew, even the sinner, can look forward to a share in *Olam Haba,* but he has to prepare himself properly for it.

❦ ❦ ❦

"It is interesting," adds R' Sholom, "how the parable with the parcel of land closely resembles the reality of creation. When G-d created Adam, the Torah says *(Bereishis* 2:7), 'And Hashem formed man from the earth of the ground and He blew into his nostrils the soul of life ...' Thus each person is a 'parcel of land' ... waiting to be cultivated.

◆§ A Father's Love

Every year during the Pesach holiday, R' Sholom delivers, at least once, a lecture that includes a deeply moving scenario about a loving father and his wayward son. It is based on a tapestry of Midrashic teachings that he has woven together from the fifth chapter of *Shir Hashirim* (Song of Songs).

Shir HaShirim itself is recited every Pesach, the time when the Jewish People first became the nation of Hashem, for it depicts the mutual love between Hashem and His nation. It is read on the Sabbath during Passover (see *Orach Chaim* 490:9). Traditionally some read it after the *seder* as well.

The words of *Shir Hashirim* are mysteriously and hauntingly beautiful. Mysterious because its literal translation does not suffice in revealing its true deeper meaning, and hauntingly beautiful for the words cry out in a yearning and longing for the closeness that we once shared with Hashem in previous generations.

In retelling this episode R' Sholom employs the *maggid's* inimitable melody which embodies this pleading and yearning, while beckoning us to repent and act like true and loyal sons to our devoted Father in Heaven.

❦ ❦ ❦

... I have drunk my wine ... Eat, O friends, drink and become intoxicated, companions. I was asleep but my heart was awake. A sound. My beloved knocks. "Open up for me, my friend, my dove, my perfect one ..."

I have removed my cloak already; shall I don it again? I have washed my feet already; shall I dirty them again? My beloved sent forth his hand from the window and my innards yearned for him. I arose to open the door for my beloved ... I opened the door for my beloved, but my beloved had turned and gone ... I sought him but could not find him. I called him, but he did not answer me. The watchmen patrolling the city found me; they beat me, they wounded me ... (Shir Hashirim 5:1-7).

A father phones his son whom he has not seen in many years and tells him that he is coming for a visit and asks his son to meet him at the airport. During his long trip the father imagines how tall and handsome his son has become, how wise and knowledgeable he has learned to be, for he remembers him only as a youngster. He is impatient to embrace him the very moment he steps off the plane.

Finally, after a long flight the plane touches down and the father disembarks. But his son is not there! What a disappointment! What hurt! "Where is he?" The father wonders. "Did anything happen to him? I was so sure he would be waiting for me ... I hope he is well." The father stands at the airport forlorn and sad.

The son, though, is home in bed sleeping ...

אֲנִי יְשֵׁנָה וְלִבִּי עֵר. — *I was asleep but my heart was awake.*

The *Midrash* teaches that this phrase refers to the Jewish People who slumber, instead of performing the *mitzvos* of their Father in Heaven. Yet, says R' Sholom, even though they were not performing *mitzvos,* in the depths of their hearts there was yet a stirring, for they were really aware of their obligations. It was only laziness that had overcome them and caused them to be negligent.

Why wasn't the son there to greet his father? He had spent the night carousing with friends and now rationalized that it would be too dangerous for him to go to the airport since he was too drunk.

שָׁתִיתִי יֵינִי ... אִכְלוּ רֵעִים, שְׁתוּ וְשִׁכְרוּ דּוֹדִים. — *I have drunk my wine ... eat, O friends, drink and become intoxicated.*

Alone at the airport the father is not concerned with his own pride. Even though he has been snubbed, he goes to his son's home. He takes a cab from the airport and rides through the city to his son's home. Once out of the taxi, he hurries to the front door and knocks, pleading that he be let in.

קוֹל דּוֹדִי דוֹפֵק, פִּתְחִי לִי. — *A sound. My beloved knocks. "Open up for me."*

The *Midrash* notes that Hashem tells the Jewish People, "Open your hearts to Me, so that I can enter. Open your hearts just a little. Give Me an opening as small as the point of a needle and I will open the doors of your heart so wide that chariots can pass through." When a person shows true interest in coming closer to Hashem, Hashem will help him along tenfold.

Still standing outside, the father calls lovingly to his son, pleading to be allowed inside.

רַעְיָתִי יוֹנָתִי תַמָּתִי. — *My friend, my dove, my perfect one.* These are expressions of love that a father uses for his one, his only child. Each word is on a higher level of affection than the previous one. Hashem's expressions of love for the Jewish People are indeed like that of a father to an only child.

The son hears the knocking, but says to himself that he cannot get out of bed to answer the door. He is already in pajamas. He has taken his shower ...

פָּשַׁטְתִּי אֶת כֻּתָּנְתִּי, אֵיכָכָה אֶלְבָּשֶׁנָּה? רָחַצְתִּי אֶת רַגְלַי, אֵיכָכָה אֲטַנְּפֵם? *— I have removed my cloak already; shall I don it again? I have washed my feet already; shall I dirty them again?*

The *Midrash* continues the metaphor and notes that Israel reacts to Hashem's knocking on the door with a perverse

> rationalization, "I have proclaimed my loyalty to other gods; how can I return to Hashem?" The commentaries explain this expression as referring to the Jews in Babylon who had become accustomed to their new country and were reluctant to endure the hardships of traveling back to their homeland.

By now the father should be furious and resentful, and should turn around and go home. His son was not at the airport, was not awake when he came to his home and even now does not have the decency to answer the pleading knocks on the door. But the father still loves his son, and makes a further effort to reach him.

Like a poor man asking for help, like a hungry man begging for food, the father puts his hand through any opening he can find.

Seeing and hearing all this, the son is finally moved. His father has tried so hard to reach him! Excitedly, he jumps out of bed and goes to the door to greet his father.

> דּוֹדִי שָׁלַח יָדוֹ מִן הַחוֹר, וּמֵעַי הָמוּ עָלָיו. — *My beloved sent forth his hand from the window, and my innards yearned for him.*

Now that the son has finally come to the door, excited with anticipation, the father is no longer there. The son stands alone wondering what happened. He does not realize why his father has gone. All he sees is the dark of night.

> קַמְתִּי **אֲנִי** לִפְתֹּחַ לְדוֹדִי ... פָּתַחְתִּי **אֲנִי** לְדוֹדִי, וְדוֹדִי חָמַק עָבָר ... — *It was I who arose to open the door for my beloved ... It was I who opened the door for my beloved; but my beloved had turned and gone.*

The son rushes out into the darkness to search for his father. He searches throughout the city but cannot find him.

> בִּקַּשְׁתִּיהוּ וְלֹא מְצָאתִיהוּ. קְרָאתִיו וְלֹא עָנָנִי. — *I sought Him but could not find Him. I called Him but He did not answer me.*

Finally, he falls prey to bandits who attack him and rob him of all his material possessions.

> מְצָאֻנִי הַשֹּׁמְרִים הַסֹּבְבִים בָּעִיר, הִכּוּנִי פְצָעוּנִי ... — *The enemy*

watchmen patrolling the city found me; they beat me, they wounded me ...

After his futile efforts, the son returns home, sad and forlorn, just as his father had been at the airport.

But, asks R' Sholom, after all his relentless efforts to find his son, why did the father disappear when his son was finally coming to greet him? He could have turned away so many times before. Why did he do so at his very moment of success?

The answer lies hidden in one extra word, written twice in the above verses. It is the word אֲנִי. In describing how he arose from bed, it would have sufficed to say קַמְתִּי, *I arose*. But the son adds the word אֲנִי, *It was I*, for emphasis, as if to say, "It was I who took the initiative." Similarly, he could have said, פָּתַחְתִּי, *I opened (the door)*. Instead, he stressed his own role by adding אֲנִי. These words imply that the entire initiative and authority belongs to the *son*, not the father. Therein lies Hashem's (the father's) reluctance to see his son. It was the father who took the initiative to see his son. It was the father who made the effort — yet in retelling the story the son audaciously claimed, "*I* aroused myself ... *I* opened the door on my own ..." taking all the credit for his efforts. This displays arrogance. There is no humility, no regret, no remorse for his disdainful behavior.

R' Sholom goes on to say that we must all open our hearts and return to Hashem, for surely He, as a devoted Father, wants to be close to us. It is we, in our complacency, who do not make the effort. But if indeed we were to do so, it would only be because He, in His infinite grace, grants us the wisdom, courage and strength to make the positive decisions to return. To think that we can do it on our own, without His assistance is an affront to Hashem and justifies His rejection of us.

We hope the time will come in our days that our total acceptance of Hashem and His *mitzvos* will signify our true return and we will be reunited with Hashem in complete harmony.

Index of Personalities

Note: Included in this index are those historical personalities who played a role in (or made a comment about) the stories. Excluded are most fictionalized names; minor characters; narrators of the stories (unless they were personally involved in the story); commentaries cited in the text; and R' Sholom Schwadron who obviously appears throughout the volume. The page numbers indicate the page on which the story begins, although the personality may not appear until later in the story.

All titles had been omitted from this index to facilitate finding the names.